FLIGHT PATTERNS

FLIGHT PATTERNS

Trends of Aeronautical Development in the United States, 1918–1929

ROGER E. BILSTEIN

The University of Georgia Press   Athens

Copyright © 1983 by the University of Georgia Press
Athens, Georgia 30602
All rights reserved
Designed by Sandra Strother Hudson
Set in 10 on 13 Caledonia
Printed in the United States of America
The paper in this book meets the guidelines for
permanence and durability of the Committee on
Production Guidelines for Book Longevity of the
Council on Library Resources.

Library of Congress Cataloging in Publication Data

Bilstein, Roger E.
Flight patterns.
Bibliography: p.
Includes index.
1. Aeronautics—United States—History. I. Title.
TL521.B53 1983   387.7'0973   83–1092
ISBN 0–8203–0670–3

For my parents,
and for Linda

Contents

Preface

Because the decade of the 1920s collapsed into a disastrous worldwide depression, the long shadow of failure often tends to obscure many fundamental trends that had their origins in the post–World War I decade and that presaged the style of modern America. One can point to the growth of the federal bureaucracy (even in the pre–New Deal era), America's initial infatuation with the automobile, the widespread fascination with radio and motion pictures, and similar manifestations of mass/popular culture characteristic of contemporary society. There are of course other patterns of progress and/or paranoia that have attracted scholarly study, ranging from skyscrapers to the Ku Klux Klan.

This book is devoted to the topic of aviation. Charles A. Lindbergh's epic transatlantic flight of 1927 stands out as one of the premier events of the decade. Most aviation histories have made much of the Lindbergh boom of the late twenties and the important technological progress of the early thirties, when the indomitable DC-3 revolutionized modern air travel. Consequently, many other important aeronautical trends have been obscured, even though earlier trends not only were basic to Lindbergh's success but also contributed to unusually rapid aviation progress of the 1930s. The present study is intended to highlight such developments, explaining how the pattern of aviation activities in the 1920s is reflected through succeeding decades to the present. At the same time, I have attempted to show the social, economic, and political ramifications of this robust new technology.

Indefatigable readers of footnotes will perceive a difference in the documentation for Chapter 1 (on military aviation) as compared to that for subsequent chapters. Aviation history buffs seem to be especially enamored of air warfare, and the secondary literature on the subject is formidable, though uneven. Fortunately, a number of studies over the past few years represent thorough research and a high level of scholarship. Although I have gratefully relied on several fine secondary sources throughout this work, I have even more gratefully turned to these military studies for my survey of military trends of the twenties, since this topic has already been mined so heavily. Elsewhere, I leaned more extensively on the periodicals of the era to get a sense of what observers of the postwar decade felt about the development and significance of aviation.

Portions of Chapters 2 and 3 appeared as an article, "Technology and Commerce: Aviation in the Conduct of American Business, 1918–1929," in *Technology and Culture* (July 1969). I wish to thank the editor, Dr. Melvin Kranzberg, for permission to use the material here. Teaching duties and other research interests diverted efforts to revise and rewrite a preliminary draft until the opportunity to spend the academic year 1977/78 as Visiting Scholar in Aerospace History at the Smithsonian Institution's National Air and Space Museum. Meanwhile, I had occasion to pursue research in American aviation of the 1920s at various times, and it is a pleasure to acknowledge the assistance and support of organizations and individuals noted below.

Professor Robert H. Bremner of Ohio State University read many early versions of the manuscript, and always commented with care, patience, and good humor. Professor John C. Burnham, also from Ohio State, offered important encouragement and advice on portions of an early draft. At the University of Wisconsin–Whitewater, I benefited from the support given me by Professor Edward J. Morgan (then chairman of the history department), and received Wisconsin University Regents' study grants during 1968 and 1969 that permitted intensive reading in the literature of aviation history. During the summer of 1969, a University of Wisconsin–Whitewater Faculty Research Travel Grant gave me the opportunity to pursue research at the Library of Congress, the National Archives, the Smithsonian Archives, the National Library of Medicine, and the Oral History Collection of Columbia University. I have also appreciated the opportunity to peruse the holdings of the Herbert Hoover Presidential Library at West Branch, Iowa; the Ross-Barnett Aviation History Collection of the Denver Public Library; and the Transportation History Collections of the Coe Library, University of Wyoming, Laramie. At the latter institution, Dr. E. V. Toy helped locate many relevant sources.

At the National Air and Space Museum, curators and staff members alike were consistently helpful. Dr. Howard S. Wolko offered early encouragement for this study and Dr. Paul A. Hanle shared insights from his research on the history of theoretical aerodynamics. Philip D. Edwards provided special assistance in locating illustrations. Dominick A. Pisano, Pete Suthard, and others of the NASM Library staff assisted me in locating miscellaneous books, files, and the like.

It is a pleasure also to acknowledge the strong support from the library staff at the University of Houston at Clear Lake City, especially Thomas O. Bates, who obtained much material for me through interlibrary loan. I also benefited from the assistance of Dr. Edward C. Ezell, NASA/Johnson Space Center; Dr. James R. Hansen, NASA/Langley Research Center; and Jay Miller, of Austin, Texas.

The occasion to spend a year at the NASM itself represented a splendid opportunity, and I wish to thank the administration of the University of Houston at Clear Lake City for granting a year's leave of absence and NASM for its generosity in providing a niche for my year in residence there. I owe a special debt of gratitude to Dr. Tom D. Crouch and Dr. Richard P. Hallion, both NASM curators, who offered invaluable guidance and suggestions and who later reviewed and commented on my manuscript.

For their careful reading and specific recommendations regarding the manuscript, I also wish to acknowledge Dr. Wesley P. Newton, of Auburn University, and Dr. Donald R. Witnah, of the University of Northern Iowa. I also profited from the criticisms of anonymous editorial referees. Mr. John H. Jennings, manuscript editor for the University of Georgia Press, rescued me from numerous oversights and errors. Ms. Lillian Kozlowski, of the NASM, and Mrs. Vel Jones, of the University of Houston at Clear Lake City, conscientiously typed and retyped drafts of this study. The errors and omissions remaining are exclusively mine. For their encouragement and interest regarding my own fascination with the world of flight, I particularly want to thank Linda, Paula, and Alex.

R.E.B.

Prologue

High over the prairies between Minneapolis and Chicago, a dozen airline patrons relaxed into cushioned seats to enjoy a motion picture. The passengers of Universal Air Lines, who introduced this diversion to relieve the tedium of travel, had ample opportunity to view the film's conclusion before they arrived in Chicago.[1] A jet plane would have landed long before the final scene, but the year was 1929, when flying still represented a comparatively unhurried mode of transportation. In addition to in-flight movies, many other innovations of aeronautics were pioneered in the first decade after World War I.

The pre–World War I era, it is true, witnessed a remarkable period of progress in aviation. There were experimental airmail flights, and the Wright brothers conducted the first air-cargo flight in 1910. Scheduled airline operations began as early as 1914 in Florida, with the St. Petersburg–Tampa Airboat Line. The origins of military aviation, including naval aviation, were rooted in this period, and World War I demonstrated the potential role of aircraft in combat. In retrospect, these events come into focus at the first, halting steps of a young technological phenomenon destined to become a modern industrial giant of unusually pervasive influence in modern civilization. During the decade of the twenties, many vague contours of aviation development coalesced into definite patterns that persist to the present.

On May 15, 1918, the United States Post Office Department began an epoch in aviation by inaugurating the first regularly scheduled airmail service in the world. The Post Office continued to operate the airmail until 1925, when the task was turned over to private contractors under the terms of the Kelly Bill. This set the stage for the airline industry in the United States. Most of the major airline systems, including American, TWA, United, and Pan American, had emerged by

1930. The Army Air Service struggled for its own identity, culminating in the highly publicized court-martial of Billy Mitchell in 1925. In the meantime, a series of outstanding long-distance military flights provided a more positive series of news headlines. The Army's round-the-world flight in 1924 presented a striking demonstration of aviation's prospects in military operations as well as in international transportation.[2] Aside from military activities and scheduled commercial operations, the twenties marked the evolution of a new aspect of flying—utility aviation or, as it is now called, general aviation. Whether treating crops, conducting photographic surveys, or carrying a busy executive to a business appointment, general aviation arrived in the post–World War I decade as a significant factor in the American aviation community.

The mid-twenties marked an interval of transition. For all of its shortcomings, the airplane, like the automobile, became increasingly accepted as a hallmark of progress. Reviewing the first quarter of the twentieth century from the vantage point of the 1930s, the popular journalist Mark Sullivan commented on the impact of aeronautics on the public consciousness. Before the turn of the century, Sullivan recalled, the impossibility of human flight had been accepted as axiomatic—an unalterable fact of nature like the progression of winter and summer, the law of gravity, and the inevitability of death. The achievement of flight represented a major dividing line in human progress. "Of all the agencies that influenced man's minds," Sullivan wrote, "that made the average man of 1925 intellectually different from him of 1900, by far the greatest was the sight of a human being in an airplane."[3] This feeling may have been shared by many thoughtful people, although others felt that the actual capabilities of aviation fell short of Sullivan's pronouncement. After his conquest of the Atlantic in *The Spirit of St. Louis*, Charles Lindbergh wrote the autobiographical *We*, which became one of the best-selling books of 1927. The book was rather short, Lindbergh explained later, for several reasons: a feeling that he lacked ability to write a comprehensive story, his shyness, and the press of time. Also, he admitted, "believing in aviation's future, I did not want to lay bare, through my own experience, its existing weaknesses."[4]

Lindbergh's flight marked the beginning of a period of meteoric growth. Indeed, the rate of progress belied Lindbergh's misgivings expressed in his book. By itself, his flight could not have created the sudden emergence of the aeronautical infrastructure that existed at the decade's end. Lindbergh's own plane, a decidedly "modern"-appearing monoplane powered by a reliable radial engine, bore little resemblance to the open-cockpit biplanes typical of World War I. *The Spirit of St. Louis* finished a nonstop transatlantic flight of thirty-three and a half hours that no plane could have matched a decade earlier. The design, construction, and engine of this aircraft represented a new level of aeronautical technology that needed only additional opportunities for exploitation. The research facilities of the National Advisory Committee for Aeronautics constituted an additional aspect of aeronautical sophistications that contributed to both past and future improvements. After the Kelly Bill of 1925 provided a financial underpinning for an expanding airline network, the Air Commerce Act of 1926 provided a regulatory and institutional framework. Plans for the influential Guggenheim Fund for the Promotion of Aeronautics were well along by 1926, and the varied roles of general aviation were already evident. While these trends and others gained momentum during the Lindbergh boom, it is important to remember that they were clearly underway before 1927.

With the catalytic influence of Lindbergh's transatlantic triumphs, the various threads of aviation progress constituted a discernible pattern of maturity that contemporary observers acknowledged by the end of the decade. Writing in the influential magazine *Aviation* in 1930, one author cited the "Law of Growth" outlined by Raymond P. Prescott in the *American Statistical Association Journal*. According to Prescott, four stages of growth occurred in industries: a period of experimentation; assimilation into social life; a stage of increasing growth, although at a diminishing rate; and a period of stability.[5] Based on this progression, the writer in *Aviation* concluded that aviation had passed through the initial stage of experimentation by 1930, and was entering the time when it could be regarded as a daily factor of social and economic life.[6] In the same year, announcing the termination of the Daniel Guggenheim Fund for the Promotion of Aeronautics, Harry F. Guggenheim put it more succinctly. "The pioneering period," he said, "has come to an end."[7]

Part One
AIR POWER
AND AIR COMMERCE

CHAPTER ONE
Air Power

The end of World War I found the role of military aviation in a state of turmoil. The Air Service was leaning more and more toward the concept of strategic bombing, and many partisans advocated the creation of an independent air force. For a variety of complex reasons, neither goal was fully realized during the postwar decade. The result was mixed: failure to gain a capable strategic bomber, and failure to gain operational independence. At the same time, important steps were taken that eventually achieved these goals in the thirties and forties. Naval aviation similarly experienced several rounds of frustrating controversy, but made progress in developing tactics, strategy, and weapons. The argument involving dirigibles versus flying boats for patrol was settled in favor of the latter. Naval and Marine aviators introduced divebombing techniques, and the fleet acquired its first aircraft carriers—a significant new weapon in naval and aerial warfare.

Army Aviation

One of the earliest advocates of strategic bombing was Lieutenant Colonel Edgar S. Gorrell, chief of the Strategical Aviation Branch of the Air Service in France during World War I. In December 1917, Gorrell talked of sending bombers to attack German communication and production centers to paralyze the German army—an important, and early, statement on the value of strategic bombing. But which bomber to use? In Europe, General Pershing backed the British-built

Handley-Page. On the other hand, an Army technical commission headed by Major Raynal C. Bolling recommended the Italian-built Caproni, superior in range and bomb load. The Army decided to use both, producing them under license in the United States. From the beginning, administrative confusion and divided energies compromised the bomber program, and set an unfortunate precedent for many Air Service controversies in the future. In any case, Caproni production was finally scrapped because of numerous diplomatic hassles as well as problems of converting Italian specifications into English and adapting Italian shop practices to the American style. Production of the inferior Handley-Page ran into a similar conversion delay, and American-built Handley-Page bombers never saw combat.[1]

Flying European equipment, American airmen made a few limited forays and the Air Service, American Expeditionary Force, became fully involved in proposals for an inter-Allied bombing force. The war ended before it was activated, but the proposals reflected another important step toward strategic bombing. The most vocal spokesman was General William (Billy) Mitchell, who became the ranking officer in command of American military aviation units overseas during World War I. Mitchell consistently argued for the use of aircraft as an offensive weapon, though he spoke in somewhat limited terms for its use against troops, communications and supply lines, and the opposing air forces. In other words, Mitchell was still thinking of a tactical air force, while Gorrell and the English military aviation theorist General Hugh Trenchard were considering the use of long-range bombing to force a military decision behind the front lines. But they were all talking in terms of independent air operations.[2]

Returning to the United States, Mitchell became assistant chief of the Air Service between 1920 and 1925, a crucial period in the evolution of Army air doctrine. Internal rivalries and jealousies hindered progress. The General Staff's interest in aeronautics was low-keyed at best, and there was much friction between Army infantry men and the Army fliers. Many junior officers in both branches of service had enlisted at the same time, but the Army Air Service officers lagged in appointments and seniority because their additional flight training postponed the date of commissioning. Not many aviation officers had gone to West Point, and they sensed discrimination by graduates of the academy. These irritants exacerbated the underlying issue involving the use of aircraft as mere adjuncts to the Army or as independent weapons. Secretary of War Newton Baker left little doubt about his own position, declaring in 1919 that he was against strategic bombing on "the most elemental and humanitarian grounds."[3]

A considerable body of military opinion supported him, if not in philosophy, at least in effect. American aviation doctrine evolved in an ironic cycle. The United States entered the war with ill-defined doctrines favoring concepts of reconnaissance and Army cooperation. Wartime producers then manufactured aircraft for this role, depriving the United States of experience with strategic or offensive bombardment. Looking back on wartime operations, postwar projections relied on existing experience. Thus, Army cooperation was stressed over independent air force roles. The General Staff further erred in proposing that the proportion of observation, fighter, and bomber aircraft should be assessed on the basis of the field strength of the belligerent powers at the time of the Armistice. By this logic, the various armed forces favored pursuit and observation planes over bombers by a wide margin. Frustrated Air Service officers pointed out that planned or projected strengths, based on wartime experience, should have been the yardstick, in which case bombers would have constituted 30–50 percent of the air forces of England, Italy, and France. The foresighted officers lost their case. Although numerous case studies of combat operations which might have rectified such erroneous conjectures by the General Staff were prepared during 1919–20, they somehow fell into limbo and were never published. Carbon copies of one such manuscript turned up during World War II—twenty years too late.[4]

The Army Reorganization Act of 1920 made some concessions to aviation, but left most fliers disappointed because tactical squadrons still operated under the control of ground commanders, although the tactical units were to be commanded by pilots. There were some benefits in the new legislation, and the Air Service appeared for the first time as a separate line unit, with status similar to the Infantry, Cavalry, and other segments. Perhaps this was the most tangible evidence of the impact of World War I on American military doctrine. Additional flight pay was authorized, and the Air Service had a unique distinction among other combatant arms in that it had control of its own training, research and development, procurement, and supply. It was a halting step toward independence, but a step nonetheless.

The confusion and debate over the role of air power in the postwar era were accompanied by a wholesale dismantling of the wartime strength of 200,000 personnel in the Air Service when the Armistice was signed. Although the General Staff recommended 24,000 officers and men for the postwar flying corps, Congress hacked away the appropriations so that the roster stood at less than 10,000 by the spring of 1920. Within a few days of the Armistice, the government canceled orders for 13,000 planes and 20,000 engines, and the director of Air Service reported in 1920 that "not a dollar is available for the purchase of new aircraft." In 1921 American air strength rested entirely on leftovers on hand in 1918: 1,500 JN-4 (Jenny) training aircraft, 1,100 DH-4B observation planes, 179 SE-5 pursuits, and a dozen Martin MB-2 bombers. Many in this collection of aging airplanes were unsafe to fly. During one twelve-month span in 1920–21, 330 crashes killed sixty-nine men and seriously injured twenty-seven more. With only 900 pilots and observers available, this casualty rate was clearly disastrous. Although the entire Army was affected by drastic financial reductions after the war, Air Service fliers were subject to additional risks in rickety, obsolete aircraft. By 1924, U.S. Army air forces listed 1,364 planes, of which only 754 were still in commission.[5]

During these postwar doldrums, the Army stretched its imagination to keep the Air Service at work in some sort of useful activity. Carl Spaatz, an experienced flier groomed to train combat pilots, instead found himself at the helm of a ragtag outfit called the Far West Flying Circus, one of several Air Service troupes organized to publicize postwar Victory Loan drives during 1919. When the Victory Bond business petered out, Spaatz became the commander of a band of military officers doing Forest Fire Patrol work, cruising western forests and scanning the woods for telltale wisps of smoke. Flying SE-5 and DH-4B aircraft, the forest patrol became useful, providing a measure of early warning and observation in remote areas that simply could not be monitored in any other way. Following a special survey above a tangled area of trees toppled by a storm in a section of the Olympia National Forest, officials wrote Secretary of Agriculture Henry Wallace that they were "exceedingly well pleased with the results obtained" from aerial reconnaissance. Another kind of aerial patrol begun in 1919, stretching from Brownsville, Texas, to San Diego, California, was flown to spot illegal border crossings and to discourage marauders along the desolate reaches of the U.S.–Mexican border. "Operations along these hundreds of air miles soon proved at least as toughening for the pilots as the missions over the mountains on the Forest Fire Patrol," General Henry H. (Hap) Arnold wrote later. "We learned a lot of things the hard way, especially regarding navigation and the need to secure accurate flight plans before taking off." Moreover, as Air Service pilots began to acquire better long-range flying skills, ground staffs evolved procedures of administration and supply for flying activities scattered across a line of operations stretching 2,000 miles.[6]

The operations that grabbed the biggest headlines were long-distance and endurance flights of the twenties, and the Air Service contributed to a significant number of these events. A quartet of frail Curtiss Jennies hopscotched 4,000 miles across the continent in 1919, gathering information for air routes and landing fields. This was followed by a 9,000-mile circuit of the rim of the continental United States made by a Martin bomber the same year. At McCook Field, near Dayton, Ohio, the Air Service worked on a turbosupercharger, developed by Sanford A. Moss of General Electric, for the Liberty engine. During the early twenties, Major R. W. Schroeder and others, using aircraft equipped with the supercharged Liberty engines, succeeded in piloting planes to altitudes above 33,000 feet, an important contribution to the development of high-altitude fighter and bomber aircraft before World War II. In May 1923, Lieutenants Oakley Kelly and John Macready successfully completed the first nonstop transcontinental jaunt, flying a Fokker T-2 transport from New York to San Diego in less than twenty-seven hours. The next month, Lieutenants L. H. Smith and J. P. Richter introduced the previously untried technique of aerial refueling, using a gasoline hose dropped by a tanker aircraft, and during August set an endurance record of more than thirty-seven hours in a DH-4 biplane over San Diego.

Simply stated, the statistics of these records do little to convey the imagination, endurance, and determination of Air Service personnel who flew these fabric-covered, wood and wire-braced planes in open cockpits. The difference between success and failure was often a matter of determination and ingenuity, as in the case of the transcontinental flight of the Fokker T-2. Macready, awkwardly controlling the T-2 from the rear cockpit, kept the plane on course while Kelly disassembled a faulty voltage regulator and repaired it en route. When the pair later attempted to retrace their route from west to east, the leakage of coolant from cracked cylinder blocks in the motor threatened total loss of the engine over Indiana. After pouring their personal supplies of drinking water, coffee, and consommé into the leaking motor, Kelly and Macready limped to an emergency landing on the Indianapolis Speedway. Similar ingenuity contributed to the success of the first flight around the world, completed in 1924. Beginning in Seattle, eight fliers began their global odyssey in four Douglas World Cruisers built especially for the mission. Elaborate advance preparations required cooperation of the U.S. Navy and the Royal Air Force, including arrangements for spare engines and other equipment around the world. Two of the planes completed the entire 26,000-mile journey in 175 days, flying with only rudimentary navigational aids.[7]

Despite the problems and delays, these operations demonstrated aviation's flexibility and long reach. Much was learned about flying conditions in the United States and around the world, and the potential of aircraft for global military operations was demonstrated. Aerial refueling, for example, became an integral aspect of military airpower in the years following World War II. More significantly, advocates of long-range bombing could point to these flights as examples of the potential of military aviation—for defense as well as offense.

The Mitchell Affair

Most American military theorists of the era still regarded sea power as the bulwark of the defense of the North American continent. General Billy Mitchell thought air power had decisively changed this traditional concept. Confronted by innumerable critics who claimed that battleships could never be sunk by airplanes, Mitchell demanded some tests to challenge the point. The result was a series of historic bombing trials held off the Virginia Capes during the summer of 1921. Mitchell's crews primarily used the Martin MB-2 bomber, a twin-engined biplane design completed too late for use in World War I. While one program was organized to drill air crews in formation-flying and bombing techniques, a second effort hastily designed and produced special bombs, including 1,000-lb and 2,000-lb armor-piercing weapons of a design unique for the time. During the first few days of the trials, Mitchell's bomber crews used smaller bombs to sink a destroyer and a cruiser—two of the three captured German warships used as targets for the bombing demonstrations. The major target was the former German battleship *Ostfriesland*, claimed by many to be unsinkable.

On July 20, 1921, the MB-2s rolled down the grassy runway at Langley Field and headed out to sea. On the first bomb run over the target, the smaller bombs did considerable damage to the *Ostfriesland* above the waterline, leaving the anchored battleship scarred but seaworthy. The next day, the first wave of MB-2s carried 1,000-lb bombs, followed by a second formation loaded with 2,000-lb projectiles. Bombs from the first wave made three hits before the Navy hastily called a halt to check the damage. Partially flooded, the ship remained afloat, and Naval inspectors decided it could still have made it back to port under its own steam. Then, the Navy team retired to watch the Air Service continue its apparently futile attacks. Seven planes, each with a 2,000-lb bomb, made the final assault. In twenty-two minutes it was all over, and the big battleship went to the bottom. Reporters noted that veteran naval officers wiped away tears as the battered *Ostfriesland* slid under the waves. Mitchell and his air crews were jubilant. Later, during the autumn of 1921, additional day and night bombing tests involving four more U.S. decommissioned capital ships sent three to the bottom; the fourth, after being subjected to a variety of aerial ordnance, finally succumbed to naval gunfire. Nevertheless, air-power advocates seemed vindicated.

But Mitchell's feud with higher authorities had just begun. Critics pointed out that the targets had been stationary, without fire-control parties or antiaircraft defenses. Mitchell and his defenders still claimed the point had been made: airplanes could sink battleships. The flamboyant Mitchell kept up a drumfire of memos, articles, and books, arguing for an expanded role for aviation and more autonomy for military aerial operations. He denounced his opponents in both the Army and the Navy. When his appointment as assistant chief of Air Service expired in 1925, he was practically banished to San Antonio, Texas, in his permanent grade of lieutenant colonel, where he served as air officer of the corps area. The same year, Mitchell's crusade for air power came to a head after the *Shenandoah*, a Navy dirigible, went down over Ohio during a September storm. The tragic loss of the airship and many of her crew during an ill-advised public relations junket had been totally unnecessary, Mitchell raged, and he authorized a press release charging "incompetency, criminal negligence, and almost treasonable administration of the National Defense." Within two weeks, President Coolidge signed the documents for Mitchell's court-martial.

Hearings during the sensational trial took seven weeks, and became a national forum for Mitchell and nearly every officer in the Air Service. The judges—a dozen major and brigadier generals—included no aviators. Their verdict was a foregone conclusion (after World War II, Douglas MacArthur said his was the only dissenting vote), with Mitchell found guilty of insubordination, contempt, and disrespect. He was suspended from duty for five years. When Coolidge approved the sentence early in 1926, Mitchell resigned from the Air Service.[8]

Opinion on Mitchell's actions was mixed. Benjamin Foulois, a Mitchell contemporary and later chief of the Air Corps, felt that Mitchell was wrong to appeal to the public, and should have persuaded his military superiors with facts and figures. Carl Spaatz, on the other hand, felt that Mitchell did no disservice to the cause of aviation, though his course of action may not have helped as much as he hoped. In any case, Spaatz said, it took the Mitchell affair to arouse public interest when earlier committees and investigative boards had not. As for Coolidge, Spaatz wryly commented that the president probably had no firm opinion one way or the other. If the president resented Mitchell, it was probably because the impetuous airman created a furor and because Coolidge had to make up his mind what to do about it. Ira Eaker, another contemporary junior officer, said that Mitchell deliberately sacrificed his own career for the cause of air power and had been vindicated. If the affair seemed to have little immediate effect on the General Staff, the increased public awareness had been a positive long-run benefit. One notable factor, Eaker recalled, was the staunch support for Mitchell from the ranks of other Air Service officers who stuck with Mitchell at the risk of their own careers. Among these mavericks was Hap Arnold, who was one of their leaders. In fact, Arnold apparently just missed being court-martialed himself. Instead, influential friends at headquarters (including General Mason Patrick) got him safely out of harm's way to Fort Riley, Kansas. Arnold became discouraged about the Mitchell affair, and considered leaving the Air Service. When he wrote Donald Douglas, Sr., about a job, Douglas replied that, although he was flattered by Arnold's interest, Arnold's future was surely in military aviation. And so, Arnold decided to stick it out.[9]

From Air Service to Air Corps

While Arnold chafed under temporary exile in Kansas and Mitchell loosed occasional blasts during his retirement, the Air Service experienced some moderate reforms. Between the end of World War I and the early 1920s, aviation and military flying was scrutinized by more than a dozen investigative boards, commissions, and committees. The two most important, the Lampert Committee and the Morrow Board, were in session during the trial of Billy Mitchell, and issued their final reports only days before Mitchell's trial concluded. The Lampert Committee, established by the House of Representatives early in 1924 to assess the Air Service, was reported to be more generally favorable to Mitchell's views on military aviation. The President's Aircraft Board, or the Morrow Board, as it was better known (after its chairman, Dwight Morrow, a well-known banker), was regarded as something of an antidote to the Mitchell furor, and Coolidge pushed for an early release of its report, submitted on November 30, 1925. But even the Lampert Committee failed to recommend a unified air arm, calling instead for adequate aviation representation on the Army's General Staff and the Navy's General Board. Similarly, the Morrow Board scotched the idea of an independent air force, although it favored upgrading the Air Service to the Air Corps, with representation on the General Staff, along with assistant secretaries for air in the War, Navy, and Commerce departments. In other details, the subsequent Air Corps Act of 1926 reflected the Morrow Board more than it did the Lampert Committee. The new legislation created the Air Corps, and implied the concept of military aviation as a discrete organization for offensive operations, as opposed to reconnaissance and auxiliary activities. F. Trubee Davison, an early Navy pilot, New York lawyer, politician, and partisan of military aviation, assumed the new post of assistant secretary of war for air. Along with this apparent new authority came various reform measures and an important authorization to carry out a five-year expansion program.

The results over the next few years were mixed. Implementation of the expansion program was set back two years for lack of funds, and consistent budget reductions, averaging about 40 percent, hampered programs during the five-year expansion period, 1927–32. The Air Corps, like the other services, faced the issue of general government retrenchment during the late twenties, a situation obviously exacerbated by the onset of the depression after 1929. Standard procedures for procurement of military aircraft proved to be a complex and frustrating issue, as Air Corps officers soon discovered. Given the terms of the Air Corps Act of 1926, procurement through "design competition" could lead to a flood of overoptimistic paper concepts, so that the promising performance of a chosen design could ultimately prove to be totally unrealistic. Also, choosing a particular design because of its low cost—"mollifying the Comptroller General"—could saddle the Air Corps with a cheap aircraft having mediocre performance. Faced with these and other quandaries, the Air Corps continued to procure its aircraft through other means, relying primarily on loopholes in the legislation that permitted sole-source procurement. The Air Corps ran afoul of heavy congressional criticism of such practices in the early 1930s, and procurement policies were revised more realistically after 1934.[10] Still, Ira Eaker considered the Morrow Board and its results a forward step, and Trubee Davison, as assistant secretary of war for air, gave military aviators a friendly partisan in the upper echelons of the War Department.

After a decade of postwar activities dogged by skinflint budgets and punctuated by controversy, American military aviation nevertheless attained a new status of operational skills and organizational effectiveness. The Air Service's Model Airways System of the early twenties linked several major air fields in the Midwest, and in five years of cargo and personnel flying (1920–25) provided ground staff and pilots with invaluable experience in logistics and flying, as well as stimulating "air-mindedness" in the communities en route. In 1926 flight training was consolidated at the Air Corps Training Center at San Antonio, where the School of Aviation Medicine was also established. Technical training was upgraded at Chanute Field in Illinois, and tactical doctrines were explored at the Air Service Tactical School at Langley Field,

Virginia. Logistics and engineering became major enterprises at McCook Field, near Dayton, Ohio. Although evaluation of experimental planes took place at several air fields, most flight tests occurred at McCook, where careful, step-by-step procedures were evolved and codified. Not a job for reckless or careless pilots, flight testing became a meticulous, technical discipline. By the end of the 1920s, standardized flight test manuals had been developed for both military and civil requirements. Additional long-distance flights and endurance flights of the late 1920s provided experience and expertise for long-range missions of the future.[11]

At the time of the Air Corps Act of 1926, the Air Corps had fewer than 10,000 personnel, well below the 17,800 authorized in 1920. The air strength of fewer than 1,000 aircraft included only sixty pursuit (fighter) planes and no bomber or attack planes considered to be modern. By 1932, the Air Corps numbered 14,700 personnel (compared to the projected figure of 16,600) with 1,709 aircraft. Fortunately, the country's stocks of World War I–vintage DH-4 planes had thinned out, and improved aircraft were beginning to enter service. Hap Arnold approvingly noted the appearance of modern appurtenances such as aircraft brakes and adjustable-pitch propellers. Still, the Air Corps remained wedded to basic biplane configurations of World War I, and open-cockpit trainers, fighters, and bombers of the postwar era were still covered by fabric, although metal ribs, spars, and formers were beginning to replace wood. A standard fighter was the Curtiss P-6 Hawk biplane, introduced in 1924 with a 400-hp "V-type" engine. Several dozen variants were produced, culminating in the 600-hp P-6E of 1932, which boasted a top speed of 198 mph and mounted two machine guns. Several bomber types were all characterized by biplane designs, usually with a pair of engines mounted between the wings and a speed of 120 mph, typical of several dozen Keystone LB-7 and LB-10 bombers (with a five-man crew) that equipped the Air Service.[12]

Although armed with aircraft of only average performance, the Air Corps continued to learn how to use them tactically and to cope with the problems of mounting large concentrations of aircraft. "We grew up," Arnold emphasized. "We had started thinking in terms of Squadrons; by now we were thinking in terms of Groups and Wings." In 1930, spring maneuvers included 250 aircraft; the following year saw

700 planes from all over the United States assembled at Dayton. Planning for such large-scale operations meant more than furnishing enough fuel and lubricants. To avoid overcrowding airfields, and to get the planes into the air in coordinated operations, flying units were scattered all over central Ohio. "That gave us some idea of the area we must contemplate using in time of war when we talked of concentrating 1,000 or 2,000 airplanes," Arnold recalled. Officers learned to schedule preparation of satellite fields, to provide maintenance support, to arrange for temporary mess and living quarters; and to set up a telephone network for communications.[13]

Still, Air Corps equipment lagged behind the service's potential, as well as doctrine and theory as expounded by Mitchell and his cohorts. The twenties became a time of gathering experience, gaining a degree of autonomy and bureaucratic influence, and establishing an organizational framework. The Air Corps entered the thirties prepared to refine tactics for fighters and bombers and to take advantage of a new generation of all-metal monoplane designs with retractable gear and other refinements to give planes a performance that made air power an unquestioned reality in modern warfare.

The Evolution of Naval and Marine Aviation

The role of Navy and Marine aviation in World War I was primarily one of patrol and reconnaissance, although pilots of both air services also made bombing raids into enemy-held territory. By the end of the war, 4,000 pilots and 30,000 enlisted men had passed through various Navy training schools, and overseas Navy personnel included more than 1,000 officers and 18,000 enlisted men. Operating from twenty patrol bases in England, the Azores, and the European continent, Navy airmen made some 22,000 flights and patrolled more than 791,000 sea miles. In combat operations, Navy and Marine air units dropped 126,302 pounds of bombs on enemy targets, and one pilot, claiming at least five planes and balloons shot down, became the Navy's lone "ace" of the conflict. By later standards, such numbers might seem minuscule, but, compared to the Navy's aviation position in April, 1917, with forty-three officers and 200 enlisted men, as well as five officers and thirty men in the Marines, the wartime achievement was eminently respectable.[14]

In the postwar era, the degree to which aviation would be integrated into the fleet became a hotly contested issue, with proponents of more active offensive operations clashing with those who still viewed aviation as best suited for scouting and patrol. In many ways, the issue reflected the debate within the Army, where many veteran combat aviators clamored for an autonomous role of broader scope. Early postwar Navy aviation made considerable progress in the development of patrol planes, including a strong move for dirigible operations as an even longer-ranged reconnaissance vehicle. A number of remarkable and successful long-distance flights gave heavy support to the flying boat for aerial patrol, and it evolved into a very successful operational status, proved in World War II. Dirigibles were never very useful. But the most significant combat development in the Navy concerned the development of aircraft carriers, along with the planes and operational techniques to make the carrier a unique naval weapon.[15]

The Navy's first big postwar headlines came in May 1919, when three Navy flying boats attempted the first aerial crossing of the Atlantic Ocean. The flying boats, NC-1, NC-3, and NC-4, came from a production batch of ten built by Curtiss Engineering Company and the Naval Aircraft Factory for antisubmarine patrol during World War I. The big, ungainly-looking planes were powered by four Liberty engines of 400 horsepower each, and carried a six-man crew. Flying for long hours in these lumbering planes with open cockpits became a grueling experience. During preliminary trials, designer and engineer Grover Loening went along during one eight-hour nonstop flight. "I thought it would never end," he confessed. "Its cruising speed was slow—80 to 85 miles an hour—and there was no shelter for 'super cargoes' like me, and it was cold and windy almost beyond endurance for so long a time." And, he concluded disconsolately, "No lunch either." For the record flight attempt, the planes were more adequately provisioned. After departing Trepassey Bay, Newfoundland, on May 15, the three ships headed for the Azores, but the NC-1 and NC-3 were forced down at sea. The NC-1 broke up and sank while under tow, and NC-3 finally limped into port in the Azores after taxiing at sea for two days. The NC-4 was the only one of the trio to fly all the way to the islands, refuel, and proceed via Lisbon, Portugal, to Plymouth, England, on May 31.[16] The remarkable flight of the NC-4 unquestionably demonstrated the potential and operational capabilities of the flying boat, a type developed by the Navy during the post–World War I decade. Seaplane tenders were commissioned to provide flying boats and other float-equipped planes with floating bases at sea. Officers worked out new tactics for patrol, navigation (including the radio compass and directional radio beams), smoke screens, torpedo attack, bombing, and gunnery.[17]

The twenties are remembered as an era of peace, although naval aviation received experience in combat conditions, specifically as a result of Marine operations in Central America. Marine aviation long remained a stepchild within the naval air forces, and generally had to contend with castoff airplanes from active Navy units. In spite of this frequently antiquated equipment, Marine pilots turned in a most creditable performance, especially during actions in Santo Domingo, Haiti, and Nicaragua. When revolutionary groups in Santo Domingo and Haiti stepped up opposition to the existing governments in 1919, the United States government dispatched Marine contingents to help shore up the shaky regimes. Marine fliers in Santo Domingo began with a half-dozen Curtiss Jennies, using them for reconnaissance over the impenetrable jungles and for making strafing runs against rebel forces. When DH-4 planes became available, these larger craft continued such missions, and were also used for medical evacuation, reducing a three-day ordeal through steaming jungles by mule and ox cart to a two-hour flight. Similar operations were conducted in Haiti, including mail and passenger service between headquarters areas and command posts.

In Nicaragua, U.S. Marines joined the Nicaraguan National Guard in sorties against a well-organized rebellion led by Augusto Sandino. Marine fliers arrived with six DH-4s early in 1927, and conducted a mission of historical significance that July, when a determined force of Sandinistas had besieged a garrison of Marines and Nicaraguan soldiers at Ocotal. With reinforcements at least a week away, the situation for the harassed defenders was grim. The Sandinistas were routed only after strafing runs by Marine DH-4s, followed by a devastating divebombing attack that reportedly left 50–70 rebels dead and 175 wounded. The rebels were forced to withdraw. The origins of the divebombing technique remain obscure; it probably was first used in combat by the Royal Air Force in 1918. Although the RAF failed to develop the technique after World War I, significant trials were made by Air Service pilots in the early 1920s, and Navy pilots made a convincing demonstration of the tactic during training exercises in 1926. But the strike at Ocotal, with its decisive results in a crucial combat situation, represents an important benchmark. The tactic was perfected by Marine and naval aviators during the years that followed, and became the basis for close-support air strikes and divebombing of enemy ships that was so effective in World War II, particularly during many engagements against Japanese forces and shipping in the Pacific.

The Marines' missions in Nicaragua encompassed a variety of reconnaissance, aerial supply, and combat sorties against the rebels, becoming so effective that the Sandinistas found it prudent to move primarily at night and during bad weather, when planes were grounded. Marine pilots also evacuated wounded, as in the daredevil flying of Lieutenant C. F. Shilt. Shilt received the Congressional Medal of Honor for his performance during action in 1928. He flew repeated missions under heavy fire into a beleaguered village, carrying in 1,400 pounds of medicine and supplies and flying out eighteen severely wounded men. Since Shilt's two-place Vought O2U-1 biplane had no brakes, waiting Marines grabbed the plane's wings to drag it to a halt, and then dug in their heels while the pilot gunned the engine to full throttle for takeoff.[18]

As one Navy officer noted years later, the experience in Nicaragua put Marine aviation on its feet, making it an integral unit of combat operations.[19] Further, the Navy Department gave closer attention to aerial evacuation of wounded from combat zones (including tests of autogyros for this purpose in 1932), and pondered the lessons of air power as a countermeasure against guerilla units, especially in jungle environments. Air strikes frequently supplied the margin of victory when Marines were surrounded by Sandinistas deep in hostile territory, and planes proved invaluable in supplying remote combat posts under enemy harassment. There were other lessons learned—and lamentably forgotten—that, although well-coordinated air attacks could make the difference in a specific engagement, indiscriminate bombing of presumed rebel areas earned only distrust and hatred of noncombatants.[20]

The Aircraft Carrier

Continuing progress in naval aviation owed much to the creation of the Bureau of Aeronautics within the Navy itself. The bill leading to its establishment was largely a result of continuous agitation by Representative Frederick Hicks of New York, who had long advocated an aeronautics bureau on an equal basis with other Navy bureaus. Hicks had trouble getting much support until the public debate generated by General Billy Mitchell raised the specter of naval aviation being absorbed into a separate unified air service. The Navy finally came to Hicks's aid, and the Bureau of Aeronautics was created on July 12, 1921. Its first chief was Captain William A. Moffett, "a suave and polished negotiator," who brought determined enthusiasm and a flair for public relations to his new post. For the next twelve years, until his death in the crash of the dirigible *Akron* in 1933, he guided naval aviation through four different presidential administrations and helped lay the basis for numerous significant developments, not the least of which was his support for aircraft carriers.[21]

While naval aviation was in the process of accumulating various kinds of patrol and combat flying experience in the postwar era, a major revolution in air power was taking shape in the form of aircraft carrier development. In the halcyon days before World War I, some energetic Navy officers built a rude, sloping 83-foot-long deck over the forecastle of the cruiser *Birmingham*, and got an adventurous pilot, Eugene Ely, to fly off it late in 1910. Elated, the officers formulated plans for a more ambitious project, and built a 120-foot deck on the armored cruiser *Pennsylvania*, anchored in the harbor at San Diego. On January 8, 1911, with Ely again at the controls of a Curtiss pusher airplane, the first landing on a ship was accomplished, followed by a successful takeoff an hour later. The perspicacious experimenters also rigged a prototype arresting gear, consisting of twenty-two lines stretched across the deck, each end of the line attached to a fifty-pound sandbag.

Between 1914 and 1918, other exigencies put continuation of American experiments in abeyance, although the British conducted several promising trials of ship-launched aircraft in 1917 and 1918. In the immediate aftermath of the war, U.S. Navy officers became concerned about the possibility of hostilities with Great Britain as a result of keen postwar competition for international trade and the rise of American sea power. If such were the case, then air power at sea would certainly be a factor. In the spring of 1918, the General Board reported to Secretary of War Josephus Daniels that "Aircraft have become an essential arm of the fleet," recommended that a Navy air service operate with the fleet on a global basis, and added, somewhat ominously, that Great Britain had already reached this capability.

The question of the types of aircraft required by naval aviation touched off a heated internal debate. The Navy had already invested heavily in flying boats and other float-equipped aircraft, and many officers opposed carriers as an untried and unwarranted expense, especially in a peacetime era of reduced budgets. Advocates of carriers pointed out limitations in the range of flying boats, and argued that seaplane operations in midocean would be difficult in rough weather and stormy seas. A key event occurred in March 1919, during a main-battery exercise involving the battleship *Texas*. An untrained observer in a spotting plane coached the ship's big guns to bracket the target with startling accuracy. Officers who considered the airplane as a mere scout to report the presence of opposing ships suddenly awakened to the usefulness of aircraft for enhancing the hitting power of the fleet's guns. The opposite was true for the spotting planes of an enemy fleet—hence the need to secure command of the air at sea. That meant aircraft carriers, equipped with wheeled fighter aircraft. About this time American strategists also surmised that a war in the Pacific would probably lead to Japanese occupation of the Philippines. A relieving naval force would inevitably have to contend with land-based fighters and bombers, superior to more cumbersome seaplanes in combat. Only wheeled aircraft of equivalent design and performance, operating from carriers, could effectively meet the challenge.

A second significant impetus to the evolution of naval aviation and carrier operations occurred during the historic bombing trials off the Virginia Capes in 1921. Captain William A. Moffett, director of Naval Aviation, was quoted in the press to the effect that "We must put planes on battleships and get aircraft carriers quickly." Moffett further advocated the acquisition of eight carriers as the Navy's minimum for a two-ocean fleet. There was considerable irony in the fact that Mitchell had hoped the bombing tests might lead to a unified air service. On the contrary, even Navy officers who remained skeptical of carriers joined partisans in arguing for naval aviation as an organic arm of the fleet. Against this background, the Navy made its first commitment to the aircraft carrier.[22]

While hoping for a thirty-knot vessel to keep pace with fast cruisers and battleships, the carrier advocates eventually had to settle for less. The General Board finally decided on the conversion of a fleet auxiliary vessel, and chose the fleet collier *Jupiter*, to the dismay of several senior flag officers who insisted that the Navy needed its collier more than it did a carrier. Commissioned in 1913, the *Jupiter* became the first Navy vessel to pass through the newly completed Panama Canal a year later, and had carried the first United States military personnel sent to Europe in the spring of 1917—the seven officers and 122 enlisted men of the First Aeronautic Detachment. Congress authorized conversion in July 1919, and the Navy's first carrier was commissioned on March 20, 1922, rechristened as the *Langley*, after Samuel Pierpont Langley (1865–1906), the former secretary of the Smithsonian Institution who was noted for his early experiments in mechanical flights. During the conversion, the superstructure was removed and replaced by a heavy wooden flight deck measuring 534 by 64 feet. A pair of horizontal smoke ducts exhausted engine gasses to the port side, leaving the entire flight deck unencumbered. The ship eventually carried a complement of twelve single-seat fighters, twelve two-place spotters, and ten torpedo planes, although the years 1922 through 1924 were spent evaluating a variety of aircraft for carrier operations and developing specifications for new airplanes. Operational procedures were evolved, and the *Langley* also tested improved cross-deck arresting gear, developed independently of a more complicated British system.[23]

In January 1925, at San Diego, the *Langley* took on planes and personnel of the first aircraft squadron specifically trained for carrier operations, becoming a full-fledged member of the American fleet. The ship's participation in additional fleet exercises helped pave the way for larger, modern carriers already in the works, including the *Lexington* and *Saratoga*. The genesis of these carriers paralleled the Washington Disarmament Conference of 1921–22. The conference agreements temporarily stabilized tensions in the Far East, but left naval experts uneasy. In the event of a war in which the Japanese seized essential island bases in the Pacific, there was grave doubt that the territory could be recaptured with the relative strength in capital ships allocated to the United States by treaty agreements. Some other means was required to maintain a balance of military strength in the Pacific, and the American negotiators won concessions for large carriers. "The readiness with which the United States acquiesced in the matter of increased carrier tonnage," observed one historian, "coupled with its reluctance to put any ceiling on numbers of naval aircraft, suggests the first, faint glimmerings that naval aviation might serve as the swing factor in resolving the problem."[24]

The *Lexington* and *Saratoga*, originally laid down in 1920–21, were converted from battle cruisers to carriers in the autumn of 1922, under the guidelines of the Washington Disarmament Conferences. A plethora of technical problems complicated the conversion process, so that the construction time rose from thirty to sixty-seven months, and the cost of each escalated from $23 million to more than $40 million, a cost overrun comparable only to some defense programs of the post–World War II era. But the big new ships caught the public's fancy, and the launch of the *Lexington* in 1925 sparked a number of favorable editorials on American air power and national security in the wake of the Washington disarmament agreements.[25] Both ships were commissioned in 1927, bringing the United States carrier fleet to three, although the pair of new carriers boasted performance and statistics that completely overshadowed the *Langley*. With a speed of more than thirty-three knots, the *Lexington* and *Saratoga* (displacing 41,000 and 33,000 tons, respectively) could handily keep pace with the best of the United States fleet, and they carried a strong defensive armament of thirteen eight-inch and five-inch guns, as well as smaller antiaircraft batteries. The ships measured 888 feet overall, and carried between seventy and eighty aircraft. Drawing on the early experience afforded by the *Langley*, the new carriers elevated aircraft carrier theory to tactical and strategic realities.[26]

The development and deployment of the Navy's carriers were paralleled by fundamental advances in the organization and activities under the direction of the Bureau of Aeronautics. During Moffett's tenure as chief, the bureau made important strides in training and support operations. The major activities involving flight training occurred at Pensacola, Florida, although additional stations, at San Diego and elsewhere, became involved, and cooperative programs with the Army were also carried out. At Great Lakes, near Chicago, the Navy conducted most of its classes in aircraft handling, overhaul, and repair, while Lakehurst, New Jersey, became the center for dirigible operations. The bureau encouraged practical research in a variety of areas, including metal tubing to replace wooden frames in aircraft construction; the use of metal in flying boat hulls, wings, tails, and propellers; and the development of corrosion-resistant materials for such equipment exposed to saltwater. Moffett also endorsed Navy support of the radial engine, one of the most significant advances of the postwar decade.[27]

As early as 1920, the National Advisory Committee for Aeronautics noted that radial, air-cooled engines would offer ship-based planes less weight per horsepower, to say nothing of increased reliability. The Lawrance J-1, developed with Navy funds in 1922, ran successfully for an unprecedented three hundred hours, at a time when an endurance of fifty hours was considered acceptable for a water-cooled engine. The radials gave tremendous confidence to Navy pilots, especially in long overwater flights, and paved the way for tactical concepts they might otherwise have shunned. The remarkable advantages of the radial were evident in a comparison of the Vought VE with a water-cooled engine and the FU, which mounted a radial. The VE's top speed was 117 mph, its service ceiling was 15,000 feet, and its range was 291 miles. By contrast, the FU had a 122-mph speed, 26,500-foot ceiling, 410-mile range.

Performance like this meant that the Navy's carrier-based fighters could hold their own in combat against land-based aircraft, an encouraging factor to naval strategists thinking about the problem of confronting Japanese air power operating from scattered island bases in the Pacific. The accretion of additional technology and technique added to the efficiency of carrier operations and to the potential of the carrier as a decisive naval weapon. Wing slots improved airplane control during low-speed landings on carrier decks; brakes improved the movement of aircraft around the carrier deck during takeoff and landing operations; the tempo of takeoff and landing intervals was continually improved; flight deck procedures were generally enhanced. The role of the landing signal officer, one of the more notable contributions of these early years, evolved by chance one day when the *Langley's* executive officer suddenly whipped off his cap and excitedly waved it to warn an incoming plane that its landing approach was too high. Thereafter, the landing signal officer, stationed near the aft deck, used a precise set of flag signals to inform incoming pilots if they were too high, too low, or off center on final approach to the carrier deck. During the 1920s, the Navy also pioneered techniques for night flying from aircraft carriers. As one historian of the era noted, "The ability to launch aircraft during darkness for a dawn attack on a target endowed carrier striking forces with a formidable advantage in the years to come."[28]

The value of this accumulated carrier technology and technique was dramatically demonstrated during the fleet exercises of early 1929, featuring a simulated attack on the Panama Canal. The defending fleet had the *Lexington*, while the attackers deployed both the *Saratoga* and *Langley*, although the latter was still being overhauled and was replaced in the exercises by a surrogate vessel with one seaplane to represent *Langley's* squadron. The key figure in the game was Rear Admiral Joseph Mason Reeves, an innovative and hard-charging officer who had introduced many successful procedures while commanding the *Langley*, and who now flew his pennant from the *Saratoga*. It had been standard practice to keep the carriers in a defensive and protected position behind the battle line, but Reeves convinced the commander of the attacking fleet, Admiral William V. Pratt, to detach *Saratoga* with an escorting cruiser and carry out an independent attack against the canal. With her escort, the *Saratoga* steamed south, wheeled back toward the canal, and penetrated the defending screen of ships in a high-speed dash during the night. Then, the *Saratoga* launched a predawn air strike that achieved total tactical surprise. Umpires assessing the action recorded destruction of critical canal locks as well as heavy damage to Army airfields in the Canal Zone, and the *Saratoga's* planes mauled the few defending fighters that managed to get into the air.

The success of this action not only vindicated the years of struggle for fast carriers and high-performance naval aircraft with radial engines but also conclusively showed the value of night flying tactics and long hours perfecting carefully detailed carrier deck operations. In the years to come, these factors proved to be decisive in the naval actions deciding the outcome of World War II in the Pacific.[29]

In addition to the United States, other nations attempted to define the role of aviation in both land and sea operations, while coping with parsimonious budgets and entrenched conservatism. For the most part, the record remained the same—halting progress, but progress that nonetheless set the stage for modernization and accelerated buildup of air strength in the late 1930s as the storm clouds of World War II began to gather. For the United States and Great Britain in particular, the respectable levels of air strength attained during World War I described a wave cycle of development, dropping to a peacetime equilibrium during the 1920s and early 1930s, and then curved upward again toward wartime levels during the mid to late 1930s.[30]

Aside from numbers and/or potential striking force alone, however, it must be remembered that the era of equilibrium witnessed specific positive developments in the United States. In addition to new bureaucratic viability, the development of improved tactics, strategy, equipment, and techniques for operational support were basic and essential trends in military aviation of the twenties. Many instances involved flight activities that demonstrated the remarkable flexibility of aircraft. During the spring of 1921, U.S. Marine Corps aviators completed highly useful aerial photographic surveys of the Dominican Republic and Haitian coastlines. In 1922, the Navy provided planes and pilots for aerial photography to pinpoint dangerous reefs in the area of Maui, Hawaii, and also supplied seaplanes for Smithsonian Institution scientists surveying mollusks in Florida waters, finishing a year's task in only a few days. Late in the winter of 1924, the Army dispatched a quartet of bombers to Nebraska to drop bombs to break up an ice jam that had raised a serious flood threat along the Platte River. Early in 1925, the dirigible *Los Angeles*, in addition to some two dozen other aircraft, carried scientists and meteorological specialists above cloud-covered New England to make observations of a total solar eclipse. In 1929, when drought created a severe hydroelectric power shortage in Tacoma, Washington, the Navy's big new aircraft carrier *Lexington* tied up at a convenient dock and supplied emergency electricity to the city.[31] Such examples, while perhaps transient, all played a part in the integration of a new technology—aviation— into national life. Additional aspects of military activity not only advanced military aeronautics but played an important role in the progress of civil aviation as well. Many of these developments will be made evident in the chapters that follow.

CHAPTER TWO
Airmail and Airlines

Near the close of World War I, many large business corporations found it desirable to decentralize their operations. Such a move was feasible because of concurrent advances in communications technology, permitting coordination of the scattered segments of the corporation's production facilities. While it may be true that aircraft did not fundamentally alter business planning until after 1930,[1] more and more commercial operations in the 1920s involved regular reliance on aviation because it was a more productive way of doing business. The role of aircraft in commercial activities was recognized by business and trade journals, supported by private and government officials in congressional hearings, and reflected in striking statistical increases for airmail, passengers, and express.

Writing in the *New Republic* just after the end of World War I, Frank E. Hill remarked on flying as a reflection of the "modern world's fever for dispatch." The most striking thing, he said, was that the commercial possibilities of aviation had slowly evolved without the public's awareness of it. Six months earlier, it had been the esoteric province of geniuses and enthusiastic partisans. Suddenly, aviation and commercial potential had arrived. "A knock has come at our door," said Hill; "we are surprised with a myth become reality."[2] Optimistic about the postwar potential of aviation, thoughtful workers in the aviation field suggested a number of functions for aircraft to perform. The designer Donald Douglas emphasized the factor of speed as an important asset of airmail, and pointed out the potential value of air express for shipping fruits, film, repair parts, and similar commodities with low weight and bulk but high value.[3] V. C. Clark, chief engineer of the Dayton-Wright Company, a wartime aircraft manufacturer, asserted that "it will be impossible to prevent aircraft from taking a serious part in the activities of the commercial world." Among other things, Clark suggested that planes could be used to deliver detailed tables and drawings required for planning business operations; these data would enhance the effectiveness of a project as well as save money over telephone and telegraph facilities without significant delay of schedules. He also predicted important advantages in air travel for high-salaried executives, enabling them to save valuable time, with a proportionate gain in working capacity and personal effectiveness.[4]

Although comprehensive transport routes and regular passenger travel lay several years ahead, one existing service already provided some of the advantages stressed by Douglas and Clark. The U.S. Air Mail, operating under the aegis of the Post Office Department, offered American businessmen an important opportunity to speed up business operations by sending correspondence and other materials via the airways.

Airmail Service

The first pilot in the United States to carry mail in an airplane was Earl L. Ovington. During an air meet on Long Island in 1911, he made several authorized flights over a route that covered ten miles, from Nassau Boulevard to Garden City Estates. The whole thing was primarily a stunt, but it demonstrated that the airplane was attracting interest as a potential mail carrier. By 1912, increasing numbers of businessmen gave serious consideration to airmail demonstrations, and the Post Office authorized thirty-one orders for airmail flights in sixteen different states. Occasional experimental and exhibition airmail flights continued for several years,[5] until the Post Office Department decided that the time had come to incorporate airmail as a standard mode of mail delivery.

On May 15, 1918, American postal authorities inaugurated the world's first regularly scheduled airmail service, between New York City, Philadelphia, and Washington, D.C., with planes and pilots furnished by the War Department. It promised to be a colorful operation, with an announced purpose of serving the public while training airmen for military duty and stimulating the fledgling aviation industry.[6] Less sanguine officials in the War Department encouraged the proceedings in order to offset unfavorable publicity about the failure of the Army Air Service to make its mark in the air war in Europe.[7] As it turned out, none of these purposes was served very effectively at the start.

In Washington, the inaugural honors were done by a small but high-level group including President and Mrs. Wilson, Postmaster General A. S. Burleson, and Assistant Secretary of the Navy Franklin Delano Roosevelt. Captain Benjamin Lipsner, who had charge of the airmail operation, was understandably concerned that all should go well, since many people still regarded the operation as a useless stunt. The nation was still gripped in a deadly war, and Lipsner was bluntly told more than once that the whole affair was uncalled for. One serious flap had already occurred when some of the twenty-four-cent airmail stamps had been printed with the center of the vignette inverted, and now the mail plane itself was late in arriving. The plane finally flew in, landed, and was ceremoniously loaded with mail for Philadelphia. Five attempts to start the engine brought only a series of coughs and a billow of black smoke, while the president and his entourage stirred restlessly. Finally, someone checked the fuel tanks, which turned out to be nearly empty. After these had been filled with gas, the engine roared into life, and Lieutenant George Boyle lifted off, just cleared the trees at the edge of the field, and disappeared from sight as the presidential party watched with approval. Lipsner, however, felt an angry pang of renewed frustration. "The first scheduled airmail was in the air," he recalled later, "but it was flying in the wrong direction." Boyle got twenty-five miles away and then had to make a forced landing near a Maryland farm.[8]

Even after the pilots got the direction of their routes properly worked out, the fledgling airmail service left much to be desired. The 218-mile run between New York and Washington was flown by Curtiss JN-4H trainers that cruised along at a sedate seventy miles per hour. Counting the period for mail collection, the trip from post office to airfield, a stop at Philadelphia for transfer to a second plane, and eventual delivery at the end of the line, the elapsed time for posting an airmail letter between New York and Washington came to about four hours—not much better than first-class rail service.[9] As one contemporary authority wryly commented, the route "had little value either as a mail transportation service or as a stimulant to commercial aviation."[10] Nor was there much activity in the way of ordering newly designed aircraft or training new fliers. For years the operations of the airmail depended on war-surplus planes as basic equipment, and the pilots were drawn from the ranks of Army-trained veterans.[11]

In spite of its erratic start, the airmail operation soon developed into a capable organization of professional airmen. On August 12, 1918, the Post Office Department took complete responsibility for airmail operations and hired its own pilots. By the autumn of 1920, a coast-to-coast airmail route had been established from New York west to Cleveland, Chicago, Omaha, and San Francisco. Flying war-surplus de Haviland DH-4s supplied at no cost by the War Department, airmail pilots finally had planes with the capacity, performance, and reliability to make coast-to-coast airmail service worthwhile in day-to-day business activities. With continued improvements in equipment, refinement of maintenance techniques, and a bold plan to develop continuous day and night transcontinental schedules, a significant new communications medium began to take shape.

The DH-4 flown by airmail pilots was something of a hybrid, since the Post Office Department extensively altered the plane to suit the department's particular needs and to eliminate some of the often fatal weaknesses of the aircraft itself. In accordance with procedures established in 1919, each aircraft was subjected to a thorough renovation that included dozens of minor changes as well as several major modifications. Gas tanks were installed in a new position away from the dangerously hot engine surfaces; the forward cockpit was completely made over to hold the bulky cargo of mail sacks; the landing gear was redesigned to bear the added weight of the payload; and the main structural members of the airframe were strengthened. As the DH-4B, the World War I "flaming coffin" became a reliable mail plane with a cruising speed of 100 miles per hour.[12] The 400-hp, water-cooled Liberty motor that powered it also came from well-stocked warehouses of Army surplus. It was a twelve-cylinder V-type engine, designed and produced virtually overnight in a six-month crash program after America's entry into World War I in April 1917. "An excellent synthesis of the state of the art" in comparison with other engines of its day, its shortcomings in the cooling system and gear mechanism were refined in due course, so that "the only weakness remaining was in the exhaust valves, which served well most of the time."[13] With thorough inspection, maintenance, and overhaul procedures, both these wartime veteran planes and engines delivered a satisfactory performance for the Post Office Department[14] and attracted a growing roster of airmail patrons. Restricted by unreliable instruments and a lack of navigational aids for night flying, pilots in the converted DH-4s let the railroad take over when darkness fell on the transcontinental run. But even with all of the stops and transfer of mail sacks, the air-rail combination time of seventy-eight hours was about a full day faster (twenty-two hours) than the best crack-train time of one hundred hours.[15]

Largely because of the time element, the banking industry was the first to employ airmail with regularity. Banks found that airmail was especially useful in reducing the amount of "float," which included idle funds such as checks and other items in process of collection. These idle funds represented unavailable cash and lost opportunities as well as slow-moving capital that accumulated expensive interest hour by hour. Raymond E. Jones, first vice-president of the Bank of Manhattan Company, stated that his company's banks had begun to use airmail with regularity at its beginning as a means to reduce the float factor in financial transactions.[16] Airplane speed could be so useful in banking activities that private air operators sometimes found eager customers in areas outside the existing government routes. Harold Bixby, the St. Louis banker who later helped underwrite Charles A. Lindbergh's transatlantic flight, contracted with a local air service, the Robertson Aircraft Corporation, to speed up the transfer of float between St. Louis and New York. In fact, Bixby's bank virtually subsidized Robertson's entire operation until the company got on its feet. "I met a lot of men who were interested in those early phases of aviation," Bixby recalled, "—remember that this was in 1923."[17]

Looking beyond their initial success in attracting growing numbers of airmail customers, postal officials realized that the real impact of airmail on business operations depended on around-the-clock schedules including night flights across the route segments handled by the railroads. Night runs by air would slash even more hours from transcontinental delivery time and yield important time savings in regional overnight transactions between cities such as Chicago and New York. The first attempt at continuous transcontinental service took place on

February 22, 1921. The severe winter weather was bound to be a problem, but officials of the Wilson administration, who had launched the Post Office's aerial service, were anxious to counter mounting criticism about the costs of mail-plane service with a convincing demonstration of the airmail's potential efficiency. The result was the historic and courageous flight of Jack Knight.

The eastbound mail originated in San Francisco, bound for New York by way of Chicago. Knight picked up the mail in North Platte, Nebraska, where darkness had already fallen, and took off for Omaha, where another plane was scheduled to carry the mail on to Chicago. Arriving in Omaha, Knight discovered that the next plane was still weatherbound in Chicago. He gambled on clearing skies and took off again for Chicago, navigating through the turbulent, icy night with the help of bonfires flickering across Iowa and Illinois. Exhausted, he reached Chicago in the early morning. A fresh pilot took over, and the first transcontinental airmail finally reached New York after an elapsed time of thirty-three hours and twenty minutes.[18] It represented a milestone of flight, but obviously required more than bonfires to function on a regular basis.

In response to this challenge, the U.S. Air Mail's system for night flying constituted a major advance in flight technology. Aided by the equipment and technique of earlier Army Air Service experiments, in 1923 the Post Office began a serious study of lighted airways to allow scheduled cross-country night flights.[19] Planes for the proposed service were rigged with navigation lights in the nautical manner. High-intensity landing lights, much like auto headlamps, were fitted under each lower wing of the DH-4B biplanes, which were also equipped with two parachute flares for emergencies. Revamping the electrical systems of the planes for the new lighting apparatus was the smallest part of the new program. Installing lighting equipment for the landing fields and signal beacons along the entire route proved to be a major undertaking. At night the main air terminals were illuminated by batteries of floodlights and marked by thirty-six-inch rotating beacons developed by Sperry Gyroscope and General Electric. Intermediate emergency fields spaced across the country at twenty-five to thirty-mile intervals had similar equipment in scaled-down versions. Tying the whole system together was a string of flashing acetylene gas beacons developed by the American Gas Accumulator Company, each with a coded flash signal to indicate the distance to the next field. On July 1, 1924, night flying operations commenced on the Chicago-Cheyenne portion of the transcontinental route, previously served by trains. The new all-air coast-to-coast mail delivery averaged about thirty-two hours, nearly three entire days faster than rail service.[20]

The night flights offered dramatic spectacles for inhabitants of towns along the route, as people flocked to watch the night mail arrive and depart. Under banks of floodlights, the plane held center stage while mechanics made it ready and stowed away the mail. Then the pilot clambered aboard, the engine sputtered to life, and the aircraft trundled into position for departure. The engine roared a crescendo, the plane sped down the lighted runway, pulled away from the ground, and dissolved into the maw of the night. En route, pilots navigated from beacon to beacon, though lighted towns along the way were important milestones, particularly in the sparsely populated West. Aviators complained that the industrious westerners went to bed too early. "The towns in Nebraska and Wyoming must all roll up and go to bed at 9 o'clock," grumbled one pilot after a difficult flight from Cheyenne to North Platte.[21]

With the aggressive leadership of Paul Henderson, second assistant postmaster general, the beacons were improved, and within two years the entire transcontinental airway was equipped for nighttime schedules, so that every major population region along the route enjoyed a new era in postal communications. "Of all American contributions to the technique of air transport operation," said the aviation expert E. P. Warner, "this was the greatest." Nothing similar to the scope of this undertaking was developed anywhere in the world for more than six years. As late as 1930, describing the system to European friends, Warner found them "politely incredulous," taking his story as "a manifestation of American bluff." America, on the other hand, had nothing comparable to the international passenger routes pioneered by European airlines during the twenties. In addition to an elaborate network within the continent itself, there were intercontinental extensions through Africa and the Middle East reaching all the way to India.[22] In the long run, the American experience seems to have been more valuable. With the advantage of thousands of miles of air routes within its own geographic boundaries, the United States was able to develop comprehensive long-range, all-weather, day and night operations unhindered by foreign frontiers and overwater hazards. Thus, when modern passenger transports such as the Boeing 247 and DC-3 were introduced in the 1930s, American lines already possessed the expertise to use such equipment to the best advantage. Superiority of technique, as well as equipment, ultimately accounted for the American lead in commercial transport aviation.[23]

As the sophistication of the supporting technology and the efficiency of the airmail service continued to improve during the twenties, the volume of banking and other financial mail began to mount. Important clients included the Federal Reserve Bank and all its branches as well as the major banks in New York, Cleveland, Chicago, Omaha, Cheyenne, Denver, Salt Lake City, Reno, Los Angeles, San Diego, and San Francisco. Paul Henderson, as assistant postmaster general, emphasized that collection time on checks was actually reduced from five days to two, resulting in saving of "enormous sums in actual interest and the release of untold millions in float" that had been tied up in the slower mails.[24] As Raymond Jones, of the Bank of Manhattan, explained, banks all over the country were well aware of the special value of the airmail service for transmitting clearances, saving interest, and reducing float, in addition to speeding the delivery of manifests, bills of lading, bonds, drafts, securities, and stocks. Francis H. Sisson, of the Guaranty Trust Company of New York, agreed. "We have found it most convenient to use the air mail," he said, "and we have found the service of inestimable value."[25]

Having established a permanent clientele and created a workable aircraft transportation system, the government acceded to growing popular sentiment and moved to transfer its operations to private enterprise. With the passage of the Air Mail Act on February 2, 1925 (otherwise known as the Kelly Bill, after its sponsor, Representative Clyde Kelly of Pennsylvania), the Post Office Department contracted for airmail service with privately owned lines. In a move that reflected the transition to another era of commercial aviation, Paul Henderson resigned his position in the Post Office Department to join National Air Transport (NAT), recently formed as one of the bidders for airmail contracts. Along with NAT, the first five companies to win a share of the new business included Colonial Air Lines, Robertson Aircraft Corporation, Varney Speed Lines, and Western Air Express. Further legislation in the form of the Air Commerce Act of 1926 created an

Aeronautics Branch within the Department of Commerce to promote commercial aviation in the United States through construction of additional lighted airways and navigational aids. The director of the Aeronautics Branch, William P. MacCracken, also had authority to license all planes and pilots, including those of the growing scheduled airlines with newly won government mail contracts. Some consolidation inevitably took place: within five years, Colonial and Robertson were incorporated into the American Airlines system; NAT and Varney became part of United Air Lines; Western Air Express evolved into Transcontinental and Western Air, Incorporated (now Trans World Airlines). Other companies such as Braniff Airways, Delta Air Lines, Eastern Air Lines, and Northwest Air Lines made their appearance during the same period.[26]

The availability of mail contracts not only encouraged the formation of viable air transportation companies but also accelerated the introduction of original aircraft designs in the mid-twenties based on the new commercial requirements of flying the mail.[27] The young companies acquired a variety of types, ranging from single-engine biplanes like the Boeing-40 series, which could also squeeze two to four passengers into a forward compartment, to the Ford trimotor monoplane, which carried ten passengers in relative comfort along with a load of mail.[28] These postwar aircraft reflected increased awareness of the significance of wing-load factors relative to payload and speed, and they were designed with a wing loading of about 15 pounds per square foot, as compared to 9.4 for the DH-4B. The cumbersome water-cooled Liberty engines also gave way in the mid-twenties to more efficient air-cooled radials such as the Wright Whirlwind and Pratt and Whitney Wasp series, which appeared in various models from 200 to 450 horsepower. These power plants gave the new commercial aircraft cruising speeds of up to 110 miles per hour.[29] Equipped with such modern planes, the recently formed airlines took over the routes pioneered by the Post Office Department and grew into mature transportation systems.

This was the era in which airline legends were born. Every company has since canonized its cast of legendary characters and acquired its own folklore. While there is no typical aviation leader or airline, the evolution of United Air Lines reflects the sorts of personalities, problems, and series of mergers that characterized much of early airline development. When the Kelly Act established routes for bidding, Walter T. Varney became one of several dozen hopeful aviators who put in an offer. A former World War I pilot, Varney operated a flying service in the San Francisco area. He won the mail contract for a route from Elko, Nevada, to Boise, Idaho, to Pasco, Washington—nobody else had wanted to bid for such an undistinguished-looking system. But Varney cajoled the Post Office into changes that realigned the route from Boise to Salt Lake City to Seattle, so that Varney Air Lines controlled a strategic route segment that linked the Pacific Northwest to important trade centers west of the Rocky Mountains.

Another strategic segment, running up the Pacific coast from Los Angeles to Seattle, belonged to Vern C. Gorst, a former Klondike gold prospector turned bus line magnate. His aggressive airline, Pacific Air Transport, acquired modern Ryan monoplanes and set up its own string of beacons for night flying. But a series of crashes and marginal airmail revenues left him short of cash. Gorst went to the Wells Fargo Bank in San Francisco for a loan to salvage the engine of a plane that had plunged into the Bay. The young banker to whom he talked, William A. ("Pat") Patterson, demurred on the scheme to salvage an engine soaked in saltwater but extended Gorst several thousand dollars for other operational expenses. Prodded by his supervisors, Patterson kept close watch on a business that many bankers, in 1926, regarded as strictly speculative. Eventually, Patterson surrendered a large portion of his monthly salary for an aerial tour of the Bay area. Aviation claimed his adventurous nature, and he eventually signed on as an executive with one of the new airlines.[30]

The catalyst in this series of events was another new airline expanding from its original contract mail routes—Boeing Air Transport. The story of Boeing's fortunes also reflects the evolution of other aircraft manufacturers. Before World War I, William E. Boeing had already accumulated a small fortune from his family's timberlands in the Pacific Northwest. Acquisition of a small boatyard in Seattle (to custom-build his own yacht) led to the discovery of float-equipped aircraft and a series of flying lessons at Glenn Martin's flight school in Los Angeles. During World War I, the Boeing Airplane Company had a contract for Navy seaplanes, but struggled along after the Armistice by turning out wooden furniture in the aftermath of postwar contract cancellations. Using a frail-looking Boeing seaplane, a test pilot and friend, Eddie

Hubbard, flew some mail seventy-four miles across Puget Sound from Seattle to Vancouver Island in Canada. From this first flight in 1919, the Boeing plane continued to carry mail for inbound and outbound ships on the Orient routes, speeding up the mail-handling process. As one of the earliest international airmail routes, it kept Boeing's name alive in aviation circles and continued to operate into the mid-1920s, giving Boeing a useful, if limited, background in airline operations.

Other developments in the early 1920s revived the Boeing Airplane Company as a manufacturer, momentarily pushing its airline into the background. The Army and Navy slowly began to upgrade and modernize their postwar air forces. From the Army, Boeing got a contract to build some pursuit planes designed by the Thomas-Morse Company (the MB-3A), and then won a contract for its own pursuit design, the PW-9. The company also received production orders from the Navy for a new trainer, the NB-1, and started work on a successful family of Navy fighter planes. When Eddie Hubbard, William Boeing's ambitious young airline pilot, wanted to bid on some newly opened mail routes in 1926, the company mustered a combination of knowledge, finances, and production skills that was hard to beat.

The new routes advertised by the Post Office in the fall of 1926 spanned the continent along the main airmail trunk line. The government offered two separate segments from New York to Chicago, and from Chicago to San Francisco. Logically, Boeing expressed interest in the western segment, even though the route passed over the formidable vastness of the towering Rockies. But William Boeing listened to his advisers, who were convinced that a new Boeing mail plane, the Model 40, possessed the sort of performance to meet the route's challenging geography. The plane's promise rested largely on an efficient radial engine, the Pratt and Whitney Wasp. Although Wasp production was dedicated to the Navy, Frederick Rentscher, president of the recently formed Pratt and Whitney organization, was an old friend of Boeing. Together they persuaded the Navy to release twenty-five engines for the new Model 40A, which turned in a dazzling performance on its trial runs in 1927.

Vern Gorst wanted to purchase some of the speedy new mail planes for Pacific Air Transport, but could not afford the Model 40A's price tag of $25,000. Instead, he took the advice of his trusted friend and banker, Pat Patterson, to sell out to Boeing.[31] The new acquisition

added the potentially lucrative Pacific coast route to Boeing's successful bid for the Chicago–San Francisco run, and helped set the stage
for a series of rapid mergers and corporate reorganization. The Boeing
Airplane and Transport Corporation appeared in 1928, and Pat Patterson left Wells Fargo to join it. A year later, Boeing joined forces with
Rentscher's Pratt and Whitney to form United Aircraft and Transport
Corporation, a holding company that picked up Varney Air Lines along
with several other airline operators and manufacturing companies. Even
though New Deal regulation later separated the transport companies
from the manufacturers, Patterson's star was set, and he eventually
became president of United Air Lines when the holding company
originally set in motion by Boeing was forced to split up (see Chapter
6, below).[32] The legacy of Varney, Gorst, Boeing, Patterson, and others like them remained in the expanding network of mail and passenger routes across the country.

Flying routes did not immediately proliferate all over the United
States, however, and there were certain instances when government
facilities were required on an ad hoc basis. In the spring of 1927, Hap
Arnold was ordered to Rapid City, South Dakota, to confer with a
representative of the White House Secret Service. Arnold learned
that President Coolidge was due to arrive in the Black Hills for his
vacation, and Arnold was to organize a special Air Corps detachment
to fly high-priority presidential mail to the chief executive's summer
retreat. Regular airline service carried the mail from Washington to
North Platte, Nebraska, where one of Arnold's Army pilots would pick
it up, and then fly north to Rapid City. Coolidge was adamant that this
special service should operate every Tuesday and Thursday, rain or
shine. Hesitant to risk his pilots in threatening weather, Arnold prudently worked out a quiet arrangement with postal officials to make
sure that Coolidge had some mail every Tuesday and Thursday, even
if Air Corps pilots remained earthbound.[33] Despite this occasional
subterfuge, these plans for airborne delivery of priority presidential
mail reflected the flexibility and value of rapid aerial communications.

Financial institutions, the first important clients of the government
Air Mail Service, consigned an even greater volume of mail to the
expanding commercial airline systems. By the autumn of 1927, to cite
one example, savings for the Kansas City Clearinghouse averaged $6,375
to $7,500 per month.[34] The *Journal of Commerce* outlined the prac-

tice in use by twenty-one leading banks in New York to speed up business with Cleveland and Chicago in an effort to limit periods of idle funds because of the Federal Reserve System deferred-availability schedule. Picking out their largest checks on Cleveland and Chicago, the New York banks put them in airmail envelopes along with individual telegrams. On delivery at Chicago and Cleveland, the telegrams were sent back to the Reserve Bank in New York, where the items were credited to the New York banks and the funds deemed to be immediately available. For the month of May 1928, the twenty-one banks saved interest amounting to $5,700 on a total of $52,000,000 in checks that met the clearing time deadlines earlier than usual. One bank soon earmarked a daily average of $750,000 in checks for airmail delivery, since that service saved a full day's interest on that amount.[35]

Meanwhile, regularly scheduled airmail service helped speed up other commercial operations in a multitude of ways. Many businesses with a trade area encompassing a radius of 500 miles and more became regular patrons of postal air service. They paid the higher airmail rates willingly in order to gain the advantages of a faster tempo in correspondence, which, in turn, yielded meaningful economies in stepping up the rate of handling goods, the application of capital, and utilization of executive time.[36] Oil shippers, from California to the Gulf coast, saved days in time and thousands of dollars annually by using airmail to forward bills of lading. In other cases, airmail proved fast enough to slice expenses in business usually handled by telegraph and wire service. Advertising agencies sent copy all over the country in mail planes rather than use the more costly telegraph. Citrus growers in California dispatched their cargo manifests by air instead of wiring them to the East. Managers of apple orchards in Oregon expedited their selling orders and railway-car tracers the same way. For similar reasons, mailings from railroads such as the Pennsylvania, Baltimore and Ohio, New York Central, Burlington, and Union Pacific poured into the airmail terminals. Millions of dollars each day were consigned to Wall Street in the form of checks, drafts, and interest-bearing securities, all stowed away in bulging airmail sacks. In 1928, New York City alone received $7 billion delivered by airmail and air express.[37] Thus the airmail continued to implement the increasing volume and pace of business activities of the 1920s with a consequent influence on American life.

At the end of the fiscal year, June 30, 1929, new aviation facilities in the United States included sixty-one passenger lines, forty-seven mail lines, and thirty-two express lines, all serving trade areas that contained ninety million people; the volume of airmail ballooned from 810,555 pounds in 1926 to 7,772,014 pounds in 1929.[38] William P. MacCracken admitted that Lindbergh's extensive air tour of the United States following his transatlantic flight had much to do with publicizing airmail and increasing the poundage in 1927.[39] There was also some skullduggery when the contract lines were struggling for survival. Since government payments were made by the pound, many contractors would send a postcard to a friend by registered mail, which required a mail sack secured by a heavy lock. "They made a hell of a lot of money on that postal card," one contemporary remarked.[40] In the latter years of the twenties, however, the climbing volume of airmail was due to its own utility. The airmail was appreciated enough that intense political pressures were brought to bear in order to secure service for areas beyond the reach of existing routes in Georgia, Michigan, and South Dakota.[41] "Use of the airmail is now such an integral part of the business machinery," asserted one contemporary author, "that if anything should arise to injure or destroy it, the hurt would be felt immediately by the commerce of the nation."[42]

Personnel and Procedures

The achievement of dependable airmail service was not without a cost, and the tenacity of the airmail fliers was resolute. When the government began to surrender operations to private lines in 1925, only nine men were alive of the forty pilots originally hired by the Post Office Department. In spite of this melancholy toll, the mail was delivered with amazing regularity: 94 percent in 1921 and 96.5 percent of all scheduled flights in 1922. Private operators were able to improve but little on that record by the end of the twenties.[43] In addition to the courage of the men who flew the mail, dependability resulted from operational procedures that slowly and painstakingly evolved. One of the airmail's most important legacies to the development of air transport concerned regular maintenance schedules that saved thousands of dollars and kept airplanes ready to fly. Along with this came the practical experience necessary for the proper care of vulnerable components that characterized flying equipment of the early 1920s. When mail planes flew through rainstorms, rain drops struck wooden propellers with such velocity that they became damaged and out of balance, and so ground crews learned to cover the leading edges with tape (and, later, metal) for protection. Another homely problem involved engine repairs. After tearing down and reassembling an engine, mechanics often found they could not realign the main bearings, a condition that suggested a bent crankshaft. The mechanics concluded that casually leaning the crankshaft against the wall of a hangar while other work proceeded was enough to put the supposedly indestructible shaft a fraction out of line (although dropping the shaft seems a more likely cause). In any case, crews built a special cradle to hold the crankshaft while overhauls were in progress. All of these seemingly inconsequential problems were lessons to be absorbed and passed on as the airmail and commercial aviation, under the relentless regimen of schedules, grew up.[44]

Ground crews also learned to labor around the clock in all kinds of weather. One author who surveyed the transcontinental run in the winter of 1926 came away with a vivid memory of the preparations at Cheyenne, Wyoming, as ground crews readied a plane to fly out the eastbound mail. It was midnight, and the thermometer read 36° F below zero as snow fell. The Cheyenne ground crew struggled in a temporary shelter, since fire had recently gutted the hangar. Working quickly, the crew prepared the water-cooled engine with sixteen gallons of boiling water and twelve gallons of heated oil. Three mechanics joined hands to pull through the prop to start the engine—carefully, since the icy footing and whirling prop made a treacherous combination. It was important to get the engine running in only a few tries; otherwise the men had to work fast to drain the oil and water, reheat it, and repeat the process.[45]

Airmail pilots, both government and contract, faced other kinds of problems. With many flights at night and during bad weather, the pilots became very much interested in instruments, but the panels of planes like the DH–4 came sparsely furnished with dials and gauges, and the rudimentary equipment usually failed to function. Altimeters rarely worked at all, and the airspeed indicator, activated by air pressure, was connected to the Pitot tube on the leading edge of the lower wing, a position that kept it constantly clogged by mud from unsurfaced landing fields. A gyroscopic turn indicator often remained the most useful for flying a straight course in cloud bank, since compasses frequently oscillated as much as 90° off the proper heading. Pilots learned to pay heed to the sound of the engine and the hum of wind through the bracing wires to determine if they were in an inadvertent climb or dive while trying to fly on instruments.[46]

Completing a successful cross-country mail run was best accomplished by careful observation of landmarks en route. Mail pilots in the twenties had no detailed flight charts, and generally relied on state road maps, although such maps normally marked only towns having post offices, with no information at all concerning hills, mountains, or other hazards poking into the air. Fliers in the Post Office Department compiled their own *Book of Directions* for major routes, a rather informal compendium describing railroad tracks, highway junctions, golf courses, and polo fields along the way. Pilots also kept up their own "little black books" with vital statistics ranging from notations about threatening church steeples to farms with telephones, useful to call for help after an emergency landing. These minute items of information were crucial for flying in bad weather, when pilots often let down to fifty feet in order to see their way from ground references. Byron Moore, a veteran of such adventures, recounted a foul-weather formula for landing at one field on his route:

> When you come to the fork in the road, get up on the left side to miss that silo; after you cross the railroad tracks pull up into the soup [fog], count to thirty, then let down—that way you'll miss the high tension lines; when the highway angles left, take the fourth dirt road and follow it to the ravine—just across the ravine is the airport.

Following railroad tracks, familiarly known as the "iron compass," was a standard ploy, though one that had to be used judiciously in some parts of the country. One airmail pilot, fighting a snowstorm, flew glued to a course just above the Southern Pacific tracks when the rails suddenly disappeared into a mountain tunnel. With the throttle wide open, the pilot jerked his plane into a steep climb, snagging a clump of sagebrush with the tail skid as the airplane skimmed over the summit. Other hazards conspired to force down pilots while en route, resulting in the classic report from Dean Smith, who sent his superiors the following dispatch: "On trip 4 westbound. Flying low. Engine quit.

Only place to land on cow. Killed cow. Wrecked plane. Scared me. Smith."[47]

The young men who flew the mail were necessarily a hardy lot, willing to pit their flying skills against considerable odds. When Dean Smith joined the government's Air Mail Service in 1920, it was "considered pretty much a suicide club." In open-cockpit biplanes, the constant exposure to cold air was one of the worst hardships, especially in winter. Even in heavy flying suits, pilots became so bitterly chilled and benumbed that judgment was impaired. Flying became a struggle of endurance and nerves. Many times, Byron Moore recalled, he remained in the cockpit several minutes after landing, for all appearances taking extra care to fill out his logbook. Actually, he was stalling for time, because he felt he could not talk evenly quite yet, and he did not want the mechanic to know he was still shaking. Whether for nerves or warmth, many pilots carried liquor when they flew, and most maintained their drinking habits when off duty. One flier of the era could remember only one pilot who did not drink— Charles Lindbergh.[48]

It would be easy to overdraw the image of the individualistic, hard-drinking, fatalistic mail pilot. Flying the mails was not the safest job in the world, to be sure, and the pilots were not inclined to embark on patently foolhardy flights. There was a growing tendency among these fliers to view themselves as professionals. During the early years of the government air mail service, fliers found it necessary to take issue with bureaucrats who insisted that the mail must go through, disregarding the fragile nature of the aircraft in service and the lack of truly reliable instruments for blind flying. During the summer of 1919, a spate of particularly nasty weather resulted in fifteen crashes and two deaths within a two-week period. A number of worried pilots agreed to support each other by refusing to fly, if ordered to do so, when the weather was too ominous. Two veteran fliers subsequently refused to take off in foggy weather with visibility down to a hundred yards. Both were dismissed. The Post Office Department then faced an incipient pilot's strike, and the affair made front-page news and stirred talk of congressional investigations from Capitol Hill. A pilots' committee finally negotiated a settlement with officials from the Post Office Department. The fliers won some concessions—improved pay, reinstatement of one of the pilots, and a more equitable arrangement for determining flying weather—but the stage was set for further disputes with management.

Following the transfer of the airmail routes to private contractors after the Kelly Bill of 1925, several groups sought to speak for the nation's commercial pilots. The most representative was the National Air Pilots Association (NAPA), formed in 1928. NAPA remained a comparatively loose organization, with an executive secretary as the only salaried official. Although many pilots kept up their NAPA dues, they still felt that the organization lagged in pressing for improved wage scales and working conditions. Yet, NAPA and similar groups of the 1920s represented "a clear pattern of organizational activity" among the airline pilots, and led to the formation of the Air Line Pilots Association in 1931. This organization became a powerful union, symbolizing the growing professionalism within the ranks of pilots during the post–World War I decade.[49]

Commercial Passenger Flying

Even before the Kelly Bill of 1925 launched successful commercial airline routes in the United States, several attempts were made to establish private airline enterprises. American promoters were evidently encouraged by activity in Europe, where, within three years after the Armistice, France boasted eight regularly scheduled lines, England three, and Germany two. National rivalries in postwar Europe spurred airline development, although disrupted surface transportation on the Continent immediately after the war encouraged airline routes. Flying also avoided time-consuming harassments when cars, buses, and trains were halted for inspection at every national frontier. Many travelers chose airlines to avoid delays in crossing the English Channel, and Americans in Europe bought airline seats for the same reasons. In fact, the majority of passengers in cross-Channel flights in the peak summer season were United States citizens.[50]

In the United States, a wave of postwar enthusiasm for airlines generated numerous plans for passenger services. One scheme was advanced by Alfred Lawson, a pioneer aeronautical publisher and promoter. During World War I, Lawson organized a small manufacturing company in Wisconsin and produced a few single-engine training aircraft at the war's end. He conceived the idea of a large multi-engine passenger airliner, and set his talented engineering staff (including Vincent Burnelli) to work on it. Completed in 1919, the Lawson C-2 twin-engine biplane could seat twenty-six passengers and boasted a range of four hundred miles. With plans to start a mail and passenger line between Chicago and New York, Lawson cannibalized the C-2 after a demonstration flight to Washington, D.C., and built an even larger passenger plane, the L-4, replete with sleeping berths and a shower bath. But the L-4 crashed during its first takeoff in 1921, and Lawson was forced to abandon his hopes for an aeronautical empire. Lawson's efforts are worth noting, for the C-2 and L-4 were the first multiengine planes in the United States designed and built as passenger airliners at a time when most aviation ventures there and abroad were attempting to utilize converted military aircraft, with cramped seating, on passenger routes. The concept of an air transport specifically produced for passenger service anticipated a major American industry of the future.[51]

Still, aviation fever infected many investors, although some airline studies suggested problems as well as potential profits. In 1922 one such project was sponsored by the Security Trust and Savings Bank of Los Angeles. The bank was considering a route from Los Angeles to San Francisco, and expected the run to appeal to businessmen, lawyers, doctors, and other travelers who wanted to save time. The bank felt that such a service would be valuable to lecturers, singers, and theatrical stars making appearances in both cities. The problem was to win the confidence of prospective patrons. As the bank's report stated, "If popular timidity of aerial flights is dispelled by ample demonstration that airplanes can fly over long distances, regularly and without accident, an aerial service established at Los Angeles should have advantages for attracting tourists possessed by few other cities." Another interested group was the American Airway Transport Company, formed by a combination of leading Milwaukee businessmen. Airway Transport tackled the problem with very serious intentions, and even arranged a special visit by the famous European designer and builder Anthony H. G. Fokker. To prepare a commercial prospectus, the Milwaukee group also hired F. W. Walker, a consulting engineer who apparently had a good reputation in transportation and engineering problems. Walker completed his study for a proposed airline in 1922, and concluded that commercial aviation could not be made to pay in the United States. The directors relieved Walker and decided to continue because they felt it was the duty of American businessmen to lend funds for the worthy cause of initial experimentation.[52]

Even though some businessmen claimed to back aviation for philanthropic reasons, it seems likely that they were lured also by the promise of substantial profits. One memorandum for a Los Angeles–San Francisco run proposed charging passengers eight dollars apiece to make the trip in a four-passenger plane. Over a twelve-month period, the organizers expected to carry nearly sixty thousand fares and realize a profit of 41 percent. But 41 percent was nothing compared to the estimate of another group for a Chicago–New York line, which expected to see a return of no less than 127 percent on its initial investment.[53]

Most of these ambitious schemes never got into the air. Travel in the United States was not impaired by inconveniences like national frontiers, as in Europe, and existing train schedules for longer American distances were better than passenger air routes, which came nowhere near the comfort and dependability of overnight Pullman service.[54] Nevertheless, a few passenger lines appeared, representing enthusiastic efforts to promote commercial aviation at a time when the government airmail was making headlines. One of the most interesting developments of the early postwar era involved Aeromarine West Indies Airways. Aeromarine inherited an experimental foreign airmail contract between Key West, Florida, and Havana from a predecessor in 1920. Equipment consisted of a trio of Curtiss-type 75 flying boats, a converted version of the Navy's F-5L patrol plane. Optimistically christened *The Nina*, *The Pinta*, and *The Santa Maria*, each plane seated a total of eleven to fourteen passengers. A contemporary description stressed the plane's passenger amenities, with "comfortably upholstered reclining chairs from which the passengers can gaze upon the underlying panorama through regular portholes fitted with curtains." A photograph of the plane's interior showed that the curtains were window shades with heavy tassels. The "comfortably upholstered reclining chairs" looked suspiciously like wicker chairs, often utilized because of their lightness. Access to the seating was probably a bit inconvenient since passengers had to use topside hatches of the plane's cabin and climb down a ladder.[55]

Still, one of the principal advantages was that of the time saved. Passengers on their way to Cuba often had to wait eight hours after getting off the train at Key West and then make an overnight boat trip to Havana; Aeromarine planned to make the 100-mile flight in seventy-five minutes. Many patrons were thirsty Americans anxious to escape the rigors of Prohibition in the United States. Besides appealing to the parched traveler in a hurry, the line expected to appeal to those wanting to escape seasickness, "while the enchantment the aerial traveler experiences aloft will offer a further inducement to go via the air route."[56]

All things considered, Aeromarine performed well during its existence. The line operated during the winter season, December 15 to April 15, making daily departures from Key West at 10:30 A.M., and starting the return trip from Havana at 3:30 P.M. the same day. Business developed so well that the line expanded into Southern, New York, and Great Lakes divisions. The following statistics indicate the extent of the airline's operations from November 1, 1921, to November 1, 1922.[57]

> *Southern Division.* 268,535 passenger miles were flown in 744 flights, and 2,388 passengers carried. The services maintained included Key West–Havana, Miami, Bimini, Nassau and Palm Beach, also special flights from New York to points in Florida and Cuba.
>
> *New York Division.* 57,658 passenger miles were flown in 807 flights, and 2,380 passengers were carried. The services maintained included New York–Atlantic City, New York–New England points, and New York–Aerial Sightseeing.
>
> *Great Lakes Division* (Detroit-Cleveland line). 412,854 passenger miles were flown in 574 flights, and 4,388 passengers were carried. The services maintained included a twice-daily service between Cleveland and Detroit; sightseeing flights on Lake Erie and Lake St. Clair; also special flights from New York to Cleveland and Detroit via Albany, Montreal, and Buffalo.

Within one year, this company made 2,125 flights and flew 739,047 passenger miles without accident to a single employee or passenger. Of special interest was the twice-daily service between Detroit and Cleveland, beginning in the summer of 1922. In spite of its short operating time, this Detroit-Cleveland service carried almost as many passengers as the other two divisions combined, even though the twenty-five-dollar rate for the ninety-minute flight from Detroit to Cleveland was high, in comparison with nine dollars by rail and five dollars by steamer.[58]

For all of its notable activity and progress, Aeromarine finally had to suspend operations in 1924. There was no big subsidy or a liberal mail contract on its routes to make it a really paying operation, and its passenger volume proved to be limited.[59] As one observer put it,

> Aeromarine hauled passengers and thereby started commercial aviation off on its left foot. The enterprise was launched on the theory that the public was ready to fly, and the public was not. . . . The normal human being is distrustful of air travel for himself, and all the comparative fatality statistics that can be compiled cannot be expected to get him off the ground for a while yet. . . . Aeromarine had the enormous resistance of human fear to overcome at the outset.[60]

Nevertheless, the story of Aeromarine West Indies Airways remains one of the most interesting in the progress of aviation in America. Through its activities, Aeromarine probably contributed more to the development of commercial air transportation than any other operation at that time, with the exception of the airmail.[61]

The failures of Aeromarine and other fledgling concerns underscored the value of adequate mail contracts from the government that paid well enough to promise a profit. The Kelly Bill of 1925 offered an invaluable cushion for companies that still looked forward to the time when carrying passengers in airliners might become a principal reason for commercial aviation. In the mid-twenties, this period of transition generally meant an awkward situation for potential passengers. By 1927, adventurous souls with $400 for the fares could theoretically piece together a thirty-two-hour transcontinental flying trip in a variety of open-cockpit two-place biplanes and enclosed-cabin four-place Boeing 40-B4s. Since the airlines' chief revenue still came from government postal contracts with payments computed on a straight poundage basis, passengers had to sign a proviso that allowed them to be dumped anywhere along the line if the company could pick up a more lucrative cargo of mail.[62] Under such conditions, many would-be patrons remained earthbound. Even the first regularly scheduled transcontinental passenger operations in 1929, like the early airmail, turned over their passengers to the railroads at dusk.[63]

But in the meantime, daytime passenger airline services on a regional basis began to develop in the mid-twenties as numerous new airlines, organized primarily to operate over the government's contract airmail routes, acquired a variety of new aircraft that could also carry two to four passengers—sometimes in enclosed cabins, sometimes not. Either way, seating accommodations were decidedly cramped. On routes that seemed likely to generate increased passenger traffic, some companies equipped themselves with larger transport planes like the Boeing, Fokker, and Ford trimotors, carrying anywhere from eight to sixteen passengers in comparatively spacious, fully enclosed cabins. At speeds of about 120 miles per hour, these planes boasted ranges of 600 to 800 miles. With the luxury of more available cabin space and longer flying times, airlines added passenger amenities such as stewards who served luncheons while en route, although "comfort stops" for bodily functions were synchronized with passenger and/or refueling stops on the ground.[64] Still, the airlines lured increasing numbers of time-pressed travelers into the sky as Americans attempted to squeeze more working hours into their crowded schedules.

The extensive use of trimotored equipment during this period reflected something of a lag in engine development. Existing power plants were neither husky nor reliable enough for large passenger transports with the twin-engine configuration in case one engine failed. In spite of the "disastrously inefficient" drag factor of the trimotor arrangement, a trio of engines provided a comforting margin of power and safety, and so the Fokkers and Fords acquired by American lines in 1926 typically mounted three 220-hp Wright J-5 Whirlwinds, with more powerful engines substituted as subsequent models of the planes were introduced.[65] Thus it was that many passengers made their first flights in one of these ungainly but workable examples of aeronautical compromise. After completing a business flight with four colleagues through a number of southern states in the spring of 1928, one pioneering passenger endorsed airplanes as a calm and fruitful way to travel.[66] It must be admitted that these adventurous companions were visiting a gentle climate in a stable season, for business flying in those early years was not always a sedate experience. It was necessary to shout to be heard in a Ford trimotor in full flight, and on cold winter days the cabin temperature hovered at 50° F. Nor would a businessman flying coast to coast include five days fogged in at Omaha as part of a "fruitful" commercial journey. Nevertheless, a traveler who had endured all these tribulations still commended the airways. One should check the safety reputation of an airline, he cautioned, but if it seemed adequate, one certainly ought to fly. "You will save a lot of time and come down safely," he added reassuringly.[67]

An engaging chronicle of one man's business trips can be found in *Records of an Airplane Passenger in 1928 and 1929*, by Frederick Arthur Poole, Jr. Poole was impressed enough by his journeys to record them in this elegant little volume that he had privately printed in twenty-five copies. The illustrations are protected with textured opaque facings, and the thirty-one gilt-topped pages have deckled edges. The text is a spare hour-and-minute record of Poole's business flights in executive and commercial aircraft, a series of impressions on the spur of the moment that evokes a picture of personal, homely aerial journeys that ended when planes began to fly across the continent at five or six miles up. Poole flew at one thousand feet and ninety miles per hour, a combination that allowed him to have fun watching as the plane caught the attention of cattle, sheep, horses, pigs, and chickens before they scattered. Pilots sometimes followed the Mississippi at a height of fifty feet, leisurely climbing to miss the bridges and then letting down again to good-naturedly buzz traffic in the river. After one flight turned back because of fog, fares were refunded, and the steward dispensed sandwiches and ginger ale all around.[68]

Despite such occasional inconveniences, an advertisement by the National City Company, bankers in New York, appearing in the *Review of Reviews* in 1929, suggested that flying on business had indeed attained a reasonable degree of prestige and acceptance by the end of the decade. The illustration depicted a man with a briefcase, purposefully striding toward a waiting plane. The accompanying copy noted that people lived at a fast tempo, reflected by this busy executive using a swift airliner to attend an important meeting.[69]

The statistics indicated a growing inclination to fly on business as the number of United States airline passengers climbed from 5,782 in 1926 to 173,405 (including 13,654 fares to foreign nations) in 1929.[70] Although commercial aviation was not really competitive with bus and

Plate 1

Plate 2

1. The Martin MB-2 bomber, mainstay of the Army's long-range bombardment capability of the early 1920s. *NASM.*

2. A phosphorous bomb, dropped by an MB-2, explodes over one of the ships sunk in bombing trials during 1921. *NASM.*

Plate 3

Plate 4

Plate 5

Plate 6

Plate 7

3. The Curtiss P-6 *Hawk.* Its "Vee-type" powerplant with streamlined engine housing, increased use of metal fuselage panels, and metal propeller were hallmarks of progress by the late twenties and early thirties. *NASM.*

4. The Navy's first aircraft carrier, the U.S.S. *Langley. NASM.*

5. The U.S.S. *Saratoga,* commissioned in 1928, launches biplane fighters during a training exercise. *Stuart Collection, NASM.*

6. A crew in Omaha loads the forward mail compartment of a DH-4 which could carry four hundred pounds of mail. *Dewell Collection, NASM.*

7. After the Airmail Act of 1926, private operators took over the airmail routes and introduced new planes such as the Curtiss *Carrier Pigeon. NASM.*

Plate 8

Plate 9

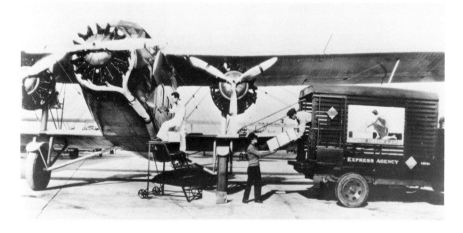

8. One of the Curtiss flying boats converted for Aeromarine West Indies Airways. *NASM*.

9. The Boeing 80A of 1929. On United Air Lines midcontinent routes, this plane could carry up to eighteen passengers and offer coast-to-coast service of twenty-seven hours. *NASM*.

rail transportation until after 1945, the airlines' clientele was an influential one. High-level businessmen comprised the bulk of airline fares, and the social effect of mobility, even in the twenties, was probably greater than the figures suggest, as more and more companies were encouraging their top men to patronize the airlines.[71] One survey in 1929 showed that most American passengers were traveling for reasons of business, and that some eighty leading corporations allowed employees and executives on company business to put air fares on expense accounts.[72] It is not surprising that most airline fares were drawn from major population centers. In the spring of 1930, one airline kept a record of the name and address of every passenger it carried, and over one month-long period it was noted that about 48 percent of the airline's business originated in seven large metropolitan areas. At the same time, the company also found a remarkably wide geographic patronage reflected in the clientele of 2,500, which was drawn from 42 states and 407 different cities.[73]

Air Express and Air Cargo

Another aspect of commercial aviation, cargo by air, had a prophetic, if unsuccessful, inauguration in the winter of 1919, when the American Railway Express (ARE), predecessor of the Railway Express Agency, loaded 1,100 pounds of freight in a converted Handley-Page bomber bound for Chicago. Frozen radiators delayed the start from Washington, and the plane was finally forced down on the way, making an ignominious landing on a race track in Ohio. Undaunted by this initial failure, the company closely followed the progress of aviation in the ensuing years, and made new plans in 1927 for the commercial airlines to fly express. National Air Transport and Colonial Air Transport offered service to the East, while Boeing Air Transport and Western Air Express covered the West. Depending on the length of the haul, rates varied from twenty-five to fifty cents for each quarter-pound or fifty cubic inches. Shortly after midnight on September 1, 1927, National Air Transport started the first run from Chicago to New York with a conglomerate consignment of newsreels, machinery parts, advertising copy, trade journals, candy, and Paris garters.[74]

The availability of air express proved to be of immediate value to American companies. Production-line shutdowns were averted when air express delivered magneto parts to Detroit and auto lamps to St. Louis. A printing plant on a twenty-four-hour schedule lost only hours rather than days when a replacement part was shipped by air from Connecticut to Illinois. There was a manufacturer who produced one of his specialty items near its normal markets, shipping out small orders to more distant points, even though he had other plants in those territories. One day he received a substantial rush order from a distant place close to one of his plants. Filling the order at the regular plant to send out as usual would involve excessive freight charges and a time-consuming rail haul. The manufacturer solved both of these problems by flying the necessary tools to the distant plant, which then filled the production order on schedule. Paul Henderson, a vice-president of National Air Transport, cited these cases to underscore the usefulness of aviation in paring inventories of small-bulk, expensive parts and materials. Occasional air cargo shipments could effect substantial economies by reducing the size and carrying charges on inventory. Retail stores throughout the country soon made everyday use of air delivery to restock supplies of light-weight items.[75] Even if a business could not use air shipments on a regular basis, it could still operate at closer inventory tolerance without extreme danger. "Not one item out of a thousand may have to be shipped by air," acknowledged the authoritative journal *Factory and Industrial Management*, "but the fact that any one of the thousand *can* be shipped by air, if it is necessary, on a few hours' notice, makes it safe to lower the reserve a little all along the line."[76]

Imaginative plans to transport various other commodities by air, including perishables, soon followed. Western Air Express equipped itself with "refrigerator" planes to fly shrimp from Mexico, where they cost ten cents per pound, to Los Angeles, where the price was sixty cents. When Pan American began Caribbean operations in 1929, the line experimented with airborne shipments of hatching eggs to Guatemala. A solid success, the trial run eventually developed into a service delivering thousands of live baby chicks all over Latin America.[77]

Airline officials were disappointed that air express did not generate anticipated revenues.[78] On the other hand, a definite upswing in volume was verification that more and more businessmen found the service worthwhile. From 45,859 pounds in 1927, air express climbed to 257,443 pounds in 1929, and topped one million pounds per year by

1931. The routes of the ARE, moreover, did not constitute a monopoly on air express. Henry Ford's private airline, which ran mainly from Detroit to Chicago, Cleveland, and Buffalo, carried one million pounds of company freight when it started in 1925, and averaged better than three million pounds annually by the close of the decade.[79] To commercial airline operators, the high volume of Ford's activity represented a broader market that remained to be exploited. But they could not get agreement from officials of the express agency, who argued for premium rates in commercial air express operations. The expense of air express probably discouraged many customers, since shipping a 100-pound cargo by air express could cost as much as $100, whereas rail express charges totaled only $4.50.[80]

There were several commercial airlines that successfully offered air express services on an independent basis. A pioneer in commercial air freight about 1920, the service of the Thompson Airplane Company in the Detroit, Lansing, and Saginaw area included the delivery of auto parts. Another interesting commercial carrier not affiliated with ARE was the Kohler Aviation Corporation, which operated three Loening single-engine, biplane amphibians in a daily shuttle of 125 miles over Lake Michigan between Milwaukee and Grand Rapids. Kohler commenced operations in the autumn of 1929, offered deferred service to prospective shippers, and soon established its freight charges close to the same level as those of ordinary rail express. Without the burden of high rates, Kohler's 125-mile run carried 13,000 pounds of freight per month and threatened to outclass the combined air routes of the ARE, which encompassed some 12,000 miles.[81]

By 1929, the vague outlines of aviation's function in commercial operations had emerged into sharper focus, vindicating the confidence expressed years before by Donald Douglas and V. C. Clark. If not a revolutionary change, the development of the DH-4B nonetheless marked a notable improvement in capability and reliability, advancing the state of the art of communications by aircraft. Despite their limitations, such second-hand types provided an advantageous service and attracted a clientele. Moreover, the DH-4B possessed the capability to benefit from the existence of the transcontinental lighted airway. The combination of these two factors—the airplane and the "guidance system"—into a twenty-four-hour operation that put the West Coast some three days closer to New York meant a signal advance in postal communications. After 1925, a new generation of engines and transport aircraft of original design created new opportunities for businessmen in terms of air express and passenger travel, in addition to business mail. Through continued development, aviation technology attracted increased endorsement from the country's businessmen. This commitment, as well as the evolution of operational skills and a firm technological base, contributed to the emergence of aviation as an integral factor in the conduct of business and established the pattern of airline development in the United States.[82]

Part Two
AIRCRAFT AT WORK

CHAPTER THREE

From Barnstorming to Business Flying

As military aviation struggled to find its place in America's defense establishment and government Air Mail gave way to scheduled commercial airline and air express service, another sector of the American aeronautical scene began to carve out a different niche in the twenties. Sometimes called "private aviation" in the post–World War I era, it is known today as "general aviation," a sort of aeronautical catchall for a variety of aircraft performing a myriad of activities. Planes in this category were generally smaller than those used on airline routes by the close of the twenties, and were flown in a remarkable variety of roles: training, pleasure, business, agricultural dusting, photography, air shows, cargo. A specific definition of the general aviation sector, therefore, was not always easy, and general aviation aircraft, even in the twenties, included airline planes like the Ford trimotor. Nevertheless, whatever the activity or size of airplane employed, the general aviation sector emerged in the twenties as a significant element in the framework of American aviation.

The Barnstormers

An airplane can be used to do hundreds of things, and the fliers who did most of these first were called the "flying gypsies" of the twenties. These gypsies were the offspring of the postwar demobilization, born in the spring and summer of 1919 when the government released its cadres of service fliers and hundreds of serviceable military aircraft. The most popular, and least expensive, surplus plane was the Curtiss JN-4, better known as the Jenny, a tandem-cockpit, two-place biplane produced as a primary trainer during World War I. More than 8,000 JN-4 types were manufactured, of which 2,600 were the JN-4D, the standard trainer for thousands of service pilots during and immediately after World War I. The JN-4D had a 90-hp engine that gave it a cruising speed of 60 mph. The planes cost the government $5,000, but were sold as surplus for a few hundred dollars. For former military airmen seeking their aerial fortunes, the Jenny quickly became the principal trademark of the flying gypsy.[1]

These aerial nomads were soon roaring over the length and breadth of America, "a lively example of a romantic profession unhampered by precedents and unrestricted by man-made law—a direct contradiction to the plea that romance no longer exists in our day," one reporter stated. The early gypsies, or barnstormers, as they became known later, generally experienced a warm welcome in towns where the arrival of an airplane was still unusual enough to warrant wide-eyed attention. Schools often declared a half-day holiday, and the gypsy's appetite was eased by the bounty of a home-cooked meal. When he was ready to fly, the pilot would break the ice by giving a free ride to one of the local belles, charging everyone else one dollar a minute—or whatever the traffic would bear. Sometimes he could make $300 in one day, but usually it was just enough to pay for the upkeep of himself, the plane, and an occasional flying companion who doubled as a mechanic and publicity agent.[2]

Working their way across the country, gypsies gave thousands of people their first rides in an airplane, making a convincing demonstration of the flying vehicle so many had read about but never seen. When Eddie Stinson, "king of the loopers," passed through Lancaster, Pennsylvania, in the spring of 1919, his aerial circus left the town in a state of aerial intoxication described as "flying mad." Eddie's troupe delivered newspapers by air—sensational enough—but it was the experience of riding in a real plane that so excited everyone. Stinson had originally planned a two-day stand, but enthusiasm was so high that he stayed on to give rides at fifteen dollars a flight, upping the price to twenty-five if the passenger wanted the added thrill of a little stunting. Stinson had to resume his tour again before the week was out, but even in the space of a few days about 250 people had paid comparatively high prices for perhaps fifteen or twenty minutes of aerial adventure.[3]

The lure of aviation captured the imagination of dozens of young Americans, and barnstorming offered a means of apprenticeship for those who had yet to learn how to fly. Charles Lindbergh performed in Nebraska as a parachute jumper and wing walker while scraping together the $500 to buy his own Curtiss JN-4 Jenny. When he took possession, Lindbergh had not had much instruction and had never soloed, but he did not have enough money for further lessons. So he gamely clambered into the cockpit and the engine was started. In his first solo attempt, Lindbergh made an erratic climb to an altitude of four feet, thought better of it, and brought the Jenny down again on one wheel and the wing skid. A sympathetic pilot generously conducted a cram course of thirty minutes' instruction that launched the young flier into a new career.[4]

Barnstorming, as Lindbergh learned, required a knowledge of other things besides flying. Some localities were not entirely hospitable to itinerant fliers, and even though the plane's wings gave some protection from the rain, spending the night on the ground under such conditions was a different matter. Lindbergh soon acquired the knack of slinging a hammock from the strut fittings of his old Jenny biplane and was able to get a comfortable night's sleep sandwiched in the shelter of the plane's upper and lower wings. The cow pastures that the barnstormers utilized as impromptu airfields made landings tricky, and there was the added hazard of cows and mules who were fond of airplane fabric. Lindbergh recalled that it was not uncommon to hear of an unguarded plane being stripped of its covering in the space of a few minutes.[5]

Another inevitable danger was an unscheduled crackup, and Lindbergh experienced a couple of these. He once ran out of gas and had to put down in the town square of a small Texas municipality. By the next day, the wind had changed, making it impossible to get out the way he had come in, and so he decided to take off from an adjacent road, if he could correctly judge the two-foot clearance between a pair of telephone poles and some tree branches. As the plane roared down the unpaved street, one wheel caught in a rut and jogged the plane a bit too far out of line. The right wing caught one of the poles, and Lindbergh pivoted squarely into a hardware store. The proprietor at first feared that he was the victim of an earthquake, but was elated to see it was only an airplane. He refused to take a cent for the damage, explaining that the publicity value would make up for the cost of repairs.[6]

When crowds became blasé about standard barnstorming tricks like loops and other gyrations in the air, promoters dreamed up new sensations to keep up a steady turnover at the gate. Unfortunately, these new stunts often held unforeseen risks. At the critical moment in completing a midair transfer from one plane to the swinging ladder attached below the fuselage of another, one leading aerial stunter, Duke Krantz, was jolted by a charge of static electricity that almost made him let go.[7] Other incidents ended less happily, and as time passed, inexperienced pilots and rickety airplanes resulted in a growing number of fatalities. The military services began to sell aircraft that were obsolete and considered unusable, giving only vague admonitions about the necessity of a thorough overhaul. Anybody who could raise the cash could own an airplane; there were no federal standards of proficiency and safety until the Air Commerce Act was passed in 1926.[8] In the absence of air laws, there was no curb to shabby flying in rundown planes that ended in the death of too many pilots and, too often, their patrons with them. "In each town visited by an aerial tragedy," aviation journalist Howard Mingos said regretfully, "the people buried their dead and consigned all flying contraptions to the devil."[9] The gypsy/barnstormers were picturesque figures, but the sensational stunts and the fatalities involved in their activities created a misunderstanding and fear of aviation that took years to erase.[10] By mid-decade, the penchant for sensational aerial showboating appeared to wane, to the satisfaction of respected aviation authorities, such as Edward Pearson Warner. "Exhibition flying is definitely, and fortunately, disappearing as a source of revenue," he wrote, noting that barnstorming "can only have had a bad effect on the popular acceptance of the airplane as a vehicle of ordinary transport."[11] Still, the gypsy/barnstormers helped make the country air-minded, and their ranks provided a nucleus for other kinds of commercial aviation.[12]

Aircraft at Work

Although stunt flying and various kinds of aerial antics continued throughout the decade, numerous barnstormers began to settle down and centralize their activities. These fliers became the local fixed-base operators whose hangars, repair shops, and maintained runways laid the foundation for general aviation and aviation services. An organization known as the Maycock Flyers, in Michigan, laid claim to having begun nonscheduled flying service all over the country as early as March 1919.[13] Such groups as these and other former gypsies worked with burning enthusiasm, in the belief that they were helping to construct the foundations of a nascent technology.[14] Their most important contribution to aviation was aerial service—imaginative application of the particular advantages of aircraft in surveying, photography, crop treatment, and emergency service, entirely apart from regularly scheduled mail, freight, and passenger service.[15]

During the deliberations of the Morrow Board in 1925, this so-called private flying sector was considered as one possible factor in the future development of the aircraft industry, but the board's report concluded that it did not promise much.[16] In this instance, the board missed the mark. Perhaps the members were most concerned about the dollar value of aircraft production, in which case the smaller airplanes used in private flying cost much less than higher-performance, larger, and more expensive equipment intended for military service and future passenger airlines. At the same time, several dozen fixed-base operators were actively at work, operating hundreds of aircraft and contributing to a lively aviation business involving all kinds of contract services. When legislation for the regulation of aeronautics was being debated in the mid-twenties, at least one observer of the general aviation scene wrote to Secretary of Commerce Herbert Hoover that pending legislation should be carefully drafted so as not to choke off the initiative of the many general aviation flying businesses. Such operations were much more active than generally realized, Hoover's correspondent warned.[17]

General aviation activities grew with remarkable rapidity from the mid-twenties onward. One source reported that local fixed-base operators carried 80,888 passengers and 208,302 pounds of freight in 1923.[18] The publisher of the periodical *Aviation* used his mailing list to run a survey in 1925 that turned up 344 separate operators who flew 6,823,730 miles.[19] Probably the most reliable statistics for 1925 appeared in the *Aircraft Yearbook*, official publication of the Aeronautical Chamber of Commerce. The *Yearbook* received written reports from 290 operators, twenty-eight of whom said they flew only for pleasure. The 290 pilots were scattered around forty-one states and owned 676 airplanes. They flew 5,396,672 miles, carried 205,094 passengers, and delivered 112 tons of assorted cargo and mail. Their reports listed a remarkable variety of services performed in a routine, professional manner.[20] By 1927, there were fifty million aircraft miles flown in the United States, with the military accounting for just slightly over half of this figure. Airmail accounted for about four and one-half million miles, and aerial services flew more than eighteen million miles. Remarking on this last aspect, the *New Republic* observed that the "business side of flying" was in a better position than most people realized.[21]

Although Bob Johnson did not start out as a gypsy, the Johnson Flying Service in Missoula, Montana, was representative of the regular fixed-base operation. Johnson was bitten by the flying bug in 1923, when an itinerant pilot came to Johnson's garage about repairs for his plane. In return, the pilot gave a little instruction to Johnson, who bought his first plane, a ninety-horsepower Swallow, in 1924. Scenic air tours gave Johnson his first income, rounded out by carrying sportsmen to remote forest areas, doing emergency work, and taking photographers aloft for increasingly popular panoramic shots from the air. Johnson became widely known for his early-morning aerial fire-detection patrols, conducted for the Forest Service as early as 1926. When he bought an enclosed cabin four-place Travel Air in 1929, all of Missoula turned out to see him fly it in. With a carpeted aisle, roll-down windows, and covered wicker seats, the plane offered luxurious contrast to the old two-place, open-cockpit Swallow. After a hangar fire destroyed the Swallow, Johnson's brisk business permitted him to replace it with two new planes. He continued his instruction services and commercial flights for local businessmen as well as other operations possible only by plane. A "snowline run" into the rugged back country maintained contact with ranchers who were running low on stock feed, and other miscellaneous deliveries included two 1,600-foot metal cables to a snowbound gold mine in the high Cascades. Landing a ski-equipped plane, Johnson picked up a seriously injured park ranger

and delivered him quickly to the hospital, eliminating a four-day ordeal by packtrain through a wilderness in the dead of winter.[22]

The speed and flexibility of aircraft proved especially useful in remote areas. The airplane became a vital link of contact with civilization in Alaska, still very much a frontier in 1924. Noel Wien flew the
fifty-five-mile run from Fairbanks to the mining town of Livengood in
forty-five minutes, a trip that took two to three weeks by the next
fastest route, the river. The various ptomaine and pneumonia victims
who traveled with Noel had good reason to be thankful for his antique
Hisso-Standard biplane, even at a fare of fifty dollars one way. Wien
later flew the old Stinson used by the famous Arctic pilot Hubert Wilkins, and then piloted a big trimotored Fokker F-3, which was shipped
from the East coast to Alaska by boat, via the Panama Canal. Wien
also had the distinction of being the first man in the world to herd
reindeer by airplane.[23]

Airplanes were obviously connected with highly inventive minds,
and this association bloomed into all sorts of intriguing operations. In
the blatantly commercial age of the twenties, the thrill of aviation lent
itself to techniques of sensation and ballyhoo. Aviation was a bold and
spectacular thing, a choice agent for splashy advertising in the form of
skywriting in mile-high strokes. A dashing Englishman, Major Jack
Savage, caught the eye of many advertising executives when he announced himself with a big "Hello U.S.A." scrawled in chemical smoke
across New York's horizon. The major was signed to a thousand-dollar-
a-day contract by the imaginative American Tobacco Company, which
quickly perceived the suggestive appeal of having a smoky Lucky Strike
inscribed in midair. In fact, the company was so delighted with this
medium of advertising that it planned to have Major Savage puff his
way across America, lettering the message over selected cities. Harassed citizens, irritated by this desecration of the daylight sky, were
hounded at night by flying neon signs. Having driven the consumer
indoors, the unrelenting admen finally resorted to airborne loudspeakers.[24] Always alert to ingenious methods of reaching the elector-
ate, politicians quickly utilized the mobility of aircraft. The Missouri
elections of 1920 were enlivened by the flying campaign of a guber-
natorial candidate with the whimsical name of E. E. E. McJimsey.[25]
Perhaps McJimsey was ahead of his time—he lost—although Governor Walter J. Kohler of Wisconsin said that the use of an airplane

allowed a wider exposure to voters and was a definite asset to his successful contest in 1929.[26]

Confronted with the increasing difficulties of covering elections and fast-paced news developments, the news media chartered planes and pilots to speed reporters and photographers to the scene of events. One early charter pilot, Clarence Jones, flew photographers to various assignments and rushed back with pictures to make the early editions. When Jack Dempsey fought in Shelby, Montana, news services paid more than $15,000 to have the fight pictures flown to East- and West-coast papers with an elaborate relay system of sixteen to eighteen planes. Jones and men like him did a considerable business in the twenties, covering all the major news events from Woodrow Wilson's funeral to Floyd Bennett's ordeal in Mammoth Cave.[27] Even the Morrow Board realized the value of such operations, remarking that "the inauguration of a President, or an important sporting event is likely to bring forth calls for airplanes which tax to the limit the resources of the operators in that part of the country."[28]

A number of well-known newspapers had their own aircraft in the twenties and even earlier. The editor of the *Detroit News* bought a plane as early as 1912, and occasionally used it in the line of business. In the prewar era, airplanes were used more for publicity than practicality, but postwar-era aircraft were used to good advantage. In the late 1920s the aviation editor of the *News*, James Piersol, found it necessary to fly as much as 20,000 miles per year on commercial airlines; in 1929 the paper finally purchased a Lockheed Vega to give Piersol more flexibility in making deadlines. The *Baltimore Sun* acquired its own plane in 1920, and in 1928 the *Des Moines Register* paid $14,000 for a five-place Fairchild, which was appropriately christened *Good News*. The red and white aircraft became a familiar sight all over Iowa and neighboring states as it carried photographers and reporters to cover stories of tornadoes, floods, and fairs; the paper's cartoonist, J. N. Darling, flew to Kansas City to record the excitement of the Republican Convention. On Saturday mornings, the Fairchild dropped off photographers to cover the leading football games, picking them up late in the afternoon with their pictures for the big Sunday sports section. Planes were new and exciting, with an aura of drama and romance suited to news reporting. The newspapers that operated aircraft served a valuable function in promoting aviation as well as boosting their own prestige. Until much of their utility was displaced by the wire-photo services, airplanes turned in a colorful perform-ance.[29]

For burgeoning urban centers of the twenties, aviation became a useful adjunct of municipal management. Beginning in 1919, San Francisco's Fire Department used hydroplanes for aerial fire patrols over the city. After experimenting with a volunteer flying patrol, in 1929 New York City equipped its police force with three planes for the work of law enforcement, including the control of reckless flying above the city environs.[30] Bergen County, New Jersey, used four planes to control flying activity over the county's airspace, and the chief him-self flew several missions in traffic control programs. One of Bergen County's flying policemen, Clyde E. Pangborn, became a well-known aviator of the thirties. The U.S. Coast Guard Air Service, born in 1926 with three Loening amphibians, represented another unit of aerial enforcement. The Coast Guard's constant battle with bootleggers im-proved with the three-plane aerial rum patrol. Seventy-five percent of the rumrunners captured by the Coast Guard were first spotted from the air, and smugglers came to identify with dismay the drone of the patrolling Loenings.[31]

Benny Howard, one of the colorful aviation figures and designers of the era, recalled an equally colorful role of general aviation in sub-verting America's experiment in Prohibition. "The thing that built aviation to start with," he recalled, "that really held its pants up for, oh, quite a few years, was the bootlegging." Barnstormers helped keep up interest in aviation, but only the bootleggers consistently put money in it, Benny claimed. He found that his airplane designs were not judged by their safe handling characteristics or even speed. The cru-cial test rested on the number of illicit cases of beverage his handiwork could safely haul out of a secluded flying strip and into the air. Aviators at least found a source of employment, even if they did get shot at occasionally, and there was always work for a pilot with a little hustle and a flexible conscience. Clarence Jones remembered that he would fly for the bootleggers one day and hire out to Revenue agents on the next.[32]

The variegated roles of aviation seemed to be limited only by the imagination of the pilots who flew the planes. Aircraft continued to be flown for diverse work of all sorts, but came to be accepted more and more as a matter of course. Harry Guggenheim, chief of the Daniel Guggenheim Fund for the Promotion of Aeronautics, asserted in 1927 that aerial service was becoming a regular aspect of modern life in the twentieth century.[33] In addition to some of the more unusual or dramatic roles of aerial service (general aviation), private flying on business became an accepted feature of American commerce as well.

Private Business Flying

Many owners, viewing their planes as vehicles for public relations and advertising, emblazoned an oversized company logo on the fuselage.[34] But the consistent value of aviation was its speed and flexibility, and this factor, more than advertising, spurred the growth of business flying. Possibilities for business flying seem to have become more widespread in the latter half of the 1920s, when the growth of fixed-base operations provided an operational basis for private aviation. Moreover, development of the airmail and the airlines around the middle of the decade helped generate the air-minded attitude that brought attention to the possibilities of air travel by personal plane.

The industrial diversification of the post–World War I era, noted in the previous chapter, also encouraged more business flying. Despite the growth of commercial airline service throughout the United States, many time-conscious executives discovered the expediency of having a company-owned or even a personal executive aircraft. In 1927, the *Magazine of Business* discussed private business flying in a series of matter-of-fact, dollars-and-cents articles—evidence of the growing awareness and appreciation of the value of aviation in a fast-paced modern world. Late in the summer of that year, the magazine's publisher, A. W. Shaw Company, hired the services of a professional pilot and bought a six-place Stinson to be used by R. L. Putman, a company vice-president based in Chicago. In spite of some mishaps, generally inadequate ground service, and a scarcity of convenient airfields and marked air routes, the Stinson still proved to be a valuable business tool. "With the airplane," Putman said, "we have accomplished many things that simply could not have been accomplished by any other means of transportation."[35] Given the rudimentary character of flying aids and services available at the time, Putman and his Stinson logged a remarkable 44,327 miles over a twelve-month period, mostly in the East and Midwest, with excursions as far south as Florida, north to Minnesota, and west to Wyoming and Colorado. Even more remarkable was the report that hundreds of acquaintances were made with other flying businessmen, including the ubiquitous oil executive, a steel man from Pittsburgh, an Ohio manufacturer visiting his several plants, a banker with a chain of outlets, an advertising representative, among others.[36]

The experience made Putman a warm advocate of aviation and its advantages in various phases of marketing. His remarks to a session of the American Management Association, in 1927, constituted a recital of air services that had already become feasible and promised future advantages. Since rapid air shipments permitted lower inventories of spare parts and numerous similar items, the economies thus realized would increase the working capital, he said. The sales and service organizations would also be affected, since the speed and flexibility of the airplane would tend to reduce the number of such facilities needed for business operations. Putman observed that his own field of publishing would be changed by aircraft, since air delivery of papers and magazines, while their news content was still fresh, would allow penetration of wider areas of circulation. Already, he pointed out, there was the saving of time and increased effectiveness of airborne executives who could make geographically scattered business appointments and return to close out the business day in the home office.[37] The experience of some businesses underscored Putman's observations. As American business became more geographically diffuse, airplanes became more useful. For example, the National Lead Battery Company reorganized on a plan that called for decentralized manufacture and distribution designed to give faster service at lower transportation costs from plant to consumer. Faced with the problem of managing production centers scattered from New York to Seattle and from St. Paul to Dallas, the company acquired a three-place plane to enable its top executives to keep in touch.[38]

In many ways representative of the patterns of business aviation, air operations from the Tulsa, Oklahoma, airport demonstrated the utility of aircraft in the petroleum industry. Around the oil fields, with widely scattered operations and a lack of convenient all-weather roads, the flexibility and speed of planes were particularly advantageous. The planes based at Tulsa also represented the changing characteristics of general aviation aircraft designs. Tulsa was the operational base for twenty-two planes, seventeen privately owned, the remaining five the property of the field manager. The private planes were of various types, including a venerable Curtiss JN-4D, but many of the ships, significantly, were similar to postwar Waco biplanes—specifically designed for private and business flying. As the field manager explained, many discarded military machines cost up to $5,000, and, in addition to "hot" flying characteristics, fuel-hungry engines, and short range, carried only one passenger in addition to the pilot. The modern types produced for the civilian market could be purchased for half as much, were more stable to fly at a level of operating costs close to that of an automobile, possessed a longer range, and carried two or three passengers.[39]

Taking notice of increased interest in flying, manufacturers of single-engine, two- to four-place airplanes began to beam an appeal to the potential market for business aircraft. The American Eagle soon made its entry into the advertisement columns of the *Magazine of Business*, where the Fairchild Company also touted the virtues of its planes for business flying.[40] Although aircraft like these could also be used for pleasure flying, they remained expensive, costly to operate, and demanding for the inexperienced pilot. As more and more individuals turned to aviation to get things done, and novice pilots entered aviation directly from civilian life rather than through military training, a market for an easily flown trainer and economical sport plane developed. A number of less complex and low-powered machines appeared during the twenties; one of the most popular was the diminutive Aeronca C-2, a squat little aircraft affectionately known as the flying bathtub. First flown in the summer of 1929, the 30-hp C-2 puttered along at 60 mph, had a range of about 300 miles, and brought the cost of flying down from more than $30 per hour to only $6. Initially developed as a single-seat sport plane for pleasure flying, the Aeronca represented an important step for private flying at a comparatively reasonable cost, setting the stage for similar designs in the 1930s, most notably the Piper J-3 Cub. Moreover, the C-2 evolved into a two-seater, becoming a very useful and economical primary trainer for student pilots.[41]

But business flying required aircraft with better speed and range, requirements that led to several designs exemplified by the American Eagle and Fairchild aircraft, as well as others. The Waco and American Eagle, for example, were typical biplane designs with two open cockpits; the forward cockpit accommodated two passengers. With 100-horsepower engines, such planes had a cruise speed of about 80 mph, landed at 35 mph, and cost between $2,000 and $2,500. The Stinson and Fairchild companies produced enclosed, five- to six-place cabin types. These designs were high-winged, 220-hp monoplanes that cruised at 100 mph, and were priced at $12,000. Aircraft like these had ranges of 500–700 miles.[42] For their time-pressed, high-salaried executives, the larger companies acquired multiengined, long-range airplanes. These impressively large, prestigious vehicles of the new executive fleet were replete with executive amenities. The interior of John Hay Whitney's Sikorsky amphibian was appointed with a lounge on one side of the cabin and comfortable chairs on the other, all upholstered in boldly patterned fabric. J. C. Graves, vice-president of the Rich-field Oil Company, posed in the company's trimotor, which was fitted with a buffet, berths for overnight hops, as well as a businesslike desk graced by a Dictaphone and vase of dewy-fresh blossoms.[43]

Despite such refinements, the svelte airborne executive suites were no less efficient and profitable than their junior counterparts of smaller size and Spartan comforts. The Ford trimotor *Stanolind*, flagship of the Standard Oil Company of Indiana, was based in Chicago, making the company's most remote office in Minot, South Dakota, as close in time as Quincy, Illinois—eight hours by train. Another company base at Casper, Wyoming, was 1,100 miles and thirty-eight hours away by rail. The air route was only 100 miles shorter, but it was twenty-four hours faster. Standard Oil figured that its directors were worth $100 a day and up. If four men flew out to Casper and back, the company had added two extra working days worth $800. The *Stanolind*'s basic price was $50,000; including depreciation and operating expenses, it cost about $24,000 per year to own. Even if company directors did not use the plane every day, numerous other high-salaried executives could. The company estimated that the *Stanolind* would eventually pay for itself and actually earn $16,000 per year during its normal life.[44]

One sales manager, in persuading his company president to buy a corporate plane, compiled figures and operating expenses from a dozen corporations who had flown their aircraft a total of 500,000 miles. The company president finally agreed to the purchase, and in its first month the new plane was flown more than 11,000 miles, carried 440 passengers, and visited thirty-two states. By making maximum use of executives' time, flying was estimated to have made a profit of $8,000 in the first six months of operation, not including the values inherent from publicity, closer supervision of company activities, and the completion of transactions that were impractical by using other modes of travel.[45]

"Even at present costs," said the editor of *Factory and Industrial Management*, "the company-owned plane is almost indispensable where fast emergency transport may at times be a matter of life and death, as in carrying relief equipment in remote mine disasters. The plane is an economy also where it can be used more or less continuously in shortening the travel time and enlarging the range of action of executives."[46] An incomplete roster of industries that flew their own planes by 1929 ran into the dozens, beginning with AC Spark Plug and continuing through the Wood Brothers Corporation in Kansas City. It included petroleum corporations, breweries, supply firms of all types, construction engineers, and mining companies, as well as familiar trade names like Jell-O, P. Lorillard, and Walgreen Drug Stores.[47]

By the decade's end, it was estimated that the sale of aircraft for business use accounted for one-third of all civil aircraft purchased in the United States. Manufacturers responded by stressing such features as speed, comfort, and safety in hopes of attracting more buyers of business aircraft. Companies such as Stearman, Fairchild, and others established franchises and distributorships that operated as flying services, but they also planned to derive a good share of income through sales to local firms who could use a business plane. Whether the distributors sold to small local companies or to large national corporations, the new business plane owners represented a variety of enterprises. By 1929, Stinson aircraft dealers had delivered planes to roofing contractors, banks, advertising agencies, a hosiery manufacturer, a public utility company, engineering firms, the Yellow Cab Company, among others.[48]

Because official government data on air travel were not compiled until the advent of the Air Commerce Act of 1926, accurate earlier passenger statistics on business flying are difficult to establish. Even after that date, statistics are likely to be confusing, since personal business flying was included as one category of general aviation, a generic term that also embraced instructional and pleasure flights. Regardless of the paucity of precise statistics, rough figures drawn from several sources indicate a surprising degree of flight activity. Secretary of Commerce Herbert Hoover testified that general aviation accounted for 80,888 passengers in 1923, and the *Aircraft Yearbook* (1930), official publication of the Aeronautical Chamber of Commerce, claimed an increase to 205,000 passengers two years later. In contrast, scheduled airlines carried a total of only 5,782 patrons in 1926. By 1929, general aviation accounted for 2,955,530 passengers annually, compared to 173,405 fares for scheduled passenger lines. The actual number of passengers in general aviation who flew for business is not known; nevertheless, it seems reasonable to assume that the dimensions of personal business flying assumed significant proportions at the close of the decade—perhaps double that of the scheduled airlines.[49]

In short, the full spectrum of private flying unfolded and flourished in the twenties, ranging from aviation as a spectator sport, to pleasure flying, to the performance of dozens of utilitarian tasks, to business flying. These aspects all employed aircraft in considerable array, numbering well into the hundreds. Other aviation developments, while not requiring nearly so many planes, nevertheless had a discernible influence on American life in the twenties and generated very respectable statistical and economical significance: aviation in agriculture and aerial surveying.

CHAPTER FOUR
An Aerial Implement

In 1918 when an invasion of the pink bollworm from Mexico threatened the domestic cotton crop the Federal Horticultural Board of the Department of Agriculture tried to check the advance by enforcing a cotton-free zone along the United States–Mexican border. Plagued by the persistent planting of small outlaw fields scattered along an extensive frontier with a few roads and an effective camouflage of wild forest, the board was intrigued by the proposal of an aerial patrol suggested by Lieutenant Harold Compere, an Air Service pilot stationed near Houston. Compere's recognized interest in science, plus the fact that his father was a well-known entomologist who had worked with the board, made the idea seem plausible. Military pilots carried out the first trial run in the fall of 1918, and spotted eight new outlaw fields in a district that had just recently been scouted by horseback and foot. The initial success encouraged the Agriculture Department, which enlisted the support of the War Department for the continued cooperation of the Horticultural Board and the Air Service. Fliers inaugurated regular patrols in the beginning of 1919, and plans to map the area by aerial photography were soon completed.[1]

The use of aircraft for the survey of diseased cotton fields represented the postwar origins of an important new role of aviation in agriculture. Aerial application of pesticides and insecticides proved to be very effective in normal farm operations as well as in forestry. But the use of airplanes went well beyond such operations, encompassing many other areas of agriculture and health. Additionally, aircraft proved unquestionably valuable in surveying, whether for the tabulation of waterways, remote forests, or urban growth. Aviation became more than a vehicle for moving mail, cargo, and people on a regular schedule. Aviation also became a highly useful tool—an implement—integral to the daily patterns of an industrial society.

Crop-Dusting

A twelve-year-old catalpa grove near Troy, Ohio, reaching maturity in 1921, was being defoliated by the catalpa sphinx and the catalpa midge. H. B. Carver started the grove, of six acres and nearly 5,000 trees, to yield post and pole timber; its defoliation not only meant a loss to the owner but indicated a serious possible threat to similar stands all over the state. The preliminary outbreak in the spring had been serious enough, but, with the second crop of foliage beginning to appear at about the same time the second brood of caterpillars was due, it seemed likely that the second wave would finish the process of denuding the grove. Prevalent dusting techniques, using conventional ground equipment, made it awkward to reach foliage of the upper tree branches. Time was also a pressing factor. For these reasons, J. S. Houser of the Ohio Agricultural Station responded to the idea of aerially distributed poison proposed by the city forester of Cleveland, C. R. Neillie. They cooperated with the Air Service personnel at McCook Field, Dayton, who furnished a Curtiss JN-6 Jenny (a variant of the famed JN-4 model), hurriedly designed the poison dust hopper for the experiment, and assigned Lieutenant John A. Macready to do the flying.

On August 2, the day before preparations were completed and the plane had flown from Dayton to Troy, the new caterpillars hatched and consumed 75 percent of the catalpa leaves in Carver's grove. It would have taken too many long hours for workers to drag tanks and hoses up and down the ranks of trees in spraying the insects in the usual fashion. Even with the Jenny's arrival in Troy the next day, prompt action became imperative to save the remaining leaves and protect new foliage. After loading the plane with arsenate of lead powder, Lieutenant Macready lowered himself into the Jenny and took off. Trailing a swath of lethal white dust, Macready made six passes over the grove and landed again in only a few minutes. Later examination

showed that 99 percent of the caterpillars above the ground succumbed to the aerial attack.

Within weeks, enthusiastic reports of the aerial dusting experiments
began appearing in aviation periodicals, specialized journals of entomology, major newspapers, and the *National Geographic*.[2] Although
the U.S. Bureau of Entomology failed, early in 1922, to get a million
dollars in federal appropriations for large-scale aerial dusting on a national basis, an economy-minded Congress recognized the need for
continued experimentation with the cooperation of the Air Service.
Supported by facilities at McCook Field, additional experimental
dusting of commercial groves, as well as dense woodland areas, was
conducted in Ohio in the spring of 1922. While these trials gave encouraging results, other test applications over rugged and uneven
woodland terrain in New England were disappointing. Among other
things, the experimenters recognized the need for more effective apparatus to distribute dust from a fast-moving aircraft. Still, aerial dusting seemed to hold great promise in other agricultural operations.[3]

The successful experiments at Troy emphasized the value of airplane dusting to control other insect pests, including those that attacked cotton. Typical cotton-growing areas were located around the
Delta Laboratory of the United States Bureau of Entomology at Tallulah, Louisiana, and in 1922 the first cotton-dusting experiments against
the cotton leaf worm were conducted there under the direction of Dr.
B. R. Coad. Coad's experiments were again supported by the Air Service, which donated pilots and all maintenance personnel for its three
Curtiss JN-6 planes. One of the planes was equipped for aerial photography; the aerial maps it furnished proved valuable aids for the
pilots to locate and study their target areas beforehand. Coad's co-
workers perfected dusting paraphernalia, formulas, and application
techniques that allowed a confident prediction for the future value of
airplane dusting on the basis of economy, effectiveness, and speed.
Depending on the location of the various fields he had to cover, a pilot
could dust from 240 to 500 acres per hour.[4] Additional work in 1923
used DH-4B aircraft equipped with improved hoppers of larger capacity, and new trials at Tallulah made Coad's group confident that aerial
dusting could also control the cotton boll weevil. To help publicize
this promising new facet of farm operations, the Department of Agriculture persuaded the Air Service to cooperate in producing a 2,000-
foot motion picture, *Fighting Insects from Airplanes*.[5]

Aerial dusting allowed the poison to be quickly applied at the most effective time just after a rain. Machines pulled by horses not only got stuck in the mud but damaged many plants, and managed to cover only thirty acres per hour. If any unexpected infestation was discovered, airplane dusting allowed rapid control of hundreds of acres within a few hours. It was estimated that one plane could do the work of fifty to seventy-five dusting machines at less cost for initial investment, operation, and depreciation.[6] There was also the added advantage that normal farm work could continue with less interference during aerial dusting since there was no drain on a farm's regular resources of draft animals and manpower. Although aerial dusting proved valuable for applications to peaches, pecans, walnuts, wheat, alfalfa, tomatoes, and peppers, the boll weevil remained the prime target for airborne operations that treated 500,000 acres of cotton in 1927.[7]

Commercial aviation groups quickly sensed the possibilities, and several airplane dusting companies began operations around the mid-twenties. Huff Daland, one of the earliest dusting organizations, was always closely associated with Coad's experiments at Delta Laboratory. Huff Daland's men were working with Coad as early as 1923, and with Coad's encouragement they developed a special airplane for the particular requirements of dusting work. The plane itself was produced by the Huff Daland Manufacturing Company, of Ogdensburg, New York, a firm that had previously built experimental aircraft under contracts with the Air Service, giving it an inside track in the new line of dusting planes. The Huff Daland Duster, an open-cockpit biplane, had an awkward appearance, but was designed for action in warm climates, and could fly at controlled speeds close to the ground. The plane also had the capability to maneuver into and out of crop fields ringed by trees and other obstructions. The Huff Daland Duster represented a new breed of aircraft. Supported by Coad's endorsement and continuing recommendations, the new planes and pilots of Huff Daland Dusters, Incorporated, of Macon, Georgia, where an enthusiastic chamber of commerce provided them with an excellent flying field and hangar facilities. Huff Daland had a total of eighteen planes at nine flying bases, operating on the principle of one plane in the air and one in reserve at each base.

The company was certainly blessed by the good will of various groups, which translated their feelings into very substantial support. Aid from Coad's Delta Laboratory and the Macon Chamber of Commerce was only a start. Recognizing that Huff Daland's activities were "of vital importance both to aviation and to agriculture," the War Department released Lieutenant H. R. Harris, head of the flying section at Mc-Cook Field, to serve the fledgling company as chief of operations for the duration of one year. Moreover, Harris was allowed to take along no less than twelve other pilots and six mechanics picked from various Army fields. With such solid credentials, the company's dusting tariff of seven dollars per acre for five applications boasted skilled flying by military pilots. An affiliate of the Aetna Insurance Company was so impressed that it offered special cotton insurance policies against not only the boll weevil but other entomological risks as well—provided, of course, that the dusting work was done exclusively by Huff Daland.[8] There was no question that the group could do an effective job. The president of the Citizens' Bank of Greenville, Mississippi, F. H. Robertshaw, became alarmed when his cotton fields were suddenly subjected to an invasion of the army worm. After a swift counterattack by the flying dusters of Huff Daland, a grateful Robertshaw wired them a congratulatory message to the effect that his 1,078-acre battle-field had been rendered 100-percent secure.[9]

In addition to Huff Daland, the Delta Aero Dusters of Monroe, Louisiana, operated twenty planes at ten bases. Their activities included dusting orchards as well as cotton, potato, watermelon, and tobacco fields. The Quick Aeroplane Dusters, Incorporated, of Houston, Texas, started in 1925, flew ten aircraft, and dusted 75,000 acres in 1928. Depending on the size of the field, prices varied from twenty-five to sixty cents an acre for each application—usually three to five.[10] Although most of the work of aerial dusting was carried on by companies in the South, the Morse Agricultural Service, of New York, ranged as far afield as Indiana in search of dusting contracts. Huff Daland even conducted international operations, beginning in Mexico in 1925. In 1927, the company crated up seven aircraft and shipped them to Peru, where the company attacked a cotton-boll-weevil infestation.[11]

Aerial dusting was not an easy operation for the pilots. It demanded a high degree of skill to maneuver a heavily loaded plane at slow speed and low altitude, twisting and climbing for each run over the field. There were other, more subtle dangers. Philip A. Love, an aerial duster of the twenties, remained oblivious to the cumulative effect of slow arsenic poisoning from the dust preparation until he finally passed out one day during a flight near Atlanta. Love survived the crash of the airplane, and dusting operators learned to exercise more caution.[12]

Miscellaneous Uses

The versatility of aircraft in dusting and agricultural observation spurred trials in a variety of other tasks, frequently involving the collaboration of military aviation services and other government agencies. In 1923, aerial dusting proved effective against a locust plague in the Philippines[13]; in the same year, air crews at the Delta Laboratory carried out promising experiments to combat the menace of malaria-carrying mosquitoes.[14] Malaria control was difficult in many areas where draining the swamps was impossible, and using oil to kill mosquitoes was slow and sometimes killed useful life. In 1927, poison dust was successfully tried in South Carolina in an antimalaria campaign carried out by the U.S. Navy and the Public Health Service.[15]

In an attempt to investigate the spread of plant diseases, the Department of Agriculture used aircraft in Texas, Nebraska, Minnesota, Illinois, Ohio, and Kentucky to capture spores carried aloft by wind currents, tracing wheat-rust spores up to an altitude of several thousand feet.[16] A similar program to follow the flight habits of insects captured various types at altitudes of from 3,000 to 14,000 feet.[17] Still another service of aircraft involved a rush shipment of anthrax vaccine to California, where cattlemen lost up to fifteen head a day during a serious epidemic.[18]

In the spring of 1919, the Bureau of Crop Estimates of the Department of Agriculture first used an airplane to improve the procedures for crop estimates. J. L. Cochrun, a field agent in Montgomery County, Ohio, took to the air in order to check the progress of spring plowing and make visual estimates of the acreage to be under cultivation.[19] Airmail also proved useful, speeding delivery of crop reports from field agents and enhancing the currency of crop estimates.[20] The Department of Agriculture later experimented with aerial photography to give a more accurate and comprehensive estimate of acreages and types of crops. The ordinary procedure of relying on thousands of individual farmer correspondents in various districts proved unsatisfactory because those doing the reporting usually gave estimates based on their own crops alone, and the estimates often proved to be inaccurate.[21] Improved crop reporting was essential, however, because estimates had a bearing on the price of farm commodities.[22] An airplane's speed and mobility made it invaluable for making a rapid check of progress during the growing season. Its ability to make a quick survey of wind, hail, and flood damage, using aerial photography when other modes of travel were disrupted, prevented wild estimates of weather damage that might have an unsettling effect on the market. For this reason, planes took off to assess Louisiana rice fields, cotton in North Carolina and Mississippi, leaf-worm epidemics in Arkansas, and wheat and rye damage in Ohio.[23]

Other agencies used aerial patrols to spot schools of fish for the commercial fishing fleets. First experiments along these lines were carried out in 1919 off Cape May, New Jersey, by the Naval Air Service. These trials had the support of the Bureau of Fisheries, which discovered that airplane spotting could be used successfully to locate menhaden, mackerel, bluefish, and other schooling species when they were invisible from a pier or even from the crow's-nest of a ship at sea. Later in the same year, on the other side of the continent, aircraft patrolled the Pacific to scout tuna and sardines off the coast at San Diego. Ships waited at the dock until a school of reasonable size was located, ending the fruitless chase of schools of fish that turned out to be disappointingly small. Air observers radioed messages to the home port, or a fleet with no radio at sea could be apprised of a more promising hunting ground by means of a message dropped in a bottle. With the ability to range far over the water and determine several particular species, one plane could serve several different companies.[24] The Coast Guard often performed such services, saving days of fruitless beating up and down the coast. A Coast Guard patrol plane finally located sizable schools of mackerel off Cape Ann in 1929 and reported back by radio to end several days of frustrated inactivity for dozens of fishermen.[25] Further up the coast, aircraft were used to search out the quarry for sealing fleets.[26]

All of these activities demonstrated certain unique virtues of aerial operations, including advantages of working in the vertical dimension and, because of the combination of height and speed, the capability of encompassing a wide geographical territory in the performance of specific tasks. These attributes led to increasingly successful demonstrations of aviation's use in forestry and aerial survey work.

Seeding and Forestry

Under certain conditions, airplanes proved to be useful agricultural instruments for seeding. In 1929, when planes were used in an emergency to seed flooded rice fields in California, the results were so satisfactory that aircraft were extensively employed thereafter with tremendous savings in time and labor.[27] Aerial seeding was valuable in reclamation projects as well. Flying over difficult terrain in the barren areas of the Hawaiian interior, the Army Air Service cooperated with the territorial Forestry Service to sow fig tree seeds to help in water preservation and drainage control.[28]

Another application of aerial seeding in the late 1920s involved logged-over areas in the Pacific Northwest, where thousands of acres lay idle. The land lay in rough mountain areas and did not have a particularly high agricultural value. Not only was it expensive to clear the debris and tangle that the loggers had left behind them, but the topsoil was also too shallow for most crops. In order to be used as a stock range, the land needed to be extensively reseeded. To do the job by hand, however, required a great deal of seed, and cost seventy-five cents to $1.25 per acre. It also demanded time-consuming labor, since foresters could cover only five to eight acres in a full day's work. Aerial seeding, on the other hand, could be more efficiently controlled to waste less seed than broadcasting by hand; it was estimated that a plane could cover up to 200 acres a day at a total cost of forty to sixty cents an acre. An organization in the region of Coos Bay, Oregon, reseeded one logged-over area as a grazing range for 5,000 head of sheep. Checking the project later, the Forest Service reported that the aerial seeding had achieved a very efficient distribution, resulting in a heavier stand of grass even though less seed was used.[29]

Other forest areas were the object of airborne operations designed to keep them intact. In 1925, when the hemlock spanworm threatened many American forests, the superintendent of Wisconsin's Peninsula State Park was dismayed to see a brown infection begin to spread through an especially fine stand of trees. The rapid progress of the spanworm attack soon accounted for a loss of 6,000,000 board feet of timber within the state forest. Heavily wooded with rugged bluffs, the park's 3,733 acres were accessible for the most part only by bridle paths and hiking trails, so that spraying or dusting from the ground was entirely impractical. Officials of the Forest Service concluded that the cost of aerial dusting might be a valid objection in a commercial forest, but in order to preserve the recreational value and the beauty of the Peninsula Park, the expense seemed more than justified. After contracting for the application of 14,500 pounds of dust in strategic locations, Forestry officers were gratified at a 60- to 95-percent mortality of the spanworm and considered the operation to be quite successful.[30]

Aviation in the twenties became extensively used by the Forest Service in forestry patrol. The first patrol group, going into operation at the start of the summer of 1919, consisted of half a dozen Curtiss Jennies and pilots supplied by the Air Service. Its task was to make twice-a-day patrols above 9,000,000 acres of mountainous wilderness contained in five different national parks. When the approach of the hunting season increased the danger of forest fires, the original force was replaced by sixteen de Havilands with longer range and greater speed to cover an increased territory of 16,000,000 acres in fifteen forests as well as an additional 5,000,000 acres of private timberlands. The Forest Service declared that air patrols were not only a valuable aid in discovering fires; the sight of the planes on constant patrols was an effective reminder of fire prevention helping to reduce the high rate of fire outbreak in populated districts. Of 442 fires located by the air patrol during the season, twenty-seven were reported ahead of other observation units.[31]

In order to lift part of the burden from the Air Service in 1920, Congress appropriated $50,000 for patrol operations to extend from California to Oregon. The Army still supplied the pilots and planes, but the Forest Service furnished observers and had charge of the reporting facilities. Paul G. Redington, district forester in California, reported that airborne observers were able to give more accurate estimates of large fires than observers in fire control towers, who had to cope with the distortions of distance and the obstacle of haze and smoke mantles from large fires. Moreover, the flexibility of aircraft proved invaluable. The Mill Creek fire in Lassen National Forest was in such remote and inaccessible country that it was virtually impossible for the ranger in charge to keep accurate check on all sides of the conflagration because it meant a three-day trek on foot. A radio-equipped plane reconnoitered the fire, cut days of travel time in ferrying fire-crew leaders to the location from other forests, and saved hundreds of dollars in follow-up fire surveillance and patrol that released men for other emergencies. In addition to its value on the job, the airplane gave a mobility to expertly trained crews all over the state that was virtually nonexistent before.[32]

The Forest Service received no funds for the air patrol in 1922, which caused some observers to criticize the false economy of President Harding's Director of the Budget Charles C. Dawes. The *Engineering News Record* pointed out that the air patrol had reported on more than 1,000 fires in California and Oregon in 1921 and should be continued. People acquainted with the program, said the *Journal of Electricity and Western Industry*, realized that savings in reducing the loss of timber outweighed the cost of patrol.[33] The Forest Service regarded the air patrol highly enough to persuade the Army to carry out some missions at the Army's expense in emergencies during 1922. The air patrol was evidently discontinued completely in 1923, although the Army again cooperated in some work the following year.[34]

Congress once more appropriated $50,000 for the air patrol in 1925, although the method of operations changed. C. S. Lind, the district forest ranger at Duluth, Minnesota, questioned the effectiveness of the airplane in regular patrol work because the smoke pall still made it difficult for aerial observers to accurately pinpoint a fire, and it was said that procedures for reporting fires were not especially rapid. Airplanes were more useful, Lind asserted, because aerial photographs could be studied at length in order to formulate more comprehensive prevention programs and fire fighting plans. Lind admitted that aerial patrol was probably more useful in the sparsely settled areas of the West.[35]

In the western districts themselves, no regularly scheduled patrols were flown from 1925 to 1927. Only nine or ten Air Corps de Havilands were on call each season in spite of the fact that their territory included widely scattered forest ranges through Montana, Idaho, Washington, Oregon, and California. Instead, the new role of aircraft was to fly reconnaissance missions after electrical storms, when fire hazards were acute, and to make fast deliveries of equipment and men where they were needed.[36] Howard R. Flint, a district inspector of the Forest Service, emphasized that the air patrol still served as a valuable arm of forestry. In Montana and northern Idaho, he pointed

out, there were 20,000,000 acres of remote forests that could be penetrated only by pack horse or by foot. One electrical storm moving
through the area could touch off as many as 200 fires in a few hours.
With only scattered observation towers and a small ground force, it
was hard to detect many fires that smoldered undetected in hundreds
of canyons and hidden slopes. An aerial patrol was able to spot these
hidden threats and return to drop a note to a ground station to send a
crew on its way in five to ten minutes after the first alarm. In other
cases, when fires raged out of control over thousands of acres of rough
mountain territory, aircraft performed an invaluable function in reporting the fire and keeping contact with several hundred fire fighters. Flint praised the pilots who had made an admirable record in
hazardous flying through severe heat and smoke in adverse weather.
"The use of the airplane in forest fire control," he declared, "is spectacular."[37]

After 1927, since the War Department was unable to furnish planes,
patrol work was carried out through commercial contract by pilots who
carried Forest Service rangers as observers. Bob Johnson of Missoula,
Montana, had done similar patrol work as early as 1926. All through
rainless weeks of August, 1928, as electrical storms sparked dozens of
fires in tinder-dry forests, Johnson and his observer flew daily fire
patrols over the mountains.[38]

In 1925, photographic maps of uncharted forest regions were pioneered by Nick Mamer, a well-known pilot in the Northwest, and
Howard Flint of the Forest Service. Huge areas of unmapped forest
were severe drawbacks in administration and protection for foresters,
who required a knowledge of the location of lakes, trails, and dead
ends in fire fighting.[39] Succeeding years witnessed increased use of
aerial mapping to fill in gaps in foresters' charts and to survey burned-
over acreage and damage from forest enemies such as the bark beetle.[40]
However, as useful as they were in forestry, aerial photography and
mapping proved even more useful in other applications.

Aerial Photography

Forward areas in World War I offered considerably less than favorable
conditions for surveyors to construct indispensable battle maps of the
front lines. Use of the aerial camera made possible adequate and up-

to-date maps of the battle areas. Peacetime aerial surveys returned similarly valuable results, as in the survey of the Mississippi River Delta, which was so marshy that it was about as inaccessible as a battle front.[41] Postwar assessments of aerial photography concluded that existing shortcomings could be corrected and that the technique could be used successfully in mapping the thousands of square miles in the United States for which no detailed maps existed. Aerial photography would also allow cartographers to keep pace with change in the constant process of revising the existing maps.[42] If nothing else, mapping done from a moving platform in midair, conjectured the *American Architect*, would at least "introduce a spirit of adventure and a lively interest into what is now a tedious and ungrateful operation."[43]

The Coast and Geodetic Survey wrestled with the constant task of revising its charts to keep up to date on seaboard cities and the everchanging coastline of an entire continent. It seemed likely that many changes could be incorporated into the existing maps and charts through the application of aerial photography, and the first experiments were carried out in the spring of 1919. Attempts to chart underwater features from the air were discouraging, but the photographs of the expanding metropolitan area of Atlantic City, New Jersey, with its adjacent sand beaches and coastal marsh areas, were judged to reveal "great possibilities." A more ambitious project was carried out in 1920; recording a 120-mile-long stretch of coastline from Cape May to Sandy Hook in a single flight was acclaimed as "a very striking demonstration."[44]

Aerial photography in original survey work seemed feasible, and a pilot project for such a program was carried out in the challenging conditions of the Mississippi River Delta. The delta area, with its particular characteristics of soil, vegetation, and stretches of marshland, pushed the costs of ordinary surveying procedure to prohibitive levels. However, the Coast and Geodetic Survey needed up-to-date charts on the changing river mouth, and the Corps of Engineers required more accurate surveys for its engineering projects along the river. A way had to be found, and the aerial camera seemed to be the solution. With the cooperation of the Naval Air Service, a satisfactory survey was carried out in the spring seasons of 1921 and 1922, a total of 513.6 square miles being mapped at a tolerable cost of $13,319.43.[45]

Aerial photography would never replace survey work on the ground, concluded W. T. Lee, a flier connected with the Geodetic Survey, but aviation did usher in a new and refreshing view of the world for the geographer and geologist that could not be matched by anything else. For the landscape gardener, the architect, and the city planner, aerial views presented an unobstructed, comprehensive perspective that allowed a project to be properly visualized in relation to its actual surroundings.[46]

An air view made the important subject the central figure of the picture, explained Lee, reducing the constriction and clutter of an earthbound vista and giving a new completeness, meaning, and drama to familiar scenes. An aerial photograph of Washington, D.C., showed the Capitol in the center of broad, converging avenues, an anchoring structure set off by the supporting roles of the Senate office buildings and the Library of Congress. Now, this could all be very easily recognized with any good map, Lee admitted; maps were important and they were precise, but they were little more than a skeleton, lacking the visual and aesthetic impression of an air photograph with its tree-shaded roads, its woods and grassy clearings. In large-scale engineering projects, he concluded, the air photograph emerged as an "incomparable tool" in sizing up true relationships, possibilities, and progress underway.[47]

The profusion of illustrations in Lee's book was appropriate to its suggestive title, *The Face of the Earth as Seen from the Air*. Aerial photographs were new in the early twenties, and they must have had an undeniable fascination apart from their function as examples to support the text. Lee's book had variously stark shots and pleasing vistas of mountains, buildings, waterfronts, coastlines, islands, and peninsulas. Nevertheless, Lee's purpose was to illustrate the usefulness of aerial photography, and a picture of the intricate, capillary tendrils of a river drainage system was a practical example. Emphasizing the fact that air photos disclosed errors in many river charts where marshy terrain made accurate surveying difficult, Lee pointedly reminded planners that airplanes presented a new way to study the incompletely understood complex of mud flats along much of the East Coast.[48]

Shifting the view from mud flats to mountain tops, Lee observed that, in order to get a picture of a volcanic crater, it used to be necessary to find a low crater and a neighboring peak that was high enough to give the photograph some degree of perspective. With an airplane, a photographer could get a full view of any volcanic chasm straight down its yawning throat. In fact, said Lee, air photographs were so admirably suited as a tool of physical geography that a "geologic renaissance" could be in the offing. A case in point was the experience of a professional American geologist in France during the war. In using military reconnaissance photographs, he discovered that he could identify and define geologic formations with such accuracy that it was possible not only to fill in gaps in existing geologic maps but to correct their mistakes as well.[49]

Lee also described the map-making experiments carried out at Schoolcraft, Michigan, a joint project of the United States Geological Survey and the Army Air Service. The Schoolcraft project yielded promising results, and the photographic records included a captivating portrait of the little community. Commenting on the picture, Lee remarked that it showed so many features that were characteristic of central and western United States: the square repetition of the section line roads tracing the dimensions set up years ago by the United States Land Office; the precise fragmentation into the smaller fields; the shady groves of trees from the seedlings brought by homesteaders. The scenario was heavily flavored with nostalgia. "The picture of the village itself might be taken as a prototype of the American village," Lee continued, "with its fairly regular layout of streets, its business center indicated by a few larger roofs along the widest street, its lawns, trees, and gardens, the bordering farm lands, and the scattered extensions of the village into points in the direction of the main roads."[50] The facing page had a regular Geological Survey map, a square of treeless white desert, tracked across by even double lines for roads, with anonymous, insectlike black squares for houses. By comparison, it was utterly devoid of vitality and life.

Aside from its scientific and aesthetic appeal, aerial photography had commercial promise, and imaginative young pilots found a growing market for their services. About 1920, Reed Chambers made an aerial catalog of one California ranch that pleased the owner so much that Chambers spent about five months photographing other ranches in the area and wound up with a profit of several thousand dollars. Chambers flew on to photograph San Jose for the city planning commission, and then did a similar job for San Francisco. There was still much to be learned about aerial photography as a profitable business,

Chambers discovered. Technical delays on the San Francisco operation ate up all his profits, and so Chambers flew airmail for a time
before going into the aviation insurance business.[51] Other flying photographers kept active. Byron Moore, who did general flying work in
the Seattle area in the mid-twenties, made regular charter flights with
a local photographer who had found a market for aerial shots of real-
estate developments, new office buildings, and apartment houses.
Moore charged the photographer a dollar a minute or fifty dollars an
hour—you had to give him credit, said Moore. In addition to the stiff
rates, he was flying in mountainous country and there was plenty of
turbulence. Still, the photographer kept coming back.[52] Many people
must have, for the aerial photographic companies did a growing business that in 1925 amounted to an estimated one million dollars per
year.[53]

Aerial photographs were generally of two types: the oblique, or perspective, view, which was a panoramic shot useful in advertising and
general planning; and the vertical, or mosaic, with matched shots to
construct a scaled map. Both techniques demanded a sharp focus of
detail and required special equipment. The bellows of ground cameras in use at the time were vulnerable to wind pressures, and had to
be redesigned with a metal cone. High-altitude, high-speed photography had the drawback of blurred images until Sherman Fairchild
came up with a rapid, between-the-lens shutter.[54] This development
undoubtedly helped raise Fairchild Aerial Surveys to a premier position in the business.

Urban and Regional Planning

Fairchild Aerial Surveys grew from four men after the war to nearly
one hundred by 1924, operating in fifteen states from New York to
Texas. The company carried out as many as thirty-two projects in New
York alone, including one for the Russell Sage Foundation, as well as
commercial ones involving publicity photos for Goodyear and General
Electric and various surveys for power companies.[55] Fairchild's most
publicized work was an aerial map for New York City, done in 1923
and 1924. Taken at 16,000 feet, the photographs used for the map
show an amazing clarity of detail, capturing every tree, bush, and
unrecorded path in the city. Fairchild's contract called for two maps of

different scales, one for 400 square miles of the city limits, and a second map of an area of 625 square miles to include adjacent sectors of New York and New Jersey.[56]

Nelson P. Lewis, a consulting city planning engineer with the Russell Sage Foundation, had already forecast the use of aircraft as a valuable tool in city planning. Writing early in 1922, before all of the techniques of aerial surveying had been refined, he agreed that accurate topographic details were essential in planning, but pointed out that such details involved much time and expense in the early stages of planning, when a general concept of the plan was so important. The details could always be worked out later. Aerial photography could give this general concept, and at a low cost.

Lewis admitted that it was possible to observe firsthand the peculiarities of any locale by riding and walking through it, tracing the valleys and ridges, judging the relation of wooded acres in parks to existing buildings. Nevertheless, the observer still ended up with an indistinct picture of important relationships. How much better it would be if the planner could see the entire region from a height of one or two miles, a vantage point that would put details into proper relationship with each other, and then record the whole scene on a photograph to have constantly at hand for referral. With the possibility of obtaining accurate information for general planning without maintaining survey crews for weeks and months of tedious work, "it is quite evident," Lewis concluded, "that a great advance has been made in a direction which will be of inestimable value to those planning for the future development, not only of cities, but of suburban and rural districts."[57]

Lewis's endorsement of aerial photography carried the weight and the prestige of the Russell Sage Foundation, and was quoted to justify the use of aircraft in the municipal planning that soon followed. Panoramic views of cities were useful in luring new industries, proved highly useful in long-range planning, and were admitted as evidence in legal questions.[58] Utilities corporations such as the Rochester Telephone Corporation used air maps to determine the rate and direction of city growth in order to estimate the location and number of telephones to be used in the next three to five years as well as to plan sites for offices and other construction in a multimillion-dollar expansion program to extend over one and a half decades.[59]

In an age of rapid urban development, aerial surveying provided a new means for tax reassessments for the benefit (and sometimes embarrassment) of taxpayers and growing communities running short of revenue. Up-to-date tax maps were essential since equalization of tax rates was necessary to maintain confidence of present and future city taxpayers. Unfortunately, the cost of mapping at a rate to keep up with cities spreading all over the countryside was prohibitive, at least until the advent of aerial photography. The use of aircraft in tax equalization was inaugurated by Edward A. McCarthy, an expert in municipal appraising, whose Municipal Service Company had experience in using aerial maps as well as older survey methods. The first city to be reappraised with the use of air maps was Middletown, Connecticut, whose forty-two square miles were mapped in sixty days at a cost of $4,000. By way of comparison, McCarthy's own home town, New Britain, had only thirteen square miles, but the old survey methods used there had cost $48,000 and took four years to complete.

Once the mapping of Middletown was over, fourteen months were required to analyze the results, which turned up some surprising and discomforting facts. For example, forty-nine of 248 stores on Middletown's main street were not on the assessment lists, and it was found that a total of 1,896 pieces of property were altogether missing from the rolls. With the cooperation of Fairchild Aerial Surveys, McCarthy's company signed contracts with four other Connecticut towns; in each case, the assessment lists swelled and the tax rate dropped. In East Haven, the cut was from twenty-eight and one-half mills to fifteen. In spite of the decline in tax rates, all of the cities derived surplus funds from their larger assessment lists, with the result that they were able to build schools and roads that the taxpayers had earlier blocked.[60]

In the spring of 1925, the *Survey Graphic* devoted an entire issue to regional planning. As a means of portraying the concepts underlying this particular issue, the editors included reproductions of etchings by Ralph Pearson, one of which was a panoramic view of a community as it appeared from the sky. "Perhaps an eagle flying into the sun has this simplified vision of earth," remarked the editors. "It is seldom that the layman or even the artist can look at his world free and detached, and arrive at an understanding of the fundamental elements of design contained in it."[61]

The comment suggested the value of aerial photography in providing comprehensive views that gave a distinctive visual impact to the text of the articles in the magazines. Lewis Mumford's article, "Regions—to Live in," immediately followed Pearson's illustrations; Mumford's article itself was illustrated with a full-page photograph (by Fairchild Aerial Surveys) captioned "A Region in the Making." This particular photo was a striking example of the use of aerial photography to portray the elements of the region. It was a broad and distant vista of a wooded mountain range emerging from the haze of a dim horizon, a wide valley marked by cultivated clearings, a network of roads, a small community, the railroad tracks hard by the factory on the waterfront.[62] It was not a fictitious relationship that was portrayed; it was not an artist's view, secondhand. This was a factual record, a firsthand, eyewitness report, and its visual significance for the reader was unmistakable. Another illustration was an aerial shot of Chicago, chosen to portray Clarence E. Stein's "Dinosaur Cities," the antediluvian urban complexes that had already played out their historic roles. The photo showed the unwieldy immensity of a huge metropolis, ribbed with interminable avenues, sprawling its way out into the horizon.[63] It was a striking picture of a design for human living that was out of date.

As "an aeroplane observer with a quite celestial eyesight," Stuart Chase found that this allegory dramatized the disheartening picture of industrial America that he saw—belabored consumers crammed into a few cities at inefficiently located railheads, which forced the wasteful process of crosshauling raw materials and finished products.[64] Mumford's view of the "aeroplane" was less allegorical. Mumford saw aircraft as an aspect of the dispersal of city concentration, "The Fourth Migration," stimulated by technological developments in transportation, communication, and electric power. Aviation, with its relatively low traffic volume of the mid-twenties, had initially developed along main lines favoring urban concentration, although an increase in air traffic volume would stimulate an aerial network with a dispersal effect. This seemed likely, said Mumford, since aircraft were less bound to linear movement than even automobiles.[65]

Aerial photography was an obvious aid in regional planning of public power and related programs. The major part of the October 15, 1920, issue of the *Journal of Electricity* was devoted to the uses of aircraft in hydroelectric projects. The magazine's frontispiece was a graphic concept of the river basin area of the entire Southwest, as an example of how hydroelectric projects would stimulate industrial and commercial possibilities of the area. An explanatory note, entitled "The Airplane: a Necessary Tool in the Development of the West," stated that the material used as a basis for the regional map was collected by aircraft.[66]

R. C. Starr, a construction engineer of the San Joaquin Light and Power Corporation, explained the role of aviation in the Kings River project, a ten-year construction program for eleven plants with a combined capacity for 500,000 horsepower. For a project of this type, an engineer needed highly accurate data on the precipitation in a particular locale, the nature of the drainage area, and the volume of runoff in order to compute the stream flow and the potential of the hydroelectric plant. It was possible to make an estimate for a proposed project by using the available records of stream flow in similar regions. Variations occurred, however, and accurate records had to be compiled before realistic estimates could be made for a given area. Aerial survey was the only method in which mountain-summit area drainage reservoirs could be economically and accurately estimated. Ground survey crews working along the trails might miss small springs and streams beyond a ridge; planes could continue work during seasons when deep snow would bring ground operations to a complete standstill; surveying parties were spared the hazardous and time-consuming negotiation of dangerous cliffs and trekking over snow fields. After using aerial photography, Starr commented, "The results obtained . . . have proven beyond doubt the value of these (aerial) surveys for preliminary studies of large hydroelectric projects."[67]

Major H. H. Arnold, commander of the Air Service, Ninth Corps Area, furnished the pilot and the camera for the Kings River job. Arnold pointed out the value of the airplane in this case, which took six flying hours to cover a territory that otherwise would have required numerous survey parties and several months.[68] One Air Service engineer projected a hypothetical hydroelectric construction job in a remote area, and estimated that the use of air freight to carry 15,000 tons of workers and supplies to the construction site, rather than the building of a road, would save about $500,000 over a two-year period.[69]

While this proposal remained to be tested, other companies made significant use of aerial surveying in power projects. When it was surveying the right of way for two new high-tension lines of twenty-five and thirty miles in length, the Pennsylvania Water and Power Company used aerial photography to plot the location of their high-tension towers, eliminating much work by preliminary surveying parties. When boundary questions developed, the air photographs not only eliminated thumbing through often inaccurate property records but actual photographs produced on the spot smoothed the negotiations in right-of-way conferences.[70] Another power survey in North Carolina was completed rapidly, including the production of accurate topographic maps constructed with the aid of a stereoscopic system to bring out the different ground contours recorded in special photographs.[71]

During the early twenties, planes used by Fairchild and others had several drawbacks, including the fact that the photographer frequently operated out of the rear seat of an open-cockpit biplane. The photographer was not only buffeted by the slipstream but also had the problem of the obstructions presented by the lower wing and assorted struts and wires. Sherman Fairchild, in particular, wanted a stable plane that would provide a broad field of vision for both pilot and photographer. Such a plane needed a roomy cabin to accommodate both crew and the bulky cameras of the era, and should be able to operate out of short, unimproved airstrips while on field assignments. With no suitable plane on the market, Fairchild organized the Fairchild Airplane Manufacturing Company and secured the services of Professor Alexander Klemin, one of the leading aerodynamicists of the era, to help design the plane he wanted. The FC-1, a prototype, first flew in 1926. This high-winged monoplane fulfilled Fairchild's primary criteria, and featured a closed and heated cabin for working comfort. Another distinction was its folding wings for ease of storage and convenience of towing behind a car or truck. A fine camera plane, the FC-1 turned out to have excellent flying and operational characteristics. Production versions of 1927, designated FC-2, were powered by a 220-hp Wright J-4 engine. These planes, as well as higher-powered variants, proved successful as camera planes, commercial transports, business planes, and as rugged aerial workhorses flown by bush pilots around the world.[72]

Natural Resources

Apart from aerial photography, one of the earliest uses of aviation was in mining operations. New mines were often located in remote areas far from existing transportation, and airplanes offered the only fast way to travel to the sites. Many mining towns had a brief life that did not justify the construction of expensive roads and railroad tracks. Planes required a small investment and could be used to survey, establish mines, service the operation, and fly out the raw product. The 1920s witnessed a number of such projects, and planes were found to be valuable in a variety of ways.[73] One plane was used to service an entire circuit of California mines with light supplies and mail in 1920, and proved useful in averting costly shutdowns. In remote districts of Nevada and Idaho, air transport was used to carry 117,000 pounds of steel pipe to isolated mines in the mountains.[74] The Bureau of Mines used airplanes to speed oxygen and medical supplies to the Argonaut mine accident in California, and a special Bureau engineer was flown to the scene of a mine explosion in Wyoming.[75]

Service and emergency work was only part of the story of aviation's role in mining, however. Mainly because of aerial photography, mining became the largest user of airplanes for industrial purposes. "Development of new mining areas has been advanced by decades," said the *Engineering and Mining Journal*, "as the airplane has been pressed into the service of prospecting, surveying, and mapping." One example was the use of aerial photography to map the growing lead and zinc district in northeast Oklahoma.[76]

The biggest application of aerial surveying was probably in the petroleum industry. The first companies to launch such programs began in 1927, and by 1929 nearly every major company doing work in the West and Southwest was using aircraft to make survey maps. Air photographs were used to pinpoint promising features, eliminating the considerable amount of time normally consumed by casting around on the ground. If it seemed worthwhile, geologists learned to follow clues of vegetation and differentiation of soil types in order to trace an exposed rock ledge that continued underground. In one case where surface indications were hard to define, geologists used aerial photographs to locate the contact point of two promising formations. The photographs revealed a definite connection that could be seen under a grainfield with a three-foot-high stand. When called for, accurate topographic features could be constructed by using the stereoscopic technique. Companies also discovered the advantages of making a quiet survey of a promising area from the air, without arousing the instincts of speculators.[77] Around the end of the decade, aerial photography was used to make the accurate survey required to lay down a 600-mile-long pipeline.[78] Fairchild Aerial Surveys had begun projects for petroleum surveys out of its Dallas office that totaled 30,000 square miles by 1933 and extended into Mexico.[79]

The rugged, remote regions of Alaska that were surveyed and mapped for the first time in 1926 and 1929 provided one of the most imaginative and dramatic tests of the usefulness of aerial photography. The Department of the Interior asked the Navy to do some aerial mapping in order to fill in the knowledge of the mineral and other natural resources of Alaska, and the project eventually included the cooperation of various government bureaus: the Bureau of Fisheries and the Lighthouse Service needed various types of information; the Forest Service wanted timber estimates; the Division of Roads in the Department of Agriculture was interested.

The man most responsible for the 1926 project was R. N. Sargent, a veteran of eighteen years with the Geodetic Survey in Alaska, who went along as the expedition's technical adviser. The Navy supplied three Loening amphibians, as well as the supporting vessels: a 250-ton freighter-lighter converted into a machine shop, photographic laboratory, office, and quarters for the expedition's seven officers and forty men; and the U.S.S. *Gannet*, a minesweeper with five officers and sixty men, to tow the lighter.

The survey, lasting from May to August 1926, had an ambitious goal of 40,000 square miles, but, with only fifteen days of flying weather, the crews had to settle for 10,000 square miles. This was a remarkable record. The area of operations spanned nearly 1,000 miles from Ketchikan to Anchorage, over impenetrable forests, mountain fastnesses, and vast glaciers, where a crash or even a forced landing left virtually no chance for escape or rescue. It was a demanding test for cameras, planes, and pilots. As if these hazards were not enough, the grumbling crews found it necessary to set up a night watch at one point because their planes were being endangered by errant ice floes.

Photographers on the expedition produced striking portraits of a magnificent wilderness in the process of recording the potential of its natural resources. The discovery of important watersheds for power sites, coupled with accurate timber estimates, prompted negotiations for new pulp mills in Ketchikan. With an estimated capacity for pulp production equaling one-third of the daily requirements in the United States, this was to be an important source of newsprint so indispensable for a civilized society. The expedition returned with a set of previously nonexistent daily weather reports for the area, and presented the chart makers with new problems of revision. One bay on Prince of Wales Island had been formerly misplaced eight miles from its true position.[80] Speaking for the Department of the Interior, R. W. Sargent said in 1929 that it would take still more years before the full results of the 1926 expedition could be evaluated, and added that it was impossible to estimate its value in dollars and cents. At any rate, it was felt worthwhile to send another expedition in 1929, this time with four planes, to map an additional 13,000 square miles.[81]

Scanty and incomplete records available for the twenties give little indication of the total number of planes, civilian and military, that were flown for agricultural treatment, forestry patrol, survey, photogrammetry, and other activities. It seems certain that the number would be much fewer than the total aircraft used in business flying, as is the case in the current aviation scene. Still, the airplane as an aerial implement found a niche in a wide variety of utility roles. In these utilitarian functions, the small numbers of aircraft available completed innumerable tasks faster and at less cost when compared with conventional procedures then in use. Because of the speed and flexibility of an airplane, the measure of its influence was not in arithmetic but in geometric progression. Within twenty-five years of the Wright brothers' first flight, the airplane's social impact was more complex than the Wrights had imagined, and the economic significance of utility aviation was far greater than might have been assumed, judging from the comparatively small number of aircraft involved. Aviation in agriculture became a widely accepted function within the United States and in international operations. The work in Alaska represented some of the most valuable assets of aerial photography: the ability to penetrate formidable geographical barriers, comprehensiveness, speed, and the added bonus of aesthetic charm.

Part Three
THE AERONAUTICAL INFRASTRUCTURE

CHAPTER FIVE
Research and Development

The progress in military and civil aeronautics during the 1920s owed much to technological accomplishments. In turn, the technical advances in airframes, engines, fuels, and assorted aviation accessories owed much to the brilliance and persistence of many individuals. While it is true that numerous individualistic personalities continued to pioneer in aeronautical developments in later years, a growing professionalization emerged as a distinct feature of aviation in the twenties. The extensive and planned research and development conducted by the National Advisory Committee for Aeronautics are only two examples. Meanwhile, new cadres of professionally trained aeronautical engineers began entering the ranks of the aviation industry, having completed specialized courses in coherently organized aero engineering departments at colleges and universities across the country. In addition, a new foundation for aviation operations evolved. Significant progress occurred in the study of meteorology and weather forecasting, as well as in techniques for instrument flying. In short, the elaboration of a distinct technological infrastructure of aeronautics emerged in the post–World War I decade.

A great deal of this new operational framework occurred as a result of the internal momentum of aviation development. At the same time, the Daniel Guggenheim Fund for the Promotion of Aeronautics, founded late in the decade, played a singular role in numerous key areas of aviation activities. The imprint of the Guggenheim Fund was clearly discernible during much of the progress in aviation during the twenties.

The NACA

The creation of the National Advisory Committee for Aeronautics (NACA) in 1915 constituted an important step toward the institutionalization of American aviation. Dr. Charles D. Walcott, secretary of the Smithsonian Institution, had suggested such an organization some years earlier, and urged the United States government to pass legislation authorizing an advisory group to engage in research and other programs to promote aviation. His idea did not receive favorable attention at first, although in 1913 the advisory committee of the Langley Laboratory was created under the auspices of the Smithsonian Institution. The Smithsonian designated the committee's members, which included government personnel nominated by the secretaries of War, Navy, Commerce, and Agriculture. With the outbreak of war in Europe in 1914, additional federal support was discouraged since there was some feeling that a government advisory committee for aeronautics had warlike connotations that would compromise the neutral role of the United States. It soon became apparent, however, that a more official body was needed to effect the best cooperation and coordinate the research activities of both civil and military aviation. Moreover, there was a legal problem because Congress had never authorized the participation of the various government officials who were involved in the work of the Langley committee. The Naval Appropriation Act of March 3, 1915, made official provisions for the establishment of a National Advisory Committee for Aeronautics, which was to coordinate the activities of the respective military and civil departments of the government. Its research reports were to be accessible to any private firm in the United States.[1]

Specifically, NACA was charged with the duty to "supervise and direct the scientific study of the problem of flight, with a view to their practical solution, and to determine the problems which should be experimentally attacked, and to discuss their solution and their application to practical questions." The dozen members appointed by the president represented the Treasury, War, and Navy departments, as well as the Weather Bureau, Bureau of Standards, and the Smithsonian, and included delegates from Stanford, Northwestern, Johns Hopkins, and Columbia universities—an indication of the committee's range of inquiry and indicative of the probable effects of its research in "application to practical questions." The initial appropriation totaled $25,000 for a period of five years. One of the first projects under the aegis of NACA was research on propellers carried out at Stanford in 1916 under the direction of Dr. William F. Durand and Dr. Jerome C. Hunsaker of the Massachusetts Institute of Technology. Hunsaker was also a leading figure in wind-tunnel research, which he had observed at England's National Physical Laboratory in 1914.[2]

The NACA eventually decided to acquire its own laboratory facilities, completed at Langley Field, Virginia, in 1918. A five-foot wind tunnel, begun the same year, was ready for operation two years later, when the Langley Memorial Aeronautical Laboratory was formally dedicated. The lab was directed by Dr. George W. Lewis, who had been professor of mechanical engineering at Swarthmore College. There was nothing unique about the five-foot tunnel, and Lewis's growing team of engineers contended with the conventional problems of trying to correlate results from wind-tunnel models with measurements from actual planes in flight. The data never seemed to correlate very well. A breakthrough came from the outstanding NACA researcher Dr. Max Munk. Munk had been an associate of Professor Ludwig Prandtl, whose original and brilliant work in theoretical aerodynamics at Göttingen, Germany, had contributed so much to German and European leadership in aeronautical science. Following his arrival in the United States, Munk probed NACA's tunnel problems, and suggested compressing the air in a tunnel to twenty atmospheres. By using a one-twentieth scale model in such a tunnel, test results should correlate to data from a full-scale plane at normal atmospheric pressure, he argued. In other words, it was necessary to compress the air in the tunnel to the degree of that in the model under test.

NACA's first variable-density tunnel went into operation in 1923, and yielded basic data for a series of pioneering NACA reports on wing improvements, setting the precedent for similar tunnels, both in the United States and abroad. The variable-density tunnel, still a five-foot design, nevertheless proved inadequate for propeller research, which led to a new tunnel with a throat of twenty feet designed to accommodate a complete fuselage, engine, and propeller. Judged by the standards of 1927, this apparatus was unusually large. It was also an unusually productive unit, contributing to, among other things, conclusive studies on the value of retractable landing gear and the alignment of engines on the leading edge of the wing for multiengine aircraft, factors that drastically reduced drag penalties. Finally, the large tunnel was used to develop one of the most successful aeronautical innovations of the twenties, the NACA engine cowling.[3]

Most American planes of the postwar decade mounted air-cooled engines, with the cylinders left exposed to the airstream in order to enhance cooling. NACA's tunnel tests revealed that this style of installation accounted for as much as one-third of a plane's total drag. Although significant work on cowled engines proceeded elsewhere, particularly in Great Britain, NACA work provided the most dramatic success. After hundreds of tests, a NACA technical note by Fred E. Weick in November 1928 detailed a cowling design that enclosed the engine in such a way that cooling was enhanced while drag was sharply reduced at the same time. During a transcontinental test flight, a 157-mph plane equipped with the new cowling averaged 177 mph. In terms of its effect on air transport, E. P. Warner wrote, the introduction of the NACA cowling was "staggering." By 1932, according to one estimate, the operational efficiency of cowled American aircraft represented a savings of $5 million.[4]

Fourteen years after its inception in 1915, the tremendous growth and complexity of aeronautics demanded an expansion in NACA's personnel and finances. In 1929, the committee's membership was increased from twelve to fifteen with the addition of Harry F. Guggenheim, of the Guggenheim Fund; William P. MacCracken, Jr., of the Department of Commerce; and the respected Edward P. Warner, editor of *Aviation* magazine. The importance and scope of NACA's activities are reflected in its statistics. Totaling $615,770 in 1929, the appropriation for 1930 was $1,508,000, including an allocation for the construction of a full-scale wind tunnel and other added facilities. In 1929, NACA distributed a total of more than 100,000 technical notes, memorandums, and circulars throughout the United States, and maintained a technical representative for Europe at the American embassy in Paris to keep informed on the latest foreign developments. The task of tracking foreign research was important for the United States, because trends and results were reported to various United

States scientific journals read by American researchers. Prandtl's various studies, for example, were acquired at the request of the NACA, translated by its staff, and circulated as one of its technical reports, "Application of Modern Hydrodynamics to Aeronautics."[5]

At its formation, the NACA embodied certain progressive goals in terms of being a pool of skilled advisers, and the agency's coordinating functions prevented duplication and waste. Moreover, the NACA was to be immune from the machinations of business and industry. But the NACA never enjoyed total immunity from political crosscurrents in Washington, and after the passage of the Air Commerce Act of 1926, the NACA focused almost exclusively on research, despite the agency's original goal of advisory activities as reflected in its name. It may be said that the NACA conscientiously avoided duplicating the sort of research carried on by the Army, the Navy, and the Bureau of Standards, but as national security seemed less pressing in the late twenties, and as civil aviation matured, representatives of the aviation industry pressed for more influence on NACA research projects. The agency held the line at direct membership on its principal committees, but instituted annual "industry conferences," beginning in 1926, and increased its attention to immediate, short-term problems such as noise reduction and safety. By 1930, the departure of forceful, research-oriented personalities such as Max Munk resulted in a more conservative style within NACA, with increasing emphasis on practical and applied research, as opposed to long-term theoretical projects. Nevertheless, in retrospect, the aeronautical pioneering and the dissemination of information by NACA have been among the most important factors of American aviation progress.[6]

Progress in Airframe Design

Along with NACA's investigations, aeronautical research by other groups and individuals in Europe and America helped set the pattern for what has been called the airframe revolution. The collective improvements in aircraft design during the post–World War I era paved the way for the economic success of air transportation. "In determining the economic status of the airlines—the role of the airplane designer has been more than influential," declared E. P. Warner. "It has been absolutely controlling."[7] Progress in the twenties led directly to the design of the

Boeing 247 and the legendary Douglas DC-3, which evolved in the early thirties and set the basic pattern for airliner design until the advent of the jet airliners of the late 1950s.

Compared to earlier biplane designs, buttressed by a tangle of supporting struts and wires, one prominent feature of the DC-3 was its streamlining, exemplified by its cantilevered monoplane wing. Attempts to achieve streamlining in order to reduce drag began before World War I, although the most successful designs were the Junkers, Fokker, and Dornier aircraft with cantilevered wings that were produced in Europe after the war. In Germany, Junkers and Dornier also pushed ahead with metal wing and fuselage structures. These examples of all-metal cantilevered monoplanes attracted the attention of the NACA early in the twenties, and influenced further examination and exploitation of these features. One important result was the Ford Trimotor of 1926, with its metal structure and cantilevered wing.

Other research involved stressed-skin construction, using the aircraft skin itself to carry more of the loads imposed on the aircraft in flight. This approach eliminated many internal trusses and braces within the wing and fuselage, and contributed to a lighter, more efficient airframe design. In Germany, Adolph Rohrbach and his collaborator Herbert Wagner represented the vanguard in this research, which became known in the United States after Rohrbach published a paper on the subject in the *Journal of the American Society of Automotive Engineers* in January 1927. Streamlining and the stressed-skin technique were evident in the Lockheed Vega of 1927, designed by John K. Northrop, who had independently devised his approach apart from German influence. But the Vega featured wooden and molded plywood construction. Metal construction for fuselage and wing structures heavily influenced United States airliner designs of the late twenties and early thirties. Two prime examples were the Northrop Alpha and the Boeing Monomail, both flown for the first time in 1930.

Both planes incorporated a number of outstanding modern design features representing growing sophistication in construction and aerodynamic refinements, such as the wing fillet, or fairing, where the wing joined the fuselage. Developed through research at the California Institute of Technology, the wing fillet markedly improved operational efficiency and flight characteristics, and has become standard for low-wing monoplanes. The Alpha, with better performance and a style of rugged wing structure later used for the DC-3, proved more successful in a commercial sense, although the Monomail occupies an important position in the evolution of modern transports. Among other things, the Boeing plane incorporated arc welding, a highly successful technique for metal-to-metal joints the company had perfected for producing a tough little fighter, the PW-9, in 1921. Unlike the Alpha, the Monomail also boasted a retractable landing gear, a feature that became standard for modern transports. One negative feature of the Monomail later turned out to be helpful. Early tests showed the need for a controllable-pitch propeller, since a propeller setting allowing the plane to operate out of Seattle at sea level was barely suitable for mail routes through Cheyenne, Wyoming, at an altitude of more than a mile above sea level. Boeing's twin-engined 247, like the Douglas DC-3 and other transports, eventually was equipped with this valuable accessory.[8]

Engines and Fuels

Although early aircraft engines owed much to automotive technology, advances in aviation were seen to have a promising influence on automotive engineering in the postwar era. This aspect was the subject of a special symposium, "Probable Effect of Aeronautic Experience on Automobile Practice," conducted in 1919 at the annual meeting of the Society of Automotive Engineers and subsequently published in its *Journal*.[9] The comments of the participants concerned wartime experience in aircraft manufacturing that could be applied to automotive engineering in the postwar decade. Howard C. Harmon, in a discussion of automobile and airplane engines, emphasized that although no radical design changes were in the offing, the experience in manufacturing high-performance aircraft engines had yielded a "multitude of engineering minutiae" that could be applied to automobile production techniques in order to give better service and improvement in engine performance. Harmon said that one of the most significant developments in aircraft engines that would be a contribution to automotive performance was the use of the steel cylinder. It would be especially effective in heavy-duty engines because of its rapid cooling qualities and its resistance to the loosening and fracturing effects of constant vibration.[10]

Henry M. Crane, vice-president and chief engineer of the Wright-Martin Aircraft Corporation, stressed the particular requirements of aircraft engine development in lighter and higher-quality bearings as well as the higher-performance characteristics of magnetos and spark plugs than would be feasible to use in automobile engines. Crane also noted that the use of composite aviation fuels had interesting promise for automobiles. Engine performance would be affected by the use of these composite fuels, which raised the ignition temperature and consequently resulted in higher compression ratios, according to O. E. Hunt, an engineer of the Packard Motor Car Company. After an especially strong assertion that no revolution in automobile design would result from the experience with aircraft, Hunt agreed that improvement in some details, such as oil control and carburetion, could be copied from aircraft engines along with the increased use of overhead valves and camshafts. The most important contribution of airplane production, he said, was the evolution of a new approach to the problems of design and manufacturing. Engineers were conditioned to think more in terms of lightness, had an increased respect for "good metallurgical practice," and discovered new concepts of high quality workmanship. "In setting up new ideals of design and workmanship," Hunt concluded, the experience of aircraft production had given an "inspiration of far greater value than any design details could possibly yield."[11]

Crane's remarks during the symposium merited more than passing interest, since he had moved from Wright-Martin to become the technical assistant to the president of the General Motors Corporation. While he held this position, he continued to affirm the influence of aviation on high-test fuels, as well as on engine design and construction techniques.[12] It seems plausible that the greatest influences of aviation on the automobile industry did in fact occur during the twenties. There is no doubt that advances in aircraft power plants and fuels were remarkable.

As significant as NACA's aerodynamic work had been to the development of aeronautics, the progress of American aircraft design in the twenties hinged on the cumulative effect of several additional technological trends. Although the radial engine at first posed something of a problem in terms of aerodynamics, the evolution of this type of power plant was fundamental to dependable aircraft operations. While most European engine manufacturers favored the more streamlined liquid-cooled power plants after World War I, the U.S. Navy evinced strong interest in the radial because of its easier maintenance and power-to-weight ratio for operations from the limited confines of carrier decks. The moving force behind the Navy's interest in radials was Captain Bruce Leighton, who supervised engine procurement for the Bureau of Aeronautics. Charles L. Lawrance had developed a very attractive radial engine design in 1921, but his Lawrance Aero Engine Company lacked the capacity for volume production. Leighton literally maneuvered the Wright Aeronautical Corporation into the purchase of Lawrance's company, which led to the very successful series of Wright Whirlwind power plants.

The Wright-Lawrance merger, however, led to some internal problems, and a dissident group of engineers decamped in 1925 to set up a new company, leading to the organization of Pratt and Whitney. In just six months, the new company developed the 425-hp Wasp, incorporating a number of important technical advances, including improved cylinder heads based on the work of S. D. Heron, then working for the Army at McCook Field. Heron, one of the most important technical innovators of the era, had come to the United States in 1918 from England, where he had done considerable experimentation on radial engine designs. Besides working on cylinder heads at McCook Field, he spearheaded the investigation of improved valve designs. Poppet exhaust valves presented a continuing problem, since they were subjected to very high gas temperatures and high gas velocities, resulting in considerable heat damage. Tungsten and chromium alloy steels helped, but Heron was convinced that liquid-filled hollow valves, to conduct heat away from the valve head, offered the best solution. Heron's researches finally led him to liquid sodium as the coolant in 1928, a solution that became standard for aircraft valves as well as those in other types of engines. In the meantime, Heron had joined Wright Aeronautical in 1926, where he had an important role in designing the Wright J-5 engine, the classic power plant that powered Lindbergh's *The Spirit of St. Louis*.[13] Together with Pratt and Whitney, Wright Aeronautical continued to introduce refined radial power plants that gave American aircraft an enviable record of efficiency and reliability, contributing to United States leadership in world aviation.

Increasingly, the successful engines of the postwar era were equipped with improved carburetors and more efficient propellers. Through the

First World War, wooden propellers had served well enough. Eventually, however, increased engine power, along with the increasing speed of propeller tips, began to surpass the safe operational limits of wooden construction, and an active search for a more suitable material began early in the twenties. Again, work at the Army's McCook Field pointed the way, where Frank Caldwell presided over the propeller test section. After a series of tests on an electrically powered test rig, metal propellers seemed the most promising—until run on a conventional piston engine. Charles Fayette Taylor, a McCook engineer during this period, ran one propeller test on a 300-hp engine. "After a few minutes at rated power," he recalled, "a blade broke off, came through the control board between the heads of two operators, climbed a wooden staircase, and went through the roof." Such tests were as destructive as they were unnerving. "The engine," Taylor added, "was reduced to junk." Vibration was the main culprit, finally controlled by 1925 by using specially treated aluminum at the base of the blades to cope with the intense shaking imparted by piston engines at full power. Also, by the end of the decade, controllable-pitch, aluminum-bladed propellers were available for optimum settings during takeoff and cruise.[14]

In the "thinner" air of higher altitudes, a turbosupercharger was required to provide the engine with adequate amounts of air at satisfactory pressures. The practical application of superchargers apparently originated with Auguste Rateau, a French engineer who had attempted to improve the performance of French fighter planes during World War I. Basically, the scheme used engine exhaust to spin a turbine that forced an increasing volume of air to the carburetor, approximating sea-level conditions. Using this principle, the British set new altitude records approaching 30,000 feet not long after the war's end. The idea was picked up in the United States by Dr. Sanford A. Moss, an engineer who had been pursuing turbine research for General Electric. The Moss turbosupercharger, installed on a Liberty-powered LePere biplane, enabled Major Rudolph W. Schroeder to set a new record of 33,113 feet in 1920. The attempt nearly took the major's life. Because of a faulty oxygen system, Schroeder blacked out and plunged toward the earth in a six-mile dive. He recovered his senses just in time to pull out at an altitude of 2,000 feet. His vision hampered by lacerated eyelids, caused by ice fragments from moisture between eyelids and eyeballs, Schroeder completed a harrowing approach and landing at McCook Field. Subsequent work by the Air Corps, the NACA, and engine manufacturers led to the highly perfected superchargers that equipped airliners and military aircraft of the 1930s and World War II.[15]

As engine performance curved upward in the twenties, the quality of aviation gasoline assumed greater significance. During the early years of aircraft development, from 1900 to about 1918, "almost anything was used in an airplane engine that would enable it to operate." Until World War I, there were no specifications for aviation gasoline as a distinct entity, and even then the main indicator of fuel quality in general was given as a gravity number—the lighter the better, since "heavy" gasoline seemed to resist efficient vaporization and combustion. For several years after the war, the main criterion for aviation gasoline was its distillation range, and government specifications in 1922 set limits for "cracked" gasoline used as aviation fuel because of problems with gum residues. Some brands of gasoline seemed to work better than others, so wise buyers preferred fuel produced from the crude oils of California, southern Texas, and Venezuela, all of which had an aromatic and naphthene base.[16] But there were many times when fliers had no choice concerning such preferred fuels. On these occasions, pilots used automobile gasoline, taking the precaution of dropping a few mothballs into the fuel tanks, since this homely additive reportedly made the engine run better.[17]

"Development of engines and fuels has not been what the layman would call a scientific process," one authoritative study commented, "it has rather been a process of cut and try."[18] The development of high-octane, antiknock fuels for aviation certainly proved the point. Important American work on the antiknock problem began with Charles F. Kettering as early as 1911. In 1916, he turned the search over to Thomas Midgely, working at Kettering's Dayton Engineering Laboratories Company (later a part of General Motors). After encouraging results with iodine, Midgely intensified his pursuit for more potent additives. Using a minuscule one-cylinder engine set up in his kitchen, Midgely experimented with numerous possibilities. When he found something interesting, he mixed up a larger batch and carried it over to McCook Field to try it out in airplane engines. By 1921, he was concentrating on metallorganic compounds, and came up with a formula based on tetraethyl lead. Additional experimental work led to a practical production method, and the Ethyl Gasoline Corporation (formed by General Motors and Standard Oil of New Jersey) was established in 1924. Within three years, both the Navy and Army began using the additive, although commercial airline companies held back extensive use for several years because of the additional cost involved.[19]

In the process of fuel research for the Ethyl Corporation, Graham Edgar worked out the octane rating scale in 1926, and aviation gasoline thereafter was sold with several octane ratings. The airlines and other commercial users generally purchased fuel with an octane range of 65–70, and such gasoline was controlled specifically for aviation use, including specifications for sulfur, corrosion, volatility, and stability. Fuels with a rating of 90 octane and above necessarily contained synthetically produced hydrocarbon additives, cost more, and were bought by the armed services. There are no reliable figures regarding the quantity of aviation gasoline produced before 1925, since the volume was too small to rate a separate tabulation. The appearance of octane ratings in 1926 helped establish categories, and more than three million gallons of aviation gasoline were produced that year. By 1929, more than 20,500,000 gallons of commercial aviation fuel were produced, and it has been estimated that the Army and Navy consumed as much as 15 million gallons of military-grade fuel in 1929.[20] The American petroleum industry found it increasingly necessary to meet the production requirements of high-test gasolines, not only for the increasing numbers of automobiles but to satisfy the needs of a growing aviation industry for special grades of aircraft engine fuel as well as an increasing demand for special types of lubricants. At the close of the decade, Skelly Oil Company was spending $2 million for a new facility to produce aviation gasoline; other companies who were serving the special requirements of the aviation business included such well-known firms as Texaco, Cities Service, Phillips, and Shell.[21]

Engineers and Engineering

The progress of aviation in the various technical areas noted above was enhanced by a growing interest in aeronautical engineering. Although the Armour Institute of Technology in Chicago reportedly offered aeronautical courses as early as 1910,[22] the best known of those pioneer programs was initiated by Jerome C. Hunsaker, who became interested in the field of fluid dynamics through his studies in naval architecture at Massachusetts Institute of Technology (MIT) in 1909. From the study of hydrodynamics in his naval courses, Hunsaker developed an interest in aerodynamics as well. Fortunately, MIT President Richard C. MacLaurin was an interested student of aviation as a new scientific art and a promising form of technological progress, and he formulated plans for a course in aeronautics around 1912. Hunsaker himself translated a book on aerodynamics, by Alexandre Eiffel, the well-known French engineer, which was used in the first course in aeronautics at MIT in 1913—taught by Hunsaker.[23] One early student was Alexander Klemin, an English engineer who took over as director of the aeronautics program when Hunsaker left MIT in 1916 to take charge of the Navy Aircraft Division in Washington. Klemin later helped establish the influential magazine *Aviation*, and did wartime research at McCook Field.[24] During World War I, the general course in aeronautics at MIT evolved into a strict discipline of aeronautical engineering. In 1925 it was taught by Edward P. Warner,[25] who became another outstanding figure in aviation.

Felix W. Pawlowski, a professor in mechanical engineering at the University of Michigan, also began to develop pioneering courses in aeronautical engineering about 1913. The course was shifted to the Department of Naval Architecture and Marine Engineering in 1915 (an interesting move in light of Hunsaker's experience and indicative of the close relationship of aerodynamics and hydrodynamics), and the course was taught at a third-year college level. Pawlowski's first candidate for the bachelor of science degree in aeronautical engineering received his diploma in 1917, and postgraduate work was offered a few years later. The University of Detroit announced the formation of an aeronautics department in 1920 under the direction of Lieutenant Thomas F. Dunn. Course work was offered beginning with the fall term of 1921, and the first bachelor of aeronautical engineering degree was awarded in 1925. In 1921, New York University offered similar course work in the new field of aeronautics; other programs were underway at the California Institute of Technology (Cal Tech), University of Washington, and Stanford University.[26]

The Daniel Guggenheim Fund for the Promotion of Aeronautics

was a tremendous stimulus to aeronautical engineering, just as it was to the dozens of other disciplines with which it became involved. Between 1926 and 1930, this private philanthropy dispensed more than $3,000,000 on a variety of fundamental research and experimental programs that influenced the growth of aviation to an unusual degree. The Guggenheim fortune, based on international mining and smelting enterprises, was controlled by Daniel, who had retired from business in 1923. In 1924, he and his wife founded the Daniel and Florence Guggenheim Foundation to promote the "well-being of mankind throughout the world." In the meantime, Daniel's son Harry had developed an interest in aeronautics and learned to fly before America's entry into World War I in 1917. Harry eventually became a commissioned officer in the U.S. Navy, helping organize United States naval air operations in Europe after America declared war on Germany. He continued flying in America during the postwar years, and was instrumental in encouraging his father to endow a new philanthropic enterprise in 1926, the Daniel Guggenheim Fund for the Promotion of Aeronautics.[27]

Even before the fund was officially established, an important grant of half a million dollars was made to New York University in 1925, establishing the Guggenheim School of Aeronautics within the College of Engineering. After the Guggenheim Fund was formally announced in 1926, this grant was followed by other awards to a number of schools, always for the purpose of furthering the study of aeronautical sciences at the university level. Stanford was the recipient of $300,000 for study and experimentation in technical problems; $300,000 were earmarked for permanent study and experimentation at Cal Tech; MIT also received $225,000 for the construction of permanent facilities; the University of Michigan received $78,000 for the completion of aeronautical laboratories and expansion of the curriculum in the field of aeronautical sciences.[28] Alexander Klemin, who had joined New York University (NYU) about 1922 and was teaching aeronautical courses when the Guggenheim School was established, emphasized the need for professionals in aeronautical engineering to maintain progress in the discipline and to help schools encompass the growing body of scientific knowledge on the subject by keeping up to date on the latest research.[29]

Klemin cautioned that aeronautical engineering should always be taught with a firm background in the general engineering curriculum, never as an entirely separate course of study. In some western universities, Klemin noted, aeronautical engineering was undertaken only at the postgraduate level. The general rule was to include it in the undergraduate curriculum before intensified research in a graduate school, as was the practice at MIT. Aeronautics courses were customarily given in the fourth year in naval architecture at Michigan or in the fourth year of a general course of engineering at Klemin's own school, NYU. By 1929, a survey by an aviation magazine reported a total of 1,400 aeronautical engineering students enrolled in fourteen schools across the United States. The University of Detroit led in enrollment, with 341 students, followed by the University of Michigan, 150; MIT, 161; NYU, 120; and the Armour Institute, 118. Smaller enrollments were reported at the University of California, Berkeley, 83; University of Minnesota, 75; and University of Washington, 60. Other schools with aeronautical programs included Purdue, University of Kansas, Stanford, University of Nebraska, and Cal Tech. With additional help from the Guggenheim Fund, Cal Tech was able to attract the internationally acclaimed aerodynamicist Theodore von Karman to direct its Guggenheim Aeronautical Laboratory. Von Karman accepted Cal Tech's lucrative offer in 1929 and arrived in the United States in the spring of 1930. His leadership at the university sparked a new era in the field of theoretical dynamics and helped the United States achieve a commanding role in world aviation.[30]

In some instances, aeronautical engineering students had the opportunity to combine their studies with on-the-job experience. The designer and manufacturer Grover Loening, in New York City, accepted a number of working students from NYU. The students accumulated university credits for satisfactory work, monitored by a company supervisor. Loening accepted several young men during the summers of 1925 to 1929, including a senior who received permission to put in a full year's work in Loening's shops.[31] But the new cadres of trained aeronautical engineers did not close out the opportunities for many of the older individuals who had literally grown up with the aviation industry. With two years of high school, one year of college, service with the Corps of Engineers in World War I, and some wartime flight training, J. H. Kindelberger joined the Glenn Martin Company's new plant in Cleveland. Shortly after the war, Kindelberger became a close friend of Donald Douglas, a protegé of Hunsaker at MIT. Douglas left the Martin Company in 1920 to work on his own in California. Five years later, with contracts for a new, aluminum-frame airplane, Douglas hired Kindelberger as chief engineer. Kindelberger represents the kind of individual who formed a bridge between the older, "untrained" group of aviation engineers and the new professionally trained designers. It is interesting to note that when Kindelberger joined the Douglas organization in 1925, he went in with a new graduate of Cal Tech, Arthur Raymond, whose pay amounted to twenty-five cents an hour.[32]

Whatever their backgrounds, aeronautical engineers were usually a colorful lot. "In those days," Donald Douglas recalled, "the most conservative type of engineers wouldn't consider going into aviation. They thought it was rather a poor affair. I suppose a person had to be a little out of the ordinary to go into it. . . ."[33] In any case, the growing pool of trained aeronautical engineers played an important role in elevating air travel to a reliable, economical, and mature technology.

In addition to university-level support, the Guggenheim Fund sponsored a drive to promote instruction in aeronautical subjects in elementary and secondary schools. Accordingly, the fund announced the establishment of the Committee on Elementary and Secondary Aeronautical Education at the start of 1928. "Because it is possible that the children of today will, upon maturity, be living in an age when transportation by air will be a common feature of life," the fund explained in its press release, "it is particularly important that the principles and methods of aviation should be familiar to their minds." The press release called attention to the fact that elementary and secondary instruction in the principles of aeronautics was necessary to foster the understanding and familiarity of air transportation inherent in the air-minded generations of the future.[34] Speaking for the fund's education committee in an address to the National Education Association, William F. Durand, of the engineering faculty at Stanford and a member of the original twelve-member National Advisory Committee for Aeronautics, stressed the need for vocational training in aviation in secondary schools. Durand warned that aeronautical studies and vocational training would promote more interest in other areas of learning and would necessitate more attention to strengthening the school curriculum in these areas. In his opinion, aeronautics was probably the most important and diversified subject in the modern curriculum, encompassing mathematics, physics, chemistry, and mechanics, not to mention numerous aspects of engineering, meteorology, navigation, psychology, and physiology. Aeronautical terminology was yet another problem. Durand reminded the audience that NACA had recently defined 565 words in current usage relating to specifically aeronautical affairs which were not yet in current dictionaries. At least 200 to 300 of these words should be a part of the vocabulary of the average man, said Durand, in order to comprehend the present growth of aviation as reported in the daily newspapers.[35]

For layman and aviator alike, many of the new aeronautical terms related to standard disciplines now receiving increased attention because of their connections with the rapid advance of aviation. This was especially true, for example, in physiology and meteorology.

Physiology and Meteorology

Pilots themselves came under increased technical scrutiny. It was essential to learn more about the effect of flight on the human body as pilots performed more functions in the sky and began to spend longer hours in the air under all sorts of arduous physical conditions. There were many unanswered questions about the ability of human beings to handle a machine as powerful and as complex as an airplane in an unknown and hostile medium. Flying an aircraft put additional demands on all normal human capabilities and required strict and unceasing attention. "The man who drives an automobile may make a mistake twice," the layman was warned, "but for the pilot his first error in judgement is only too often his last."[36] The airman was subject to the psychological and physiological effects of high altitude compounded by the added factors of high speed, severe vibrations, and deafening noise, all of which exposed his senses to an unaccustomed strain. In order to be better informed in the selection of pilots and to maintain a constantly high level of fitness for aviators, it was considered imperative to develop some standards of aviation medicine suitable to the requirements of human beings confronted with a new set of environmental factors that were bewildering and full of dangers.[37]

Again, it was the emergency of war that spurred the beginnings of research in the field of aviation medicine. In 1917, the Army Medical Research Board organized a special research laboratory for aviation medicine at Hazelhurst Field, Long Island. Lieutenant Louis H. Bauer, an M.D. from the Harvard Medical School, took over the laboratory in 1919. The lab became the School of Aviation Medicine in 1922, with Bauer as Commandant, and moved to Brooks Field near San Antonio, Texas, in 1926, where the school provided instruction for the Navy as well. Both services emphasized physical examination of student pilots, rather than the theory of aeromedical problems. For this reason, the literature of aviation medicine remained somewhat sparse during these years, with occasional articles appearing in the *Military Surgeon* or in the *Journal of the American Medical Association*. The only specialized textbook available was *The Medical and Surgical Aspects of Aviation*, written by Dr. H. Graeme Anderson, an RAF officer, and published in England in 1919. But Bauer had been gathering material for his own book, based on his observations during the war and later experience as commandant of the School of Aviation Medicine. His *Aviation Medicine*, issued in 1926, was the first such text published in the United States, and became the standard text for many years. Reflecting the medical philosophies prevalent at Brooks Field, the book emphasized the procedures relevant to physical requirements and examinations of pilots.

Nevertheless, the growing group of flight surgeons, especially the Brooks Field contingent, began probing theoretical problems of aviation medicine, and devised early equipment to predict instrument reflexes and aptitudes of candidates for pilot training. One of the most vexing problems of early aviation was the inability of pilots to do blind, or instrument, flying, in smoke, fog, or clouds when it was not possible to see the ground clearly. When they were unable to orient themselves in relation to the horizon or to the earth below, pilots found that they were subject to a total loss of the sense of their flight attitude—a complete confusion of lateral and horizontal position. Through original research in aviation medicine during the mid-1920s, however, Captain David A. Meyers and Major William C. Ocker explored the physiological principles and helped furnish the basis for the techniques of instrument flying.[38]

The transition from theory to technique owed much to the Guggenheim Fund's Full Flight Laboratory (FFL) and to the aeronautical skills of Lieutenant James H. Doolittle. The FFL was established at Mitchell Field, Long Island, in 1928, and engaged in developing proce-

Plate 10

Plate 11

Plate 12

10. The American *Eagle,* typical of the biplanes favored by barnstormers and early fixed-base operators. The forward cockpit held two passengers. *NASM.*

11. The Stinson *Detroiter,* capable of carrying six passengers, served as a corporate plane and also equipped some early airlines. *NASM.*

12. For both sport and business flying, enclosed-cabin monoplanes such as the four-place Curtiss *Robin* became more numerous by the late twenties. *NASM.*

Plate 13

Plate 14

13. Aerial crop dusting became viable business during the twenties. Huff Daland at work in Georgia, ca. 1925. *NASM*.

14. Huff Daland Dusters, off on international business. This crate is part of a shipment of seven airplanes sent to fight the cotton boll weevil in Peru in 1927. *NASM*.

Plate 15

Plate 16

15. The reliable Fairchild FC-2W, widely used in photographic work and favored by many bush pilots. *NASM*.

16. Major Rudolph Schroeder pilots the LePere biplane, with supercharged Liberty engine, over McCook field during an early phase of high-altitude test flights in 1919. *NASM*.

Plate 17

Plate 18

17 and 18. Progress in flight technology. The Lockheed *Vega* with its internally braced wing and wooden skin; the metal Boeing *Monomail* with retractable landing gear. Both had improved radial engines. *Both from NASM.*

dures for fog dispersal, deicing equipment, and new systems for instrument flying. The fog-dispersal and deicing experiments were only partly successful, but the FFL's contribution to instrument flying was monumental. Doolittle had already become interested in instrument flying as a result of his record transcontinental flight September 4/5, 1922, when he became the first person to fly coast to coast in less than twenty-four hours. Doolittle prudently equipped his DH-4 with a recently developed turn-and-bank indicator, designed by Elmer Sperry, Jr., and the instrument literally saved Doolittle's life when he had to fight his way through a turbulent storm during the night. "This particular flight," Doolittle asserted, "made me a firm believer in proper instrumentation for bad weather flying." A highly personable officer, the colorful Doolittle was known for several other pioneering aeronautical exploits, including his victory in the Schneider Cup Race for 1925, in which he set a world's record speed for seaplanes of 245 mph. Behind the sensational headlines and apparent flamboyance, Doolittle combined sound airmanship and a thorough understanding of aeronautics, represented by the Doctor of Science degree in aeronautical engineering he acquired from MIT in 1925. When the Guggenheim Fund's FFL began, Lieutenant Doolittle was temporarily detached from the Air Corps to head the operation. The Air Corps also furnished additional personnel and facilities.[39]

Typical navigational instruments of the era were rudimentary at best: airspeed indicator, altimeter, and magnetic compass. The latter two were especially subject to error, and both lacked the accuracy required for safe instrument approaches and landings. Even the turn-and-bank indicator lacked the precision necessary for low-speed landing approaches on instruments since it yielded information that was more qualitative than quantitative. Over a period of several months, Doolittle and a highly qualified staff at the FFL refined the necessary equipment. One was a workable radio homing range with visual cues enabling a pilot on instruments to fly an accurate course to the landing field. Elaborating on a preliminary sketch made by Doolittle, Elmer Sperry, Jr., designed and built a pair of new instruments of fundamental value to instrument flying: the Sperry Artificial Horizon, and the Sperry Directional Gyroscope. The Artificial Horizon provided a pilot with precise visual cues, displaying a winged airplane symbol so as to represent its relative altitude against a background of the earth's horizon. The Directional Gyroscope effectively eliminated the variation inherent in the magnetic compass, with its tendency for a northerly inclination. Doolittle also cooperated with the Kollsman Instrument Company in perfecting a much more accurate barometric altimeter that eliminated the fluctuations of older designs, ranging from fifty to one hundred feet, and gave readings that varied by only five to ten feet. Finally, the staff at the FFL considered the visual designs of instruments and carefully plotted the location of these new instruments in relation to normal gauges and dials in the instrument panel in order to enhance effective scanning, thereby reducing pilot stress and fatigue.

A series of experimental flights verified the usefulness of the newly developed instrumentation as installed in a Consolidated NY-2 biplane that had been purchased by the FFL. The plane's rear cockpit contained the full array of instruments, and had a hood that completely blocked Doolittle's vision during the test flights when Lieutenant B. S. Kelsey occupied the forward cockpit as a safety measure. The first complete blind flight occurred on September 24, 1929. With Kelsey along, ostentatiously holding his hands visible outside the forward cockpit, Doolittle settled into the rear seat under the blind-flying hood. Using the radio beam and instruments, Doolittle took off, made a pair of 180° turns, and landed without once seeing the ground. When the Guggenheim FFL began its work in 1928, blind landings through fog or heavy clouds were made only in extreme emergencies or by foolhardy pilots. Within ten months a major breakthrough had been accomplished, and within a decade military and civil fliers alike were engaged in blind flying by instruments on a routine basis. The essential instruments and techniques have since remained basic. Few obstacles to safe flying have been so quickly or so conclusively resolved.[40]

Progress in radio represented a similarly sophisticated contribution to flight operations and navigation. Although organized research into the problem of two-way communication between ground stations and airborne planes dated to military projects in collaboration with the Bureau of Standards during World War I, little was accomplished until the mid-twenties. From its inception in 1926, the Aeronautics Branch of the Department of Commerce considered radio communication to be essential, and again called on the Bureau of Standards for help. Taking advantage of recent advances in radio technology, the bureau developed promising prototype apparatus by 1927; during 1928, the Aeronautics Branch opened its first seven stations, rigged with improved equipment capable of two-way voice communications within a range of at least 150 miles. The Aeronautics Branch also began to install a new system of teletypewriter gear for more reliable transmission of weather bulletins and other relevant flight information. Finally, the Aeronautics Branch fostered development of the four-course radio range, which operated as the basic American air navigation aid from the late twenties until after World War II. Once again, the Bureau of Standards and the armed services made steady progress in the early twenties, adapting techniques pioneered in Europe. As it evolved by 1928, the American system employed aural signals (although research on visual instrumentation continued). A pilot flying directly on course heard a steady monotone signal; if he strayed to either side, he heard a Morse code signal for A (dot-dash) or N (dash-dot), depending on his direction of flight. Additional signals from a radio marker beacon assisted the pilot in plotting the distance he had traveled along the airway. Auxiliary services markedly improved, bringing detailed aviation maps, improved navigational equipment such as sextants, and more sophisticated navigational techniques that not only enhanced service on domestic flights but also set the stage for more adventurous regular transoceanic routes and long-range navigation for military bombers during the decade of the thirties. For commercial aviation, the striking advance in radio facilities—despite the occasionally balky equipment—proved the most important. It meant that air transports could begin to fly long distances without ever seeing the ground, maintaining regular schedules through the night or during cloudy weather (when beacons became only marginally useful). Airlines could not only begin to compete with express trains on a twenty-four-hour timetable but could fly at higher altitudes above an overcast to take advantage of more favorable winds and smoother air. The increasing safety and regularity made possible by radio navigation and communications were important in attracting a growing clientele among tourists, as well as schedule-conscious businessmen, whether they themselves were flying or depending on airmail to beat a deadline.[41]

The technical progress in aircraft and increase in aircraft performance forced continuous revision of old precepts, created new problems, and prompted new standards. The passage of the Air Commerce

Act in 1926 meant added pressure by the federal government to establish the most rigorous requirements for the selection of pilots engaged in air transport as well as encouragment of further studies to ensure passenger comfort and safety. As one early source observed, authorities finally awoke to the realization that "flight in aircraft could and should be accomplished without exposing both passengers and pilots to the deafening roar of high powered motors, paralyzing cold, the stupefying effects of the rarified air at high altitudes, the deadly fumes of carbon monoxide, and the blistering effects of winds of hurricane velocity."[42]

In 1926, Louis Bauer resigned from the Army to take over as medical director of the Aeronautics Branch of the Bureau of Air Commerce. Under Bauer's direction, progressively stricter standards were established for three classes of fliers generally recognized at that time: private pilots, industrial pilots, and transport pilots. Bauer also named the first medical examiners officially designated to test and certify pilots, and his system of examinations by designated physicians in selected cities across the country became standard. Bauer's influence on the professionalization of the discipline of aviation medicine was reflected in his key role during the formation of an association and a specialized periodical. The Aero Medical Association of the United States, organized in 1929, included both military and civilian members, and its annual meetings provided the setting for informal exchanges of information as well as an opportunity for the presentation of formal research papers. The first meeting of the association in 1929 included a paper on "Relation of Hypotension and Aviation," a study of airline pilots by the medical adviser of Boeing Air Transport. The meeting helped provide material for the first issue of the *Journal of Aviation Medicine*, which made its debut early the following year. Both the association and the *Journal* succeeded, acquiring international stature and membership in the decades ahead.[43]

The foundation of the Aero Medical Association and its *Journal* reflected the trend toward increased professionalization within the aviation community, and marked the emergence of aviation medicine as a recognized branch of science. A spokesman of the Mayo Clinic, looking back over the previous two decades of aviation medicine before 1941, remarked how the term "flight surgeon" had become an accepted term of military nomenclature, with hundreds of physicians specializing in flight medicine. It was significant too, he said, that so many leading medical schools included or were expanding their curriculum to offer instruction in aviation medicine and that a number of well-known universities were sponsoring path-breaking research in the field.[44]

Research on the condition of man in the air was paralleled by an increasing interest in the air itself. The intensive study of meteorology was an outgrowth of wartime requirements, although many significant advances in techniques were due to the stimulus of aeronautics in the postwar decade. Increased knowledge of the upper atmosphere grew out of the progress of aviation. For example, the "great circle" routes to the Orient that took aircraft over the Arctic helped focus attention on polar regions, which, in turn, led to better understanding of weather theory.[45] Willis R. Gregg, chief of the Aeronautical Division of the Weather Bureau, praised the ability of aircraft to gather accurate weather data for early-morning radio broadcasts in the mid-twenties. The Weather Bureau had followed the practice of releasing balloons with instruments attached to collect data on conditions in the upper atmosphere. The balloons did not always yield satisfactory results. Their uncontrolled ascent and flight path limited their value in gathering precise weather data at significant altitudes over important geographic regions; calms and storms limited their capacity for routine data collection on a regular frequency; prolonged balloon flights were acceptable for research purposes, but had little utility for daily weather broadcasts early in the morning. An airplane, taking off at 8 AM, could fly a comprehensive weather mission in rapid time to gather the relevant factors at the best altitude, including the air pressure, temperature, humidity, visibility; define the extent and altitude of the cloud layer, and check any unusual conditions in the process. All of this information would be analyzed and prepared in time for the first weather broadcast at 9 AM—exactly one hour after the plane was rolled out of the hangar.[46]

This procedure recalled an earlier condition when pioneer balloonists had enhanced man's knowledge of the upper atmosphere. Balloonists and, later, aircraft pilots served meteorology for a time until the techniques they pioneered were incorporated into newer and more sophisticated instrumentation of various weather devices that replaced them. The situation then reversed itself, and the meteorologist evolved into the position of advising the pilot. Nevertheless, aeronautics had a fundamental effect on the advances in meteorology and the science of weather prediction; it was the increasing activity of aviation that necessitated more accuracy in forecasting as well as a greater knowledge of the vagaries of weather. When the Air Commerce Act of 1926 went into effect, the services of the Weather Bureau were placed under a new schedule of operations around the clock in order to supply the passenger lines with indispensable weather information. Before 1926, up-to-the-minute weather reports had been issued for special events such as air races and long-distance flights; never before had accurate forecasts been immediately at hand for regular airline operations.[47] Then too, up-to-date forecasting was important to farmers, ranchers, construction engineers, resort owners, fishermen— dozens of people whose work was affected one way or another by cloudless or stormy skies, and who were grateful for the Weather Bureau's daily warning or promise of better days to come.

The requirements of scheduled flight services fostered a closer attention to the study of surface weather conditions in general—fog, rain, sleet, snow. Revised standards to estimate visibility and cloud frequency were developed. For the first time, information of this type, including wind characteristics as well, was systematically collected for the Plains states and the Pacific coast where such data were sketchy or had never been available in a comprehensive report. The nature of general weather trends and development over the entire continental United States came into sharper focus as the Weather Bureau encouraged stations across the country to send in standardized reports to be summarized in a meaningful compilation.[48] "Aid to American aviation," wrote Donald Whitnah, a historian of the Weather Bureau, "has involved more innovation, technological development, and opportunities for expansion of Weather Bureau facilities than any other field of weather service."[49]

Meteorology in the twenties cannot be discussed without crediting the Daniel Guggenheim Fund for the Promotion of Aeronautics. Concerned about the lack of an organized weather service, a shortcoming that had been a severe handicap to planning the Lindbergh transatlantic flight, Harry Guggenheim engaged the fund in various meteorological projects. Among these new programs was preparing a scholarly text on meteorology for aviators, operating a Model Weather Service in California, granting funds to the University of Michigan to support an expedition to Greenland for research and studies in forecasting storms, and developing a program of course work for professional training in aeronautical meteorology.[50] Although the department of geophysics in the St. Louis University's Institute of Technology had offered instruction in meteorology as early as 1925, course work on a professional level for aeronautics was first inaugurated at MIT in the autumn of 1928 under the auspices of the Guggenheim Fund.[51]

The first courses were taught by Carl-Gustaf Arvid Rossby, a transplanted Swedish expert and a veteran of Guggenheim's Model Weather Service. He delivered his first lecture in the Guggenheim Aeronautical Laboratory, the legacy of the fund's earlier concern with aeronautical engineering. The three-year program was carried out on the graduate level until 1940, when it became a separate department of meteorology. Early in the thirties, MIT carried out the first serious research in collecting and utilizing upper air data through the development of the radiosonde, a device to measure humidity, temperature, and air pressure at high altitudes that grew out of Rossby's experience with the Model Weather Service. This fundamental contribution to meteorology was followed by the formulation, in cooperation with the Department of Agriculture, of the five-day weather forecast, which was to have a substantial value for agriculture, industry, and the general public.[52]

Other Technical Patterns

The remarkable technological progress in aeronautics during the twenties presents a kaleidoscopic pattern in which some pieces can almost be overlooked, even if by accident. As an example, one might point to the growing interest in the somewhat peripheral discipline of rocketry. Although rocket researchers on both sides of the Atlantic recorded significant progress, a major milestone occurred when the American pioneer Robert H. Goddard successfully launched the world's first liquid-fueled rocket on March 16, 1926. Goddard conducted his historic experiment in an apple orchard near Auburn, Massachusetts, and the rocket climbed to only 184 feet in its two-and-one-half-second flight, but from such humble beginnings a new chapter in the exploration of our universe began. Another innovation, relegated for a time to amusement parks, had a major impact on flight training—for astronauts in the future as well as for aviators. In 1929, Edward A. Link patented the first electrical-mechanical flight simulator, built with considerable imagination and miscellaneous components from the Link Piano and Organ Company, owned by his father. Although the Navy bought a flight simulator in 1931, and a handful were sold to various aviation-related firms, amusement parks acquired several dozen and remained the biggest market for several years. In 1934, the Army ordered six flight simulators, and the Link Trainer soon became ubiquitous at flying schools around the globe. After World War II, flight simulators became increasingly complex, keeping pace with sophisticated new military and commercial aircraft, and provided invaluable experience in preparation for manned space flight.[53] Other technical contributions of the twenties may seem ephemeral in retrospect, even though they served as important components in developing a firm foundation for aeronautical growth. For instance, the Guggenheim Fund encouraged a program to paint directional arrows atop large roofs of barns, factories, and other buildings that provided rudimentary information about a town's identity, the nearest airfield, and the direction of true north.[54] In the days of frequently erratic radio communications and incomplete aerial charts, homely navigational aids like these were a godsend.

As a manifestation of other ancillary aerodynamic trends, one might point to the evolution of rotorcraft, such as the helicopter and the autogiro. While a number of helicopter designs achieved partial successes before World War I, the first entirely successful helicopter, designed by Heinrich Karl Focke of Germany, made its initial flight in 1936. During the twenties, attention focused on the concept of the autogiro as designed by the Spaniard Juan de la Cierva. Unlike the helicopter, whose rotor blades are turned under power, the autogiro's rotor blades rotated freely, while a conventional engine and propeller provided forward motion. But the large rotor blades did enable the autogiro to make steep takeoffs and landings within a limited space. Cierva's first autogiro took to the air during 1923 in Spain, followed by promising development in England during the late twenties. In the United States, Harold F. Pitcairn made the first autogiro flight on December 19, 1928.[55] Although the autogiro never became the aviation wonder that Pitcairn and other visionaries hoped for, it offered the public a tantalizing example of the aerial flexibility to come with the helicopter. Fascination with dirigibles comprised another instance of aeronautical technology that flourished during the late twenties in particular but eventually lost out to more substantial improvement in transport aviation. As noted in Chapter 1, above, the Navy's early interest in dirigibles for long-range patrol waned as the performance of propeller-driven aircraft advanced. American plans for commercial airship lines during the twenties took place against the background of apparently successful operations of the majestic German dirigibles like the *Graf Zeppelin*, whose eighteenth flight over the Atlantic brought her to America for the first time in 1928. But in spite of America's monopoly on helium (as opposed to the highly inflammable hydrogen used in German dirigibles), helium remained expensive, and the costs of construction and operation of giant rigid airships doomed them to extinction.[56]

Still other hallmarks of technical progress during the twenties reflected overtones of promotionalism and commercialism, even though certain of these trends highlighted growing reliability and demonstrated the airplane's capacity for increasingly higher speeds. Reliability, in fact, was a featured value during the Ford Airplane Reliability Tours begun in 1925. These tours, hopping from city to city across the United States, not only acquainted the public with a variety of commercially promising aircraft but also highlighted their potential usefulness as transport vehicles. Avowedly promotional in nature, the Reliability Tour and its imitators helped build an air-minded public.[57]

Among other prominent aeronautical features of the decade, air races stand out. This aspect of aerial competition unquestionably demonstrated the airplane's virtue of speed, displayed new technical refinements, and, judging from the attention generated in newspapers and magazines of the era, certainly kept the reading public air-minded. Flying meets and air races flourished in the pre–World War I era, but postwar races became major media events. The aerial exploits of combat fliers during the war seemed to infuse flying with danger and a dash of glamor that found new expression in postwar racing, and the obvious gains in flying speeds exercised a magnetic appeal for many Americans. After the war, a number of American businessmen, with the tacit support of military figures, decided to sponsor trophies and put up cash awards for air races as a means to catch up with European aviation. Ralph Pulitzer sponsored one of the first events in 1920, and the outstanding success of the initial Pulitzer Trophy Race placed it among the premier annual aviation competitions of the era. Similar aviation events in America, such as the National Air Races, also began during the early twenties, and United States planes and pilots successfully competed in international meets such as the Schneider Trophy Contest for float-equipped racers.

The significance of the competitive quest for higher speeds remains somewhat speculative. To be sure, some of the planes entered in competition incorporated technical embellishments that later became standard. During the 1923 Pulitzer races, the Verville-Sperry R-3 monoplane featured a low-mounted, cantilevered wing, retractable landing gear, a cowled engine, and a streamlined propeller spinner. The R-3 lost that year to the Navy's Curtiss R2C-1 biplane before winning the Pulitzer in 1924, but the 1925 race belonged to another Curtiss biplane, the Army's R3C-1.[58] It could be said that many technical racing features were too far advanced (or temperamental) to gain widespread application in the workaday world of commercial—or even military—flying. Some knowledgeable engineers, such as Charles Fayette Taylor, pointed approvingly to races; Taylor claimed that Curtiss engines, developed for the specialized air racing circuit, spurred development of the Rolls-Royce Merlin of the 1930s. On the other hand, an experienced fuel and power-plant engineer such as S. D. Heron remained skeptical of racing's influence on aeronautical progress. Heron, an active researcher during the twenties, felt that the fascination with exotic fuels and hybrid engines for racing had led power-plant and fuel engineers down too many unproductive paths—the "pestering," as he called it, that interfered too much with reasonable and workable engine/fuel combinations. It is interesting to note that military participation in such events began to wane during the 1930s, apparently because military leaders decided that little could be gained.[59]

The fallout from air races may have been as much in publicity as in technology. In any event, there were a number of less publicized organizational and institutional trends that may be considered more fundamental to the long-term health of aviation than transitory speed records.

CHAPTER SIX

Industry and Institutions

The elaboration of an aeronautical infrastructure not only encompassed technical foundations such as engineers and engineering but also involved the rationalization of operations formerly conducted on an ad hoc basis, such as the layout and operation of airports. The maturing aeronautical infrastructure became evident in terms of a recognizable manufacturing and corporate phenomenon that began to attract the increasing interest of the investment community. Attendant issues such as insurance coverage, a legal framework, and the prospect of federal regulation led to concrete developments within the decade. Distinctive, aviation-related associations became more prominent in national activities.

This institutionalization of aviation marked it as a mature technology, with increased public visibility and supported by its own self-interest groups. It developed its own unique financial, legal, administrative, and regulatory identity.

Trends in Manufacturing and Finance

In 1929 Victor Selden Clark, author of a comprehensive survey of American industry, declared that the manufacture of aircraft occupied a position of "minor importance" in the hierarchy of American enterprise. He acknowledged that the value of aircraft manufactures had doubled from $7 million to $14 million between 1925 and 1927. Such growth had promise for the future, Clark said, but in his opinion the main value of aircraft manufacture to the engineering industry was in terms of innovations in engineering technique.[1]

Judging the industry by its peak of wartime achievement compared to its postwar record in 1929, the prospects of aircraft manufacturing may have seemed wanting. From April 1917 to November 1918, American producers had delivered 13,984 planes valued at $113,721,043, with the capacity to turn out 21,000 aircraft per year at the time of the Armistice.[2] The war's end choked off the lucrative military contracts, and just 780 planes were built in 1919, all but eight of them for the military. Until the situation at middle of the decade, the military services continued to claim most of the production, but the development of commercial aviation suggested new possibilities. The effects of the Kelly Act of 1925, which turned over mail routes to private contractors, is seen in a comparison of production figures in 1925, when 445 of 789 planes were manufactured for the armed services, and 1926, when they claimed only 478 of 1,186. In 1929, after the Air Commerce Act and Lindbergh's transatlantic flight, 779 military types were produced in contrast to 5,414 civilian aircraft,[3] for a total value of $70,334,107 for all aircraft, parts, and equipment.[4] As an increasingly accepted mode of modern transportation, aviation was assisted by this momentum to weather the troubled economic climate of the 1930s. In spite of the depression, the book value of the three main sectors of the transportation industry indicates a steady increase by aviation. The following figures emphasize the dominant position of the automotive industry, but show that the aircraft industry experienced a significant rate of growth, even in the depressed thirties.[5]

	1919	1929	1937
Total book value	$2,480,000	$3,476,000	$3,672,000
Motor vehicles	$1,936,000	$2,742,000	$2,792,000
Locomotive and railroad equipment	$523,000	$616,000	$680,000
Airplanes	$19,000	$118,000	$201,000

Indicators of the rising strength of the aviation business during the twenties encouraged enthusiastic reports by the aviation press, business journals, and investment houses. An aircraft show at Detroit in 1928 excited the reporter of the *Magazine of Business*. The exhibition cataloged 100 exhibits in all, evidence of the expanding foundations of the aviation industry and a yardstick promising a sound potential for

growth. There was a definite feeling of modernity, novelty, and challenge. "A new industry," said the writer. "Striking new vehicular forms.
A new nomenclature. New firms." Yet the new aviation industry was
strongly rooted in a sound structure of modern technology, resting on
a foundation of firm although comparatively modern enterprises such
as B. F. Goodrich, Standard Oil, AC Spark Plug, and Westinghouse.
These contemporary giants exhibited at the aircraft show too, and their
presence lent an atmosphere of stability and practicality to the vehicles of the future.[6] The *Magazine of Business*, reviewing the emergence of the aviation industry, noted that its fund of experience extended
back more years than was generally realized, and that the manufacturing techniques, methods of construction, marketing, and record of
production to date all added a "sense of solidarity" to the new airplane
business.[7]

The enterprise of aeronautics was further buttressed by a growing
myriad of manufacturers, subcontractors, suppliers of parts and accessories. The ranks of subcontractors and vendors came into the aviation
business during World War I. Caught in the postwar doldrums, many
persisted, and a review of the trade journals during the twenties shows
their steady growth throughout the decade. Sometimes such firms were
dedicated solely to the aviation industry; sometimes a firm served
aviation requirements, as well as marine, automotive, or other industrial activity. Whatever commercial mode they followed, such businesses represented another important factor in the aeronautical
infrastructure—unmistakable evidence of aeronautics as a mature enterprise able to attract a broad spectrum of vendors. Pynchon and
Company, members of the New York Stock Exchange, published an
eighty-page review of *The Aviation Industry* in 1928; it was a surprisingly extensive catalog of the dozens of firms in one way or another
involved in aeronautical manufactures.[8]

Pynchon's publication, however, was less an admiring tribute to a
new technological phenomenon than a gambit designed to engage the
interest of potential investors in aeronautical securities, a topic that
Pynchon further detailed in later discussions of the subject.[9] Pynchon
was not the only institution to try to catch the eye of the prospective
stargazers in aerial securities. Another member of the Stock Exchange, Pask and Walbridge chronicled *The Development of Aviation
in the United States* in a sixteen-page pamphlet that included a schol-

arly outline of the history of American aviation, a résumé of the expansion of mail and passenger lines, and other statistical progressions that were intended to underscore the potential investment value of the industry. A more specific title issued by Pask and Walbridge surveyed *The Development and Outlook of the Fairchild Aviation Corporation and Its Subsidiaries*. After sixteen pages of optimistic yet conscientiously objective analysis enlivened by several attractive photographs, Pask and Walbridge inevitably concluded that the Fairchild Aviation Corporation was a sound investment that "possesses merit as a speculation." Those who sought up-to-date information on promising aeronautical securities could avail themselves of the services of the *Aero Analyst: A Financial and Technical Review*, published from time to time in New York. Founded in the spring of 1929, the high-flying *Aero Analyst* had a short-lived existence, wiped out by the nose dive of the stock market crash.[10]

Before the crash, the Commercial National Bank and Trust Company of New York reported that $500 million had been "made available" to aeronautical development from 1927 to 1929. The company's own investment information listings had more than doubled from 230 to 600 entries as of July 1929, which stirred the firm to issue a new 156-page *Financial Handbook of the American Aviation Industry*.[11] The bank was only reporting a trend, however, for the real investment deluge was yet to come. Beginning in March 1928 and running through December 1929, $1 billion of aviation securities were traded on the New York Stock Exchange. By 1932, the value had sunk to $50 million—an investment loss that returned only five cents for every dollar.[12]

The big market in aviation stocks reflected the general bullishness in securities, although it was certainly abetted by the overconfidence radiated by the brokerage houses as well as the public press. Leading magazine publishing companies such as Crowell and Curtis carried dozens of articles, all predicting a sound evolution of aviation in the future, and published their own respective studies of the airplane business. Admittedly, there was something of an ulterior motive involved in these reports. *Collier's*, the leading organ of the Crowell organization, put forth an evaluation of *The Aviation Industry and Its Market*, which not only tabulated the usual statistics of production, flying fields, and so on, but also outlined the role played by Crowell publications in influencing the buying public.[13] The same idea was implicit in *The Aviation Industry*, a more extensive publication originating in the Curtis Publishing Company. The Curtis volume includes an interesting item about advertising revenues that once more indicates the relatively small size of the aviation business as compared to the automobile industry. Manufacturers in the aircraft sector spent slightly more than $400,000 with Curtis, while the automobile companies spent $6,500,000 for advertising.[14]

Nevertheless, the significance of these two leading publications as well as brokerage houses expending so much attention on aeronautics should not be overlooked. After the hysteria of fortune hunting had blown over, the useful information of these articles and brokerage reports helped create the foundations of an intelligent and realistic approach to aviation. It is also necessary to give Crowell and Curtis credit for publishing a number of constructive and informative articles on the problems as well as the progress of aviation. Not all of their stories were the glamorized, stereotyped sagas of dashing airmen and dangerous aircraft. The *Saturday Evening Post*, in particular, performed a valuable service in printing articles by Charles A. Lindbergh and Howard Mingos, the latter a leading aviation spokesman who was editor of the *Aircraft Yearbook*. Other able, common-sense pieces on aviation were contributed by Ralph D. Weyerbacker and the *Post's* associate editor, Wesley W. Stout.[15] While these essays may have whetted the appetites of many individuals with a craving for choice morsels among aerial stocks, they also imparted an important fund of knowledge to the general public.

The aviation industry, like so many other elements of American business in the twenties, experienced considerable consolidation through acquisition and merger. The trend was evident in the evolution of airline companies as well as in manufacturing. In most instances, the operators remained separate from the manufacturers, although several extensive combines emerged. One of the largest, and most broadly based, was United Aircraft and Transport Corporation, organized early in 1929 and underwritten by the National City Company, a subsidiary of the National City Bank of New York. In addition to Boeing Air Transport, Inc., and the Boeing Airplane Company, the United combine swallowed up Pratt and Whitney, a leading power-plant manufacturer, along with two propeller manufacturers renamed Hamilton

Standard Propeller Corporation. United's interest in the private plane sector was represented in the acquisition of Stearman, in Wichita, Kansas. By the end of the year, United's various properties included four other airlines and three other aircraft companies, including those of Chance Vought and Igor Sikorsky. United emerged as an integrated aerial octopus, building a complete range of civil and military aircraft, running its own airlines, and supplying itself with engines, accessories, and miscellaneous services.

Much has been made of the intense interest in aviation following Lindbergh's transatlantic flight in 1927, and the Lindbergh boom in aviation stocks and mergers, like United's, was fueled by the bullish Wall Street market of the twenties. Other combinations followed, such as North American Aviation and the Aviation Corporation, known as AVCO. General Motors also invested several millions in various aviation firms during the closing years of the 1920s. "The result of all this activity," noted one historian of the feverish activity in aviation stocks, "was that in 1929 . . . aviation stocks rose to heights that distinguished them even in the speculative market of that year."[16]

This is not to say that the big mergers put all of American aviation in the hands of all-powerful monopolistic interests. Clyde Cessna kept building planes in Wichita; Donald Douglas on the West coast and Leroy Grumman on the East coast continued to preside over strong independent companies that survived the mergers and even the depression. The stock market crash of 1929 ruined many aviation companies, along with many other Wall Street favorites, but it was the New Deal that delivered the most telling blow to the big aeronautical combines of the late twenties. Following the Air Mail Act of 1934, manufacturing and transportation were permanently divorced, and the New Deal's antipathy to overintegrated business kept them that way. The structure of the American aviation industry has continued in this pattern, with a basic separation of aircraft, power-plant, and transport companies. The corporate legacy of the merger era continues, however, in the form of the companies that continue to play a leading role in domestic and international aeronautics. The United combine, for example, was split into Boeing Aircraft, United Airlines, and United Aircraft Corporation, basically an engine and component manufacturer that included Pratt and Whitney along with Hamilton Standard.[17]

Geography and Location

Whether a company belonged to a corporate family or remained independent, the growing labor requirements of the aviation industry became significant in several states during the twenties, and resulted in definable patterns of industrial location. The aviation industry developed into a factor of industrial location that created different types of jobs in traditional centers of manufacturing and brought new opportunities to other areas that were particularly suited to the special requirements of aircraft production. Some companies, such as Boeing in Seattle, were content to stay where they were. Many manufacturers preferred to remain in the East, close to transportation centers and points of distribution. The East also provided the skilled aptitudes of machinists for engine manufacture as well as furnishing a pool of workers and shops for the specialized production of sensitive instruments and aircraft fittings. The western prairies, characterized by areas of level plains, implying fewer topographical hazards to airplanes plus reasonable weather, attracted some of the pioneer designers and manufacturers who liked the promising flying and testing conditions there. Moreover, Wichita, Kansas, the locus of a Midwest oil boom, generated a source of risk capital tapped by aggressive aeronautical entrepreneurs. Famous names such as Stearman, Beech, and Cessna have been associated with Wichita since the early part of the twenties. Promise of extended periods of flying weather, as well as the topographical conditions and growing labor supply, attracted more manufacturers to California, whose climate had special advantages. The facilities for aircraft production necessitated large buildings with plenty of space to accommodate the growing wing span and fuselage length of modern planes. Such buildings for aircraft construction and assembly required less heating expense in California, and were subject to less depreciation resulting from attrition due to weather.[18]

Aviation seemed so promising that some cities advertised themselves as potential production sites, apparently hoping for new investment and new jobs. Atlanta, Georgia, tried to sell itself as a center for the aviation industry and touted the availability of its production facilities. Lamentably, the era's racism tainted Atlanta's promotion; the city's propaganda proclaimed special advantages in the well-known skills of "Anglo-Saxon workers."[19] Promotion on the West Coast, on the other hand, stressed climate, terrain, and international route possibilities. West Coast boosters argued that the prevalence of favorable weather on the southern California coast permitted consistently longer hours of flying time, invaluable for evaluation of aircraft. It also meant that manufacturers could derive more utility from their investment in fields, equipment, and other paraphernalia that remained useless in winter weather elsewhere. Coastal winds were even less variable than those on the plains, so that there was a smaller element of danger in takeoffs and landing. Numerous flat, brushless areas along the Pacific coast allowed a safer margin in emergency landings, the argument ran on, and this feature also made it easy to lay out an airfield in the most practical location relative to a city. In addition to all this, it was necessary to keep in mind that Latin Americans were tremendously impressed by the achievements of American aviation; the Pacific coast location was a favorable locale for situating airfields in support of Latin American air routes.[20] In 1929 the Los Angeles Chamber of Commerce sponsored a full-page advertisement in *World's Work* that pointed out that the West coast, especially Los Angeles County, had indeed arrived as a center of aeronautics and supported its claim by citing statistics. The United States Department of Commerce was quoted to the effect that 32 percent of all flying activity in the United States originated in southern California, and that no fewer than twelve major aircraft and engine manufacturers operated in the same area.[21]

New York nevertheless remained the industry leader. Noting the rapid growth of the aviation industry, the Bureau of Labor Statistics undertook a survey in 1929 to ascertain the size and importance of this segment of business enterprise. Aside from manufacturing, the bureau reported, there would be direct and indirect influences on employment through: factory and airfield construction; openings for pilots, mechanics, and ground crews; and side effects on component industries such as metals, rubber, and petroleum. The bureau sent questionnaires to, and received responses from, more than a hundred known aircraft and engine companies in twenty-nine states, compiling a set of figures from January to May 1929. As for aircraft, the production total in 1928 was 4,886, with 1,020 produced in New York, 858 in Kansas, and 821 in Ohio. A total of 22,082 workers were listed on the payrolls, led again by New York with 4,396, California with 1,605, and Michigan, Washington, Kansas, New Jersey, and Ohio all reporting more than 1,000 each. These results led the bureau to make an optimistic, if judicious, forecast. Keeping in mind that aviation was a relatively new industry, the bureau said, the outlook was encouraging that aviation would have an effect of "material importance" on the job market.[22]

Airports

The bureau's inclusion of airport construction, although it promised jobs for workers, not only highlighted growing problems for cities in selecting and maintaining airport sites but also posed serious questions for many city administrations as to whether it was feasible to invest in airport construction. Aviation was growing, to be sure. Was it growing rapidly enough to warrant airport construction? On the other hand, if a progressive city did not spend the necessary sums for an airfield, might it not run the risk of becoming a second-rate commercial center, losing its position to a more foresighted neighboring metropolis? Many cities accepted the challenge.

In doing so, cities received minimal assistance from the federal government. There was virtually no national civil airway program before the Air Commerce Act of 1926, and the act itself, while providing aid for air navigation facilities, specifically excluded airports. In drafting this legislation, Congress apparently relied on the report of the Morrow Board of 1925, which drew, in turn, from the recommendations of Secretary of Commerce Herbert Hoover. Hoover based his view on the analogy between the "dock" concept of maritime commerce and air commerce. In the former, docking facilities for shipping were provided by private enterprise or by municipal funding. The federal government had responsibilities for providing a legal framework, along with charts, marking, and similar supportive services. The same pattern, Hoover argued, should obviously apply to air commerce. Until 1933, when Franklin Delano Roosevelt's depression-era administration committed millions of dollars to airport construction as part of a national recovery program, private and municipal investment accounted for the overwhelming share of airport funding. Between 1911 and 1932, funding was divided as follows: private, 49.7 percent; municipal, 47.6 percent; state, 2 percent; federal, 0.7 percent (mostly accountable to the Air Mail Service). The most active period of airport development occurred between 1927 and 1931, when the number of municipal fields jumped from 240 to 636, and the total number of all fields in operation increased from 1,036 to 2,093 in the same period.[23]

Clearly, both private and municipal planners were suddenly faced with complex problems in the design, construction, and operation of airports. Solutions to these difficulties came from diverse sources. To those who were interested in 1926, the Westinghouse Lamp Company supplied a forty-page pamphlet devoted to the single subject of *Airport and Airway Lighting*, a useful analysis of the location and types of equipment as well as of the various systems of lighting to ensure the highest degree of safety and efficiency.[24] Civil engineers plagued with unknown dimensions about laying and building landing strips could consult a volume put out by the Ford Motor Company in 1927, *The New Era of Transportation*. Although written in all seriousness, this overall handbook on the subject of aeronautics included several passages of unintended humor. In the chapter reviewing some "General Information about the Landing Field," the author imparted the colorful axiom that a terminal field is one "where the planes stay at night," a phrase that conjures up a sort of technological barnyard where aircraft, like other denizens of the air, could roost until the dawn. The best surface for the landing field, after all, was alfalfa or heavy grass. Other solemn specifications included tested principles of engineering evaluation. "The surface of the landing field," advised the text, "should be hard enough to support the plane during all seasons and so smooth that a motor car can be driven at fifty miles an hour over any part of it without throwing the passengers out of the seat."[25]

A more professional discussion was given by a consulting engineer, Ernest Payton Goodrich, in 1928, in the *National Municipal Review*. Goodrich's article represented a significant analysis of the problems of airfield planning to allow for the requirements of the safe operation of aircraft in relation to the landing field's size, location, design, and so on. He already recognized the difficulties in situating fields so as to allow the necessary margins of operational safety while retaining convenient and quick access to the heart of a city. Voicing a complaint that echoed the plight of generations of future airline patrons at many airports around the world, Goodrich noted that airfields on Long Island and in New Jersey were already so far from Manhattan that it took as much time to get downtown as it did to fly from Boston.[26] A professor of political science at the University of California, Austin F. Mc-

Donald, nevertheless reaffirmed, in 1930, the necessity of cities to maintain modern airports, not only to attract new businesses but also to keep firms in residence from moving away. McDonald wrote his timely article as a Simon N. Patten Fellow of the American Academy of Political and Social Science, which had granted him funds for this special research project and printed his findings in its *Annals* in recognition of the scope of the airport problem and the importance of airfields to modern cities. In spite of the irritating complexities of airport management, McDonald found that the public accepted municipal ownership, and that the chief fields were municipally, rather than privately, owned.[27] The increasingly specialized requirements of operating flying fields were reflected in *Civil Airports and Airways*, with each chapter written by an expert on a specific subject such as runway surfacing, lighting, shop management, and administration. The book itself was edited by a professional consulting aeronautical engineer, Archibald Black. As a part of its City Planning Studies, Harvard University published a special monograph in 1930, *Airports: Their Location, Administration, and Legal Basis*; another example of the growing technical literature in this field was a book, published in 1927, by Donald Duke, *Airports and Airways: Cost, Operation, and Maintenance*.[28]

Airports were not always profitable items for municipalities. Encouraged by the Lindbergh boom and spurred by a civic desire to keep up with other cities, Columbus, Ohio, passed an $850,000 bond issue in the fall of 1927 for the construction of an airfield to be known as Port Columbus. Port Columbus seemed a likely success because it was one of the terminal points of the combined air and rail service between New York and Los Angeles offered by Trans-Continental Air Transport and the Pennsylvania Railroad. Inaugurated in July 1929, the forty-eight-hour trip failed to offer a considerable time advantage over crack trains, and faltering revenues cracked further under the strain of the depression.[29] Although Port Columbus made no profits, its losses at least compared favorably with those of other airfields; it earned 56 percent of its expenses in 1929 and as much as 62 to 86 percent in succeeding years. Some American airports, however, not only made their expenses but even earned a modest return. Cities fortunate enough to have such profitable fields included Cincinnati, Cleveland, Kansas City, Lincoln, Salt Lake City, and Newark.[30]

Newark was the crucible for a number of pioneering airport schemes. Begun early in 1928, Newark's airfield was built up with hydraulic fill in a marsh area near the city. Newark had its eye on developing a first-class airport in order to become the major air terminal for the New York metropolitan area, and succeeded when the Post Office Department designated Newark as the eastern airmail terminal. The airport claimed the first hard-surfaced (asphalt) runway for a commercial field in the United States, and tested the feasibility batteries of floodlights for night flying. Newark also experimented with a series of lights implanted down the center of the runway as an aid to night landings, and tried out several other innovative airport operational aids. The landing field developed a growing amount of passenger travel, in addition to mail, especially after completion of the Pulaski Skyway, an express road that ran directly to the airport from the Holland Tunnel. In 1929, Newark reported 28,000 arriving aircraft and, five years later, had more takeoffs and landings per day than the combined traffic of international European airports such as Croydon (London), Le-Bourget (Paris), and Tempelhof (Berlin).[31]

Insurance and Law

City managers and engineers were not the only persons presented with unique problems brought about by the growth of aviation. Insurance agencies had to develop new procedures for underwriting the new risks of flying—"a veritable insurance adventure hardly inferior to that of aviation itself."[32] An Englishman reportedly wrote the first aeronautical policy in 1912; the postwar interest in aviation in the United States caught the interest of several groups. Unfortunately, inexperience resulted in some extremely dangerous ventures that ended in considerable losses, with the result that most companies refrained from issuing any comprehensive policies until the Air Commerce Act in 1926 enforced more stability in aviation. In the meantime, there were other attempts to create reasonable standards. Soon after World War I, a group of insurance companies formed the National Aircraft Underwriters' Association, and enlisted the cooperation of the Underwriters Laboratories (UL) to open a new department to certify aircraft. Higher quality of new aircraft construction caused UL requirements to be eased around 1923, permitting some planes to be accepted for insurance without UL certificates. A few companies also paid for the services of qualified aviation engineers to act as underwriters in order to build up expert departments to deal with aviation insurance covering fire, theft, and storm protection as well as public and passenger liability. [33]

Rates were originally high enough to lend credence to the assertion of an insurance magazine that excessive insurance costs were a deterrent to air travel. [34] In 1920, one large company put a limit of $2,000 on the amount of air travel insurance it offered for a duration of one year—and charged $90.00 for each $1,000 of insurance. Three years later, restricted coverage was available to passengers or pilots who engaged in limited flying at a cost of $25.00 per year for $1,000. [35] By 1929, insurance for scheduled airline flights could be obtained for $0.75 to $1.50 per $1,000 of insurance, and Pan American included a $500 accident insurance policy in its fares. Some companies offered a special year-long policy for flying travelers at rates of $15.00 per $1,000; Mutual Life covered its regular policyholders, with an added premium for occasional fliers; Bankers of Iowa charged no extra premium if a policyholder flew only occasionally; Equitable had no restrictions for airline passengers. [36]

Some observers blamed weaknesses in insurance coverage on the lack of a legal framework and of regulation of aeronautics. The truth was, one critic acidly commented, "any inexperienced pilot with any second-hand plane, who can induce a passenger to go into the air with him is free to do so, a condition unthinkable at sea." [37] Actually, American courts of law had begun ruling on aeronautical matters nearly a century earlier, when a balloonist made an unplanned landing in a garden patch. The unfortunate aeronaut was immediately made partner to a suit for damages he had caused in landing his craft and extricating the wreckage. The gardener won. As early as 1911, Governor Baldwin of Connecticut proposed federal control of aviation in a message to the American Bar Association. Although he failed, soon afterward Connecticut became the first state to pass aeronautical legislation, followed by Massachusetts. After November 1918, various legislative proposals circulated in Congress, though none was ever reported out of committees. In 1920, the Conference of Commissions on Uniform State Laws and the American Bar Association cooperated in approving a uniform state law policy, and released a joint statement endorsing a

program of federal legislation two years later.[38] Federal action, however, failed to follow.

In the face of this inability to achieve any encouraging results, other
influential voices were beginning to advocate the idea of federal control of aeronautics. Secretary of Commerce Herbert Hoover convened
an air law conference in the summer of 1921.[39] Even though the conference had no immediate results, Hoover's influential position and
the identification of the Commerce Department with the idea of legislation leading to a legal framework were important developments.
The highly respected Edward P. Warner emphasized that it was imperative to pass federal legislation for the regulation of aircraft and to
set up a Bureau of Aeronautics to help pave the way for articulated
development of American aviation. Airmail, he continued, should be
carried by private firms under contract to the government, which should
also lay out and maintain a system of regular airways. In addition, said
Warner, the goverment ought to ratify the International Air Law Convention, written at Paris in 1919, "to put us in line with the rest of the
world."[40]

A joint report of the American Engineering Council and the Department of Commerce in 1925 reaffirmed the necessity of American
participation in the International Air Law Convention, pointing out
that most of the major countries of the world were already members,
and further recommended the formation of a Bureau of Civil Aeronautics in the Department of Commerce.[41] In the wake of the controversy
over aircraft and national defense, centered on Brigadier General
Mitchell, the report of the President's Aircraft Board (the Morrow Board)
included recommendations that helped the passage of the Air Commerce Act in May 1926 creating an Aeronautics Branch in the Department of Commerce, an important step toward a legal framework.[42]

When the passage of the Air Commerce Act was being considered,
the publicity surrounding both the Lampert and Morrow boards seems
to have been the catalyst for the origin of several aviation bills in Congress during the mid-1920s, although the prestige of the NACA and
of Herbert Hoover, as secretary of commerce, was influential in keeping the issue of air regulation alive. The diverse individuals and groups
advocating some sort of legislation all seemed to want an organization
to fulfill several goals: to bring order out of chaos; to provide federal

aid to aviation similar to the support historically extended to shipping, railroads, and highways; to improve the existing air transport network; and to promote aviation as a matter of national security. Obviously, the new Aeronautics Branch needed a director of outstanding energy as well as of legal and bureaucratic instincts. Hoover found his man in William P. MacCracken, Jr.

A native of Chicago, MacCracken attended the University of Chicago, and took his law degree there in 1911. He learned to fly as an Army pilot during World War I. Returning to the law after his discharge, MacCracken became appalled by the lack of information concerning aviation law, and took a strong stand on the subject within the American Bar Association. Personable, energetic, and bright, he became closely involved with other individuals and organizations (such as the National Aeronautic Association) that, like himself, leaned toward some sort of federal regulation to give American aviation direction and momentum, and emerged as a leading figure in the congressional infighting and legislative compromises that led to the passage of the Air Commerce Act.

As assistant secretary for aeronautics, MacCracken needed all the energy and tact he could muster during the chaotic early months of his new office. For the first fiscal year, the Aeronautics Branch received little more than $550,000 and had a staff of less than a hundred people. Inundated by thousands of applications for licenses as transport pilots, as industrial pilots, as private pilots, and as mechanics, the Aeronautics Branch finally began to hit its stride in fiscal year 1928, with a budget of $3.8 million and an expanded work force for the field inspection team and the licensing section. At the same time, Mac-Cracken and his dedicated crew began to frame the first set of Air Commerce Regulations, ranging from requirements for flight training to proficiency standards for airline pilots and copilots. The branch also established a program of medical examiners, and worked out procedures for the certification of both engines and airframes. There were projects involving safety, acquisition and dissemination of statistics, public relations, and airport development. In addition, the Aeronautics Branch made major contributions to technical progress, such as more comprehensive beacon-lit air routes and the successful development of radio navigation facilities that became standard around the country in the 1930s. For the era of the 1920s, however, the Aeronautics Branch had its biggest impact in terms of bringing long-needed standards of safety and consistency to the American aviation scene.[43]

By the end of the decade, the body of laws and regulations of the air was complemented by the creation of the Air Law Institute of Chicago under the auspices of Northwestern University. The plan for such an institute apparently originated with Professor John W. Wigmore, dean of the law school at Northwestern. Wigmore was motivated by the desire to make Chicago a more air-minded city, and an occasion presented itself on the impending return of Northwestern's Professor Frederick D. Fagg, who had been an exchange professor at the Air Law Institute of Königsberg, the only one of its kind in Europe.[44] Wigmore solicited the aid of a friend, Reed Landis, to encourage Jerry Land of the Guggenheim Fund to support the proposed institute. Both Land and Harry Guggenheim indicated their interest,[45] and the Air Law Institute was incorporated in August 1929, with one-third of the initial cost of $35,000 subscribed by the Guggenheim Fund. As stated in the announcement of its opening, the purpose of the institute was to furnish information on air law in the United States and abroad, to build up a library of air law, to publish a journal, the *Air Law Review*, and to engage in other appropriate activities.[46]

The spate of congressional hearings and the creation of organizations such as the Aeronautics Branch and the Air Law Institute, with their ancillary activities and publications, all underscored the growing recognition of aviation in modern life and reflected the trend to institutionalization of a mature technology. In the same context, one can also point to the formation of the Air Line Pilots Association in 1931. There were additional indicators of maturation in other areas. Although the Aero Club of America dated back to 1905, it retained the aura of a private club for leisured amateurs. Internal dissension led to its demise in 1922, being succeeded by the National Aeronautic Association (NAA), still a somewhat genteel organization but connected to the Federation Aeronautique International, which had worldwide authority for the official certification of all flying records. Another transmogrification occurred when the wartime Manufacturers' Aircraft Association, established to rationalize national and international patent and production agreements, eventually spun off the Aeronautical Chamber of Commerce (ACC), established in 1921. Although the

ACC included major manufacturers, its more broad-based membership of operators and suppliers, running into the dozens, gave it a
more varied field of interest. Among other things, in 1919 the ACC
assumed responsibility for publishing annual editions of the *Aircraft
Year Book*, which became a valuable reference work about production
figures, major trends, case histories, and general information about
nearly every facet of the aviation industry.[47]

But congressional hearings, federal agencies, and trade associations
represented only minor manifestations of aviation technology as a
modern institution. Other groups approached aviation as a permanent
facet of contemporary civilization, and considered both the promises
and challenges inherent in the new phenomenon. Representative of
heightened public interest was a study entitled *Civil Aviation*, published in 1926 as a joint effort by the Department of Commerce and
the American Engineering Council. A year later, the American Academy of Political and Social Science dedicated the entire May 1927
issue of its *Annals* to the topic of "Aviation." This prestigious scholarly
journal presented commentary on the full spectrum of civil and military aviation, including manufacturing, service, and operations. Contributing authors included General William Mitchell, William P.
MacCracken, and Alexander Klemin as well as industry executives
and leading aviation figures from the Post Office Department and the
Weather Service.[48]

The most publicized review of flight occurred in 1928, when President Coolidge hosted the International Civil Aeronautics Conference.
Coolidge called the meeting "to provide an opportunity for an inter-
change of views upon problems pertaining to aircraft in international
commerce and trade," and to honor the twenty-fifth anniversary of the
Wright brothers' historic first powered airplane flight. Officials from
thirty-four nations accepted invitations, and a total of 441 delegates
participated in conference programs that lasted from November 26 to
December 18. Following a round of receptions in New York City, the
official delegates and others departed for Cleveland to inspect the city
airport, toured an international aviation exposition in Chicago, and
then visited Army aviation labs near Dayton while paying tribute to
the Wright brothers. Formal presentations and sessions followed during a four-day colloquium in Washington, after which additional tours
included the Bureau of Standards and NACA labs at Langley Field.

The entourage arrived in North Carolina by December 17, to observe commemorative ceremonies at Kitty Hawk, and then returned to Washington for adjournment.

The four-day session in Washington, where many papers were presented, resulted in two substantial publications. The *Proceedings* included conference miscellany as well as twenty-eight supplemental papers. The principal volume, the *Papers*, ran to 669 pages and included the sixty-two major presentations made during the conference. These presentations covered a remarkable spectrum of aviation topics, and were accompanied by résumés in both English and French. All in all, the conference conveyed the image of modern aviation, and the papers constituted a significant review of the state of the art for reference as well as guidance on new policy.[49]

While it is true that these trends in industry, finance, and related areas tended to involve specialists, technicians, and executives already in more or less direct contact with aviation, there were other indicators of increased awareness by the general public. Moreover, the social significance of aviation was increasingly viewed in both continental and intercontinental terms.

Part Four
NEW PERSPECTIVES OF FLIGHT

CHAPTER SEVEN

Symbolism and Imagery

In the 1920s aviation entered the American consciousness as an integral component of life and culture. Not surprisingly, aeronautical themes soon intruded into those indicators of American culture, Tin Pan Alley, comic strips, and movies. Aviation became a topic that momentarily dominated the book trade in the late twenties, especially in the wake of Lindbergh's flight. It generated its own specialized literature and a host of practitioners and aficionados. Further, aviation offered new perspectives for Americans to view their environment, and stimulated additional assessment of the airplane as an icon of the postwar technological age.

Cultural Themes

Increasing numbers of clues indicated that aviation was becoming a firmly fixed phenomenon in American society—an accepted artifact within contemporary American civilization. Thomas Hart Benton, the popular American painter fascinated by rural themes as well as the nation's commerce and industry, became one of the first recognized artists to utilize aeronautical symbolism. *Bootleggers* (1927), a comment on one of America's most nefarious commercial enterprises, nevertheless portrayed up-to-date rumrunners transporting illicit hootch via aircraft. Aviation received more positive representation in Benton's series of murals completed for the New School for Social Research in New York City (1930–31). *The Changing West* showed a soaring plane as part of the modern technological influences shaping life in the American West. More to the point, *Instruments of Power* delineated a concentration of electrical gadgetry, gears, and other industrial artifacts, out of which burst new machine-age implements such as the airplane.[1] Also representative of this symbolism of technology and flight was one of the illustrations chosen for Charles and Mary Beard's *The Rise of American Civilization*. A chapter entitled "The Machine Age" featured a lithograph comprising an industrial montage, with a swift airplane slicing across the top of the illustration. In their text, the Beards listed aviation as one of the monumental forces at work in American society. "More fraught with social destiny than . . . mass production of things in dazzling variety," they wrote, "were the radical departures effected in technology by electrical devices, the internal combustion engine, wireless transmission of power, the radio, and the airplane—changes more momentous even than those wrought by invention in the age of Watt and Fulton."[2]

Even though published in 1934, the Beards' assessment captured the public's growing fascination and awareness of aviation in the decade following World War I. It is an inescapable fact that Lindbergh's Atlantic triumph of 1927 triggered much of this popular acclaim. But even thoughtful contemporaries realized that all the publicity lavished on the Lone Eagle just as surely made the American public more aware of aviation technology. The esteemed science writer Edwin E. Slosson made this point in discussing aeronautical progress, especially after Lindbergh's triumphal American tour of 1928, during which the idolized aviator flew *The Spirit of St. Louis* to eighty-two cities in forty-eight states (under the auspices of the Daniel Guggenheim Fund for the Promotion of Aeronautics). Slosson's observation deserves comment, since it appeared in a long-respected historical study, *The Great Crusade and After, 1914–1928*, published by his son Preston W. Slosson in 1930. This was part of a multivolume series, *A History of American Life*, edited by Arthur M. Schlesinger, Sr., and Dixon Ryan Fox; all books in the series shared the same endpaper illustration depicting historic trends in American life, culminating in a plane and dirigible soaring aboue a modern city of skyscrapers.[3]

In a variety of themes, then, aviation became an ubiquitous facet of American culture. Considering music as a mirror of the times, it is worth noting that the earliest aeronautical ditty, "Chanson sur le Globe

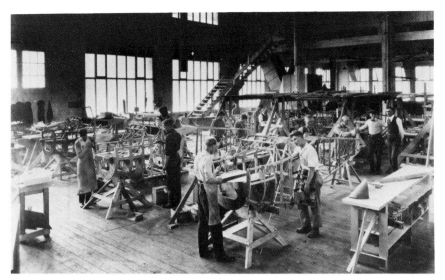

Plate 19

Plate 20

19. Aircraft workers at the Boeing factory in 1922. *NASM*.

20. The airplaine business. A Waco dealer merchandises his product. *NASM*.

Plate 21

21. Newark airport as it appeared in 1928, showing its battery of floodlights. According to a contemporary press release accompanying the photograph, the airport "will have the latest modern devices for night landing and will be up-to-date in every respect." A Ford tri-motor, popular airliner of the era, is parked at left; a Bellanca CH *Pacemaker* at right. *NASM*.

Plate 22

Plate 23

22. A DH-4B carries the mail high over the prairie west of Cheyenne. Airmail pilots on the transcontinental run developed a new sense of distance and time. *NASM.*

23. Sport and recreational flying drew a variety of people in diverse flying gear. This group included recreational fliers as well as pilots on the payroll of the New England Aircraft Co., Inc., of Hartford, Connecticut. *NASM.*

Plate 24

Plate 25

24. A Boeing 40-B-4 skims the mountain crests. Planes like these, built for commercial airmail service, also symbolized aviation's ability to surmount age-old geographic barriers. *NASM*.

25. The Navy's NC-4, first plane to fly successfully across the Atlantic, taxies in the harbor of Lisbon, Portugal, in 1919. *U.S. Navy*.

26. General William (Billy) Mitchell, the dapper, jaunty, and pugnacious aviator whose books argued for a new conception of national security in an air-age world. *NASM.*

27. During 1928, Pan Am began service between Key West and Havana with Fokker F-VII trimotors. In January 1929 Charles Lindbergh joined the company as a technical advisor. He is seen here in the cockpit in Havana in February of that year. *NASM.*

Plate 26

Plate 27

Aerostatique," appeared in 1785, published with a cover depicting a Montgolfier balloon rising from the Tuilleries in Paris. This piece of sheet music (and some 1,500 other aeronautical titles) eventually lodged in the collection of Mrs. Bella C. Landauer, who started collecting such musical miscellany in 1922, partly because she was an indefatigable collector and partly because her son was a pilot. Many of the early songs dealt with balloons and dirigibles, though airplanes made a strong appearance with tunes like "Come, Josephine in My Flying Machine," a smash hit in 1910. A variety of popular songs in the Landauer Collection denote interest in aviation of the twenties, either in terms of assorted flights and heroes or as a dimension of romance. The biggest surge came in 1927, when Lindbergh's flight hit the tunesmiths of Tin Pan Alley like a shot in the arm; the Lindy Hop enjoyed frenetic popularity on dance floors across the country in the early thirties. The Landauer Collection includes sixty pieces devoted to the hero of the hour, most of it eminently forgettable ("Like an Angel You Flew into Every One's Heart") and at least one Lindbergh ditty, with Arabic lyrics, from Syria.

Some well-known composers also used aviation themes. At the request of Admiral Moffett, John Philip Sousa composed a march in 1930 dedicated to naval aviation, *The Aviators*. In a more serious vein, the Landauer Collection contains scores of several piano solos, each running to several pages, and each attempting to reflect various dimensions of aeronautical themes. Among these is the *Airplane Sonata* (1922), written by the modernist composer and pianist George Antheil. Unorthodox and iconoclastic, Antheil delighted in the accolade "bad boy of music," a sobriquet he chose as the title of his autobiography, published in 1945. *Ballet Méchanique*, which he composed in 1923/24, featured a score for airplane engines and propellers (along with doorbells and typewriters) to create Antheil's musical conception of modern life. When the work premiered in Paris in 1926, a riot ensued, although the American première at Carnegie Hall the next year passed less tumultuously. The work, while not a standard in orchestral repertoires, has persevered; the composer rescored it in the 1950s to include the taped rumble of jet engines. Among other ambitious compositions to incorporate aeronautical themes, Kurt Weill wrote *Der Lindberghflug* in 1927 as a cantata for radio broadcast. The piece was conceived as a work for orchestra, chorus, tenor, baritone, and bass, with the libretto supplied by Bertolt Brecht. The cantata dramatized Lindbergh's vicissitudes in combatting weather and exhaustion during the transatlantic flight, although an unimpressed reviewer who heard it at the Baden-Baden music festival said, in the *Musical Courier*, "Pathos is completely lacking in this cantata of the American hero."[4]

Flight as a token of American popular culture emerged in the mass media of the twenties as well. Hollywood quickly recognized the airplane as a potential box-office draw. Feature films such as *The Airship Fugitives* and *The Air Pilot* appeared as early as 1913. Since directors frequently called for airplane crashes as part of the new genre of aerial thrillers, early Hollywood stunt pilots learned to equip themselves with football pads and helmets, the latter additionally padded with inch-thick felt on the inside as well as thick chunks of cork attached to the outside. Some stunt fliers added a twenty-foot coil of rope to this paraphernalia, winding it over the helmet and around the neck to reduce the chances of a snapped vertebra. The post–World War I era included a growing number of films that either featured aviation or included flying as dramatic elements of the plot. Commenting on the state of American aviation after the war, Grover Loening's brother Albert reported to C. G. Grey in London that California seemed to be a good place for pilots to find a job because the movie industry regarded airplanes as a profitable gimmick in attracting patrons.[5]

Caught up in the flying mania, Walt Disney put Mickey Mouse in the cockpit for *Plane Crazy* (1928), in which the diminutive aerial mouse evoked the image of Lindbergh. Hollywood churned out a number of high-flying feature epics in the twenties, including several combat thrillers based on the aerial duels fought in the skies over Europe during World War I. Some of these productions attracted the talents of leading Hollywood directors and stars: *Wings*, directed by William Wellman, won an Oscar during the first Academy Award ceremonies in 1928; Howard Hughes produced and directed *Hell's Angels*; and Howard Hawks directed Douglas Fairbanks, Jr., in *Dawn Patrol*, released in 1930.[6] But there were other themes, contemporaneous to the twenties. The exploits of the aviation branch of the Post Office unquestionably popularized mail pilots, resulting in a Paramount film, *The Air Mail*, released in 1925. Starring Warner Baxter, Billie Dove, Mary Brian, and Douglas Fairbanks, Jr., the film became so popular among flying buffs that the magazine *Aero Digest* listed all of the Paramount ticket offices in the New York area to aid patrons wanting to know where and when it was playing.[7] Drawing on news stories of Marine aviation during Nicaraguan operations, *Flight* was released by Columbia in 1928. Billed as "the great American epic of the air," the film featured Jack Holt and was directed by Frank Capra, who also supplied the dialogue. The hero of the film, Lefty Phelps (played by Ralph Graves), bungles a football play for Yale and loses the crucial game of the season to Harvard. Distraught, Lefty joins the Marines as a flying cadet, determined to become the next Lindbergh. Lefty and his pal (played by Holt) eventually wind up in Nicaragua fighting the Sandinista rebels; Lefty takes over a battered plane from his wounded friend and makes a spectacular landing; Lefty is finally vindicated, and the pair deliver important combat information to headquarters.[8] Between the various romantic tangles of both films, the airplane emerges as a useful and significant form of technology in communications and modern warfare.

In addition to films, aeronautical imagery appeared in other formats of mass culture. During the twenties *Ace Drummond*, a cartoon strip, ran in more than a hundred papers. Wartime ace Eddie Rickenbacker wrote much of the strip's continuity, loosely based on his military flying experiences. Bud Fischer, creator of the *Mutt and Jeff* cartoon series, got into the act with a strip showing the indefatigable pair setting off in their own plane, *The Exclamation Mark*, in an attempt to beat an endurance record (1929) recently set by military pilots Ira Eaker, Carl Spaatz, and Elwood Quesada, in a plane called *The Question Mark*. A variety of cartoons in the editorial section of papers across the nation addressed issues of national security, flying safety, and aviation progress.[9] Even advertisements in magazines and newspapers picked up aeronautical themes. Some were didactic and self-serving. During the late twenties, the Ford Motor Company, obviously with an eye to sales for its trimotor, sponsored an ambitious series in national mass-circulation magazines such as the *Saturday Evening Post* and *Literary Digest* which stressed the benefits of aviation to the general public. The *Literary Digest* even ran its own advertisement early in 1929, making a direct pitch to potential advertisers within the aviation industry to buy space in the magazine.[10]

Other advertisements of the era appeared to trade on the modern image of aviation and aeronautical workmanship in design and performance. In one instance, the publicity department of the Ford Motor Company pointedly combined two of its fine products in a photographic ad that displayed an impressively sized Lincoln against the backdrop of an airfield stocked with Ford trimotors. The aerodynamic connotation was no doubt contrived to complement the "speed and strength . . . inherent in the graceful lines of the new Lincoln body," described in the advertisement's caption. By accident or design, a full-page color advertisement from the Franklin Automobile Company appeared on the facing page, proclaiming that its mechanical vehicles exhibited a quality of performance just like the "craft of the air." "Smoothly, swiftly, powerfully, they slip through space. And the Franklin too," the company boasted. Not only that, but italicized emphasis was given to the fact that the Franklin also had "airplane feel"[11]—an indication at least that Packard's O. E. Hunt had been partly right ten years earlier when he told the Society of Automotive Engineers that aeronautical engineering would stimulate new concepts in design and workmanship.

Periodical readers who might skip advertisements nevertheless encountered aviation as major news items, as ancillary aspects of other stories, or in regular columns. The sources cited in the present study alone are indicative of the variety and scope of aviation topics presented in all kinds of magazines. At least one leading humorist and essayist of the era, Will Rogers, made aviation a recurrent theme in public appearances and articles. Rogers, who frequently flew as a passenger to meet his hectic travel schedules, continuously toasted aviation during his radio broadcasts as well as in frequent pieces in the *New York Times* and the *Saturday Evening Post*.[12] Even before Rogers's one-man campaign and Lindbergh's flight, the *Literary Digest* carried regular aeronautical notes in its "Motoring and Aviation" column during the early twenties; *World's Work* announced a special "Aviation Bureau" to dispense intelligence about planes, airlines, airports, and the like in line with the purpose of *World's Work* to interpret progress to its readers; at the decade's end, *American City* launched an "Airports and Aviation" column edited by aviation consultant Archibald Black; and *Cosmopolitan* hired Amelia Earhart as its aviation consultant. In a move symbolic of the times, an announcement in the *Magazine of Business*, by McGraw-Hill Publishers, the parent company, proudly informed readers that it had added the trusted magazine *Aviation* to its publishing empire.[13]

Aviation fever infected youthful readers as well. Even a cursory review of the *Reader's Guide to Periodical Literature* reveals a growing interest in aeronautical topics within juvenile periodicals, to say nothing of juvenile books. And, in the late twenties, the *Boy Scout Handbook* included a drawing intended to portray the heroic individuals of the American way. A clean-cut Scout appeared in the foreground, with background figures suggesting his sturdy, honorable American heritage and, presumably, a type of life style to copy. These heroic figures included Daniel Boone, Abraham Lincoln, Teddy Roosevelt—and Charles A. Lindbergh.[14]

Indeed, readers of all ages could avail themselves of a growing tide of books on aviation. Before 1925, one reviewer observed, a general survey of aeronautical literature would have been an easy job. By 1929, a complete survey meant a Herculean task to wade through a flood of histories, war stories, textbooks, and just plain propaganda. Most of the books, the reviewer added, were pretty trivial.[15] On the other hand, the outlook for book publishers was extremely bright. One trade journal approvingly noted a statement by Roy Howard, chief of the Scripps-Howard chain, that stories on aviation, flyers, and flying commanded more reader attention than any other items his papers printed. The message for book publishers was clear. Although the trends indicated that the reading audience was evincing a higher degree of selectivity, a vast market in aviation literature still loomed ahead. The publisher George Palmer Putnam forecast a decline in the popularity of individual accounts of long-distance records such as Lindbergh's *We* and Chamberlin's *Record Flights*. The new emphasis centered on adult and juvenile fiction in addition to an increasing demand for textbooks and technical studies. Apparently to a man, every garage mechanic in America decided to catch up in the new field of aeronautics. The Ronald Press, publishers of a special "aeronautic series" with no less than twenty-three generally technical titles, reported an unheralded demand for books on the subject. Without doubt, asserted a writer in *Publishers Weekly*, the hottest subject in America was aviation, and bookstores who failed to take action were missing a "phenomenal opportunity."[16]

Flight and Feminism

Although the vast majority of Americans in the twenties had to settle for vicarious aeronautical thrills in movies and reading, an increasing number took up personal flying as a form of recreation. For those who could afford it, sport aviation became a growing movement. Flying caught the fancy of the smart set, both men and women, "taking its place in country life along with other outdoor diversions."[17] As early as 1923, Detroit boasted of its plans for a thirty-one-story Aviation Town and Country Club. In glowing prose, the club's official magazine described its special aeronautical facilities—the very latest conception, belonging to tomorrow as well as today.[18] The new diversion developed its special brand of literature such as the *Sportsman Pilot*, a magazine of generous format and slick, high-quality pages full of the latest aviation gossip. One section featured graceful photographic portraits of leading woman aeronauts to be—"Fair Devotees of Flight." To merit such an accolade, it was not necessary to have a flying license; just to be a candidate was enough.[19] In 1929, Aviation Country Clubs were formally organized with a national board of governors and a national committee on admissions. The clubs were originally intended to promote aviation in general,[20] but, for the most part, magazines such as *Sportsman Pilot* were devoted to matrimonial affairs of the aerial elite and style notes on how the well-accoutered aviatrix should appear at the airdrome. The club also sponsored a national tour by Ruth Nichols, a well-known flyer, to publicize the idea of Aviation Country Clubs as a means of promoting aviation.[21]

Miss Nichols's aerial jaunt across the country underscored the continuing role of women in advancing aviation. In the early days of flying, when the appearance of any person in a flying machine became a sure attraction for photographers and reporters, the public seemed even more enamored of the aviatrix, a term popularly applied to women who took to the air in the halcyon years before World War I. Since there was no required federal licensing system, the total number of female flyers is unknown; the Aero Club of America had issued certificates to ten women by 1917, although there were apparently many more in the United States, and women set a number of distance and endurance records. During the war, Ruth Law barnstormed the country in support of Red Cross campaigns and Liberty Loan drives; Katherine and Marjorie Stinson did the same while operating a flying school for American and Canadian military air cadets. While much prewar and wartime activity of women fliers could realistically be called promotional, one study of the era noted that their fame "did not spring entirely from the novelty of women as pilots but from the genuine respect they had earned by their exploits."[22]

In aviation, as in other fields, women continued to play a notable role during the postwar era.[23] The idea of a woman in a plane still endeared females to many promoters as an out-of-the-ordinary news item (as in the case of Ruth Nichols). Amelia Earhart also hit the headlines as the first woman to fly the Atlantic—as a passenger—on June 17, 1928. Aboard a Fokker trimotor, Earhart accompanied Wilmer Stultz, pilot, and Louis Gordon, mechanic, on a flight from Newfoundland to Wales, one of the many transoceanic ventures sparked by Lindbergh's epochal flight the year before. Amelia's presence aboard the plane was planned strictly for publicity although she was already an accomplished pilot with an unofficial altitude record for women. Still, as one biographer pointed out, she "epitomized . . . the venturesome spirit of a sex newly liberated from ancient restraints." Four years later, in 1932, Earhart soloed her own plane across the Atlantic. In the meantime, while continuing to set other records, she played an active role in the aviation community as aviation editor of *Cosmopolitan* from 1928 to 1930, consultant to several emerging airlines around the turn of the decade, and in the mid-thirties became associated with Purdue University as a career counselor for women.[24]

Amelia Earhart represented a significant new image of women emerging in the twenties—dignified, poised, feminine, but highly capable in mastering the complexities of the age. The press responded warmly to Earhart's personality, expressing opinions that her aeronautical ventures in no way compromised her femininity. In his perceptive study of the era, *Another Part of the Twenties*, historian Paul Carter noted that Anne Morrow Lindbergh also played more than the role of diffident passenger as she accompanied her famous husband on several demanding flights in the late twenties. Mrs. Lindbergh "serviced, navigated, and co-piloted her husband's aircraft—strenuous, physical, mechanical, 'masculine' activities—without causing any eyebrows to be raised."[25] Male chauvinism did not seem to be so stultifying for women seeking careers in the post–World War I decade as it became later. In 1927, Ruth Nicols received one of the first transport licenses to be issued; she and others continued to fly and set aviation records. Further, a number of women entered aviation in other areas during the late twenties, eventually establishing successful careers as engineers, airport and flight school managers, public relations experts, airline executives, and aviation consultants.[26] At the same time, the publicity attending the flights of Ruth Nichols, Amelia Earhart, Anne Lindbergh, and others in the twenties still suggested an undercurrent of defensiveness about aviation—a covert message that if women could do it, so could anyone. Aviation still carried the image of a hazardous activity. Years later, recalling her tour on behalf of Aviation Country Clubs, Ruth Nichols remarked that she made it a point to appear only in casual hats and dresses to help dispel the public's notion that flying was dangerous. Commenting on the success of Amelia Earhart, one reporter remarked that Amelia's career demonstrated that anyone could learn to fly.[27]

The Aesthetics of Flight

The ability to make a comfortable flight in an enclosed-cabin plane, allowing passengers to travel without irksome flying suits and goggles as Miss Nichols had, suggests the progress of aviation in ten years. In 1919, when most planes featured open cockpits, the noted designer Grover C. Loening had exhorted his colleagues to be "brutally frank" and admit that it was not altogether a pleasure to fly. Loening reminded his associates that there was "a disappointing absence . . . of the sense of buoyant exhilaration which almost everyone looks for on his first trip. Airplanes are very material," he emphasized, "their vibrations are very evident, their grip on the air almost ferocious, and frequently oil, exhaust, and the cold rush of air add to a feeling of utter subordination to a mechanical power." Goggles, helmets, and flying suits were of small help. "The general nature of flying," he admitted with reluctant candor, "even as a passenger, uses up nervous energy." Nevertheless, Loening added, there was enjoyment in flying, including the pleasures of magnificent views from a vantage point high in the air.[28]

For all of its discomforts, the airplane provided a new perspective of the world that was stimulating and exciting. In 1924, Lieutenants

A. W. Stevens and John A. MacReady made a photographic tour of the United States, recording an aerial panorama of America that was uniquely new for the generation of the twenties. In a remarkable series of portraits, the two fliers presented an entirely new face of America. A canyon in Death Valley became an abstraction, with an optical trick of approaching and receding cliff lines. Sand dunes assumed the graceful, elegant folds of heavy brocade. From the air, the tailings left from a gold dredge working in a river took the peculiar pattern of squeezed toothpaste. Farm fields strewn across the landscape suggested a cubistic canvas of heroic proportions. The craggy shoulder of a mountain curved upward to a lofty summit that lost itself in yet another world—a world of the sky's infinite horizon, ethereal clouds and soaring spires in an endless space. Lacking equipment for night photography, Stevens and MacReady attempted to write about the memorable sight of New York City at night—an awesome stretch of winking lights that suggested a metropolis burned to the ground, leaving a sea of glowing embers in which multilighted skyscrapers took the form of towering, white-hot cinders thrusting into the dark night sky.[29]

Although increasing numbers of airline passengers enjoyed plane travel because of the thrill that came from having performed one of humanity's persistent dreams—flying—they also appreciated these new perspectives of the earth, recalling their impressions with enthusiasm and verve. A flight across the United States became a dramatic reminder of the geographical diversity and variety of America. Travelers who terminated their journey in California were rewarded with a special sight—a sea of color to greet them as they cruised among the clouds above the mountain tops: "Miles upon miles of flowering orchards, filling the valleys and sloping up green hill-sides in a surge of pink and white blossoms . . . here and there foot-hills lying crumpled between drifts of deep-piled velvets and velours, carelessly spattered with petals. Deep greens and light greens, emerald and sea greens, with the rich brown of the earth showing through fields of waving young grain . . . We high riders reigned alone in this unreal realm, this sky kingdom, with a hidden world there at our feet."[30]

The experience of flight made its imprint on the imaginations of professional fliers as well as those of laymen. One Army Service pilot, recording his sensations during a survey of airmail routes, was particularly impressed by a segment of the trip over an arid district in the West. "The course lay above a country that God had seemingly forgotten," he wrote. "Ugly waterless gulches wandered lost in the cracked and cauterized earth, and the whole bleak, lifeless landscape simmered in the fires of an unconsoling sun. The last outpost of civilization seemed to have receded beyond recall while we hung like a suspended speck, an ineffectual wavering thunder, at the heart of an oppressive mystery."[31] He also recalled the sense of disengagement and introspection that took hold of him at certain times in night flights. He seemed to float, like a lost soul, through a dark, uncharted sky marked only by phantomlike clouds and clusters of wandering stars. Experiences like that, he remarked, with a haunting fusion of reality and illusion, had colored his "sentiment of existence" in a way that was difficult to define.[32] Charles Lindbergh also commented on this sense of solitude and the paradox of this emotion recurring while borne aloft by a creation of the machine age. "I may be flying a complicated airplane, rushing through space, but this cabin is surrounded by simplicity and thoughts set free of time. . . . Here, in the *Spirit of St. Louis*, I live in a different frame of time and space. . . . How detached the intimate things around me seem from the great world down below. How strange is this combination of proximity and separation. That ground—seconds away—thousands of miles away. This air, stirring mildly around me. That air, rushing by with the speed of a tornado, an inch beyond. These minute details in my cockpit. The grandeur of the world outside. The nearness of death. The longness of life."[33]

Comments from veteran military fliers, airmail pilots, and other experienced aviation professionals repeated these examples of retrospection and introspection, exhilaration, and visual impact. As former mail pilot Dean Smith wrote emphatically, "It was so alive and rich a life that any other conceivable choice seemed dull, prosaic, and humdrum."[34]

Social Effect, Symbolism, and Imagery

Aside from the unique sensations of flight, a number of writers began devoting more attention to the social consequences of rapid airline routes linking all areas of the country. The *Independent* gave editorial support to an enlarged air transportation system, and pointed out that air transport would have the same effect as other rapid transportation in bringing together the respective benefits of rural ease and urban commerce and culture.[35] Following his conquest of the Atlantic, Lindbergh's air tour of the United States once more caused the *Independent* to predict an even closer feeling of community between the East and West Coasts. Eventually, said the *Independent*, aviation in the form of airmail and passenger transportation would do more than the train, telegraph, and radio to reduce sectionalism in the United States.[36] Aircraft represented one of several modes of transportation in the twenties that bound America more tightly together. Even though aviation's statistical size did not compare with the railroad industry or the revolution wrought by the automobile, its subtle effects were being felt and recognized. In 1929, analyzing the concepts of "spatial distance" in the scholarly journal *Sociology and Social Research*, Roderick McKenzie evaluated the social influences of travel and rail transportation and commented on the potential effects of aeronautics. The most important impact on time and distance factors, he pointed out, had been made by the automobile and the airplane, which had, respectively, created new scales for local and long-distance travel. As the automobile had helped to erase urban-rural boundary lines and give rise to metropolitan areas, the airplane promised to have a somewhat similar effect on a larger scale.[37] The newspaper columnist Heywood Broun criticized such trends. Fulminating at the invasion of privacy by airborne loudspeakers and other aeronautical improvisations, Broun saw no advantage in the further shrinkage of the United States that would promote even more standardization and conformity. As to the enjoyment of flying, there was no beauty in a blurred countryside, he added truculently.[38]

Will Durant, on the other hand, scorned the critics who wanted to turn back the clock. That meant a return to the age of cobwebs, bugs, snakes, dirt, and chores, he said, and we need have no more of it. Durant recited a litany of praise for the machines and tools that liberated man—microscopes, radios, tractors, and telescopes. The airplane he regarded as another mark of progress for a better world. Nor was romance lost in the saga of machines. From the dream of Icarus, to the detailed sketches of Leonardo da Vinci, to the persevering Wright brothers and the astounding realization of an ageless quest—one could not ask for a more romantic story of achievement. "We move over the land and the air with the freedom of timeless gods," wrote Durant. "Mere speed is useless: it is a symbol of persistent human will that the airplane has its highest meaning for us; long chained, like Prometheus, to the earth, we have freed ourselves at last, and now we can look the skylark in the face."[39]

Other observers speculated that the "freedom and exhilaration" induced by travel in the sky would influence art. "Aircraft may carry forward the deep-lying constructive forces that are the essence of real art purpose," said one writer. "The aircraft in itself is a stimulating, inspiring thing."[40] Still another literary critic pondered the effect of aviation on poetry, lamenting that poets seemed to maintain a "respectful distance" in dealing with the machine age—a relatively new phenomenon, after all, with implications for mankind that were sometimes murky. Fortunately, as the poet and critic Babette Deutsch reported, recent work indicated that poets were coming to grips with the problem, proving that it was impossible to write unpedestrian poetry about machines. Miss Deutsch cited the poem "Clouds," by Frank Ernest Hill, as a happy example:

Earth dies to haze below, the cables sing
The motor drones like some gigantic fly,
A monstrous mound of vapor bathes my wing
And backward with the wind goes sweeping by;
Above the voids white crags go sharp and dim,
Oaks wave, the discs of rootless islands swim.
And arches climb and crumble in the sun
Over gray dinosaur and mastodon.
Earth, dim and fluid, seals the ragged spaces
Where misty islands meet and part below;
Cities that mask eternal hungering faces,
Black wood and water mingle in its flow.
Down, down ten mountain heights beneath this floor
Of marble-smooth and marble-solid air,
The shout and pride of color are no more
Than moon-faint mottlings. Distance does not spare.
They are the clouds now. Icy-lipped I ride
A window-floor immeasurably wide,
Firmer than rotted stone. And through its glass
I watch their formless, sunken shadows pass.[41]

Indeed, to many people, the swift, high-flying airplane epitomized the promise of a technological age. Driving to the airfield to watch the preparations for the 1927 transatlantic flights, the essayist and literary critic Gilbert Seldes followed the highway through a gritty, bleak industrial area, succeeded, in turn, by the "tasteless monotony" of colonies of workers' homes. It left him depressed until suddenly he reached the flying field. An airplane, said Seldes, never failed to take hold of his imagination; his spirits lifted at the sight of a sky alive with aircraft. Each time one rose into the air he always wished he were a part of it. An airplane possessed fragility and grace—and dazzling speed to whisk it over the horizon. A dwindling speck, it turned; a polished surface of the wing reflected a waning ray of daylight like a window flaming in the setting sun. An aircraft embodied an anomaly of the prosaic notations of equations, wood, fabric, engine, and gasoline that produced the wonder and thrill of throwing off the bonds of earth. Even when reduced to the dollars-and-cents process of making a living, the nobility of aircraft in flight rose above the inanity and grossness of commercialism. "There is no ugliness, no monotony, no grasping," proclaimed Seldes. "They represent one of the ideals toward which commercialism and industry and mechanical progress can move; they are a triumph of applied science and a triumph of the human spirit at the same time. Watching them, you can forget mean streets and mean bickerings. Here is something better than machinery and better than man."[42]

Denying the charge that the machine age was eroding historic skills of the workman, Stuart Chase, a trenchant observer of the urban scene, reminded critics that, even though a certain number of trades were made obsolete, the advance of technology spawned new jobs as it proceeded. Moreover, Chase continued, the personal skills of the workman continued to find a place in the modern age. The aviation technology of the twenties, for example, put a high premium on the craftsman's intimate technique. Building an airplane required the homely vocations of cabinetmakers, tinsmiths, coppersmiths, and even seamstresses. The careful work they lavished on each "plane" imparted to it an individuality compounded of skilled craftsmanship, knowledge, and love. In a supreme compliment to these workmen of the machine age, Chase commented reflectively, "Somehow they put me in mind of the builders of Chartres." Then he admitted with regret, "It is sad to think of mass production hanging, like a sword of Damocles, above their heads."[43]

Even though the skills of the airplane workmen were doomed to give way to the spreading regimen of assembly-line technique, Chase hastened to reassure the pessimists that it was not wise to become too maudlin. In spite of the massive standarization of volume production, modern technology had the promise of producing a sound airplane that was practically priced and foolproof to boot. Moreover, "a standardized airplane need send no hostages to loveliness." The medium of the sky in which an aircraft functioned demanded the precision of a micrometer and the glossy finish of a buffing tool. It was possible that these machines could turn out a more appropriate and graceful ship than craftsmen ever could.[44] Individualism? It lived on in an age of power and the machine. The qualities of individualism had not been obliterated, they were recognized now in relation to the machine age. Charles Lindbergh, tending a machine over 3,000 miles of open sea, was so closely bound to his plane that he spoke to audiences not of himself alone but of "we." He felt a sense of kinship with his plane, said Chase, and people loved him the more for it. Nobody called Lindbergh a robot.[45] Social critic Lewis Mumford repeated an aspect of these sentiments in terms of aviation's relation to other fields of engineering. Although he commented that surface travel from outlying airfields to the city center consumed valuable time and worried about military aviation as an element of heightened international tensions,[46] aviation represented a positive facet of modernity. Aeronautical engineering set the standards for refined and exact engineering, ranging from bridges, to cranes, to the steel sinews of twentieth-century skyscrapers.[47]

Thus, most Americans seemed to accept the airplane as a symbol of technology, the result of the mating of two sciences, theoretical and applied, with engineers acting as godfathers and reaping additional qualitative benefits. Lindbergh's flight could be interpreted as an aspect of the promise of the machine age while encompassing elements of the traditional concepts of the American heritage of individualism. Lindbergh epitomized the daring pioneer, striking out alone, an underdog challenging and conquering the hostile elements of nature and escaping the limitations of society. He was the self-sufficient individual who had settled the United States—the new technological citizen cast in the mold of the independent, moral Yankee character. Lindbergh's flight symbolized individual achievement within the framework of the age of technology. There were new frontiers to conquer in the contemporary world. The challenges of that world were met by society adapting itself to the technological discipline of the machine.[48] Lindbergh's conquest of the Atlantic became a metaphor for the mastery of the complexities of the twentieth century.[49]

CHAPTER EIGHT
International Skyways

The multidimensional world of air travel not only suggested new aspects of commerce and international relations but caused Americans to rethink geographical concepts. A series of intercontinental goodwill flights usually resulted in enhanced international bonds of friendship. But many people also became concerned about aviation's effect on traditional American bulwarks against foreign threats: the Arctic bastion, and the great distance across the Pacific and Atlantic oceans. Aerial links between the United States and Latin America acquired serious political significance. Collectively, these benign and worrisome influences of global dimensions sparked a growing interest in what came to be called air-age geography.

Linking Hemispheres and Continents

The popular tumult in the wake of Lindbergh's transatlantic flight not only tended to obscure earlier Atlantic flights and other intercontinental efforts but also obscured earlier postwar hopes for aviation as a vehicle for improved international relations. "We have been speeded up during the last decade by the steamship and the railroad," observed the editor of *Aerial Age* in 1919, "and the speed that we will realize by the aeroplane air route will bring that commingling of nations we are all striving for, and when we secure it we will have culminated the greatest barrier to civilization—warfare—and will have closely approached a condition of modern Utopia on this earth." In fact, he added, nations will probably have to develop a universal language.[1]

As the world entered the post–World War I decade, partisans of aviation regarded the airplane as a definite factor in promoting international contacts leading to international peace and understanding. Many flying veterans of the war such as Gill Robb Wilson and Eddie Rickenbacker left the service with a wholehearted belief that the airplane would become a vehicle to eliminate geographical boundaries and bind mankind together.[2] "There will . . . be no east or west," wrote an observer, "and with the new aerial age will come a new internationalism founded on speedy intercommunication and good will toward all mankind."[3]

Even though the first airplane flights over the Atlantic occurred in 1919 (the American NC-4 in May; the British in a converted bomber in June),[4] most Americans read little about the impact of aviation on international relations until the U.S. Air Service completed its globe-girdling tour in 1924. Lowell Thomas compared the flight to the voyage of Magellan, opening new avenues of commerce and ushering in a new era of civilization binding all nations closer together.[5] In an address to the Franklin Institute in Philadelphia while the flight was in progress, Major General Mason M. Patrick, chief of the Air Service, remarked that it had more than military significance. Aviation, he said, could also be a great boon to international communications, allowing people from the remote corners of the earth to come together and know each other better. Understanding was the result of knowledge, continued Patrick. Airplanes, the most destructive military weapon ever made by man, could well become important vehicles to promote peace throughout the world.[6] Later, Patrick reaffirmed these sentiments at the conclusion of the flight, and continued to emphasize this role of the Air Service and its aircraft in succeeding articles and a book.[7]

But it was the odyssey of *The Spirit of St. Louis* (not only non-stop but solo) that crystallized the image of aviation as a factor of global friendship. The airplane became a symbol of a new human spirit of internationalism. This aspect of Lindbergh's flight impressed Harry Guggenheim most of all. "No appeal of science to man's reason could have accomplished in a period of years what Charles Lindbergh's appeal to heart and imagination accomplished between the dawn of May

20th, and the night of May 21st," he wrote. "The world was impressed with the significance of the airplane not only as a lessener of the distance between the habitations of men, but between the minds of men as well."[8] Writing for the *Review of Reviews*, J. J. Jusserand, the French ambassador to the United States from 1902 to 1925, remarked on the wild acclaim and unabashed joy with which the clannish Parisians welcomed Lindbergh as one of their own. On this occasion, Jusserand recalled some thoughts expressed in an essay by the chemist Pierre Marcelin Berthelot just before his death in 1907. Of all the inventions destined to make great changes in the world, Berthelot had written, surely one of the most significant was the airplane. In the mastery of the air, there would be no more frontiers to separate nations. Just so, said Jusserand; Lindbergh and *The Spirit of St. Louis* had inaugurated a new state of human relations.[9] Myron T. Herrick, the American ambassador who received Lindbergh in Paris, commented particularly on the feeling of international good will generated by Lindbergh's flight over the Atlantic[10]—a feeling so strong that it affected negotiations between the United States and France that led to the successful conclusion of the Kellogg-Briand Pact of 1928. As the diplomatic historian Robert Ferrell assessed the flight many years later, it was "an adventitious event of breath-taking interest to the entire world, an event which tightened remarkably the hitherto loose bonds of Franco-American amity."[11]

The flight of *The Spirit of St. Louis* colored American relations with other European countries as well as France. Lindbergh's rapid tour of European capitals and his exposure through the European press corrected the image of Uncle Shylock that was not compatible with this appealing, forthright, competent young man. Successive transatlantic flights improved the situation. Clarence Chamberlin and Charles Levine, landing their *Columbia* propitiously near Martin Luther's home at Eisleben, Germany, helped heal the scars of war between the United States and its former enemy.[12] David Lawrence, foreign correspondent for the Consolidated Press, reported that the Germans were highly complimented by the route chosen by Chamberlin and Levine. German public reaction surpassed the French reception of Lindbergh. The Berlin *Allgemeine Zeitung* approvingly acknowledged the feeling of good will apparent in the wake of the Chamberlin-Levine flight, and the *Tageblatt* conjectured that, as space was so easily negotiated, it was possible to expect more and more national barriers to go down. "The ethereal bridge traversed by the *Columbia* thus is certain to become a span of peace between nations," wrote the editors.[13]

Flights of *The Spirit of St. Louis*, *The Columbia*, and others of the late twenties generated international amity largely through serendipitous consequences. The value of such flights in promoting international relations did not escape some shrewd diplomats seeking a dramatic gesture of American good will. E. W. Burgess, professor of sociology at the University of Chicago, noted that the first premeditated project to promote international friendship through aviation was Lindbergh's Latin American tour in 1928. Burgess overstated his case somewhat, since the Army had already mounted two good-will flights in Latin America in 1924 and again in 1926/27. The 1924 effort involved a trio of military planes in Central America, and the more ambitious 1926/27 project involved a flight of five military aircraft through both Central and South America. Despite public announcements that stressed international amity, these missions admittedly had long-range commercial interests, and both were undertaken against a background of concern for the issue of American national security vis-à-vis the Panama Canal. Moreover, the 1926/27 mission encountered many frosty receptions, especially in Mexico.[14] The Lindbergh venture, on the other hand, demonstrably represented a nonmilitary excursion, even though Lindbergh later commented about future airline routes in the wake of his tour. In any case, Lindbergh's Latin American sojourn certainly enhanced America's image in that part of the hemisphere.

Latin American Routes

Dwight Morrow, the American ambassador to Mexico, had been searching for some action to improve deteriorating Mexican-American relations, which had recently sunk to a dangerously low ebb. The electric effect of Lindbergh's Atlantic flight on Franco-American relations greatly impressed Morrow. When Lindbergh returned to the United States, Morrow spoke to him about a similar flight to Mexico.[15] Lindbergh was indeed interested. He already had an urge to fly through South America for the enjoyment of it, and he was intrigued by the prospect of pioneering a route for future airlines through the area. His plane and its engine were still in fine shape after his transcontinental

United States tour. When Morrow's influence finally resulted in an invitation from Mexican President Calles, Lindbergh accepted at once.[16] On his arrival, December 14, 1927, Mexico welcomed Lindbergh as a national hero. In a remarkable gesture of esteem generally reserved for native Mexicans of extraordinary attainments—and never foreigners—the Mexican Chamber of Deputies convened in "solemn session" to receive the American visitor. Charles W. Hackett, professor of Latin American history at the University of Texas and an experienced observer of Mexican-American affairs, characterized Lindbergh's visit as "the capital event in the development of Ambassador Morrow's new diplomacy."[17] Lindbergh proceeded to embark on an aerial odyssey through Central and South America, making one triumphal entry after another in thirteen capitals. Climaxing a two-month tour, he arrived in Havana, Cuba, February 8, 1928, to appear before a session of the Pan American Congress. Dispatches from correspondents of the *New York Times* all along the route testified to the emotional response to his trip, which helped create a tremendous feeling of good will toward the United States,[18] and aroused a new interest in its northern neighbor.[19]

Returning from the Pan American Conference, former American Secretary of State Charles Evans Hughes warned an audience at Princeton that United States relations with Latin America were facing increasing difficulties because of increased contact of European and Latin American statesmen in the League of Nations and the World Court. Although Hughes qualified his remarks as being nonpolitical, he nevertheless proceeded to suggest the future value of aviation in redressing this balance of relations in favor of the United States. He pointed out that airlines from the United States to Latin America were more practical since they could be planned to reduce the interminable stretches of open-ocean flying that made transoceanic routes so hazardous. Modern developments meant that old barriers were falling, to "create a new feeling of intimacy among the American states." Aviation, Hughes continued, should cause Americans to look for a more "realistic conception of our relations to the American states and our duties and privileges."[20] Other commentators also drew attention to the role of aeronautics in promoting amicable relations with Latin America, and added that it could serve our national interest at the same time.[21]

From the first, Latin America seemed a likely field for the use of aviation because of the propaganda value of aeronautics in spreading proof of a nation's technical ability, thereby bolstering its prestige. But this was also true for European governments. As aviation developed, technologically advanced nations perceived their airlines as extremely valuable weapons of commercial competition,[22] and the United States took alarm at European aeronautical activity in South America in particular. Against this background of aeronautical competition, Senator Ransdell of Louisiana began agitating for airmail routes to South America as early as 1925. Obviously interested in the business value to his own state, the senator's correspondence with other individuals indicated an awareness of the commercial possibilities in various quarters. The Bureau of Foreign and Domestic Commerce of the Department of Commerce cited the increased speed of business correspondence as a valuable asset in foreign trade, and a St. Louis businessman spelled out the definite advantages of airmail to facilitate handling of small cargo shipments.[23] Publicity generated by contemporary long-distance flights and Lindbergh's Latin American tour focused even more attention on the business prospects of aviation in promoting additional trade. Although an extensive correspondence by air might not be required to maintain established trade lines of sugar and coffee, proponents admitted, it was nonetheless necessary to open new markets and speed up business transactions concerning other types of goods. Advocates of air transport argued that the timely advantage of airmail would give the United States a compelling advantage over European competitors.[24]

The eventual development of South American routes evolved against this symbiotic background of commercial interest and national security, with strong support from the government in Washington. Although tentative studies of Latin American airmail service undertaken by the Post Office Department during 1923 and 1924 were not completely optimistic about profitability, one report, emphasizing service to Central America and the Canal Zone, observed that military and political factors "merit consideration of the question from a broader viewpoint." When a pair of flying boats from the Sociedad Colombo-Alemana de Transportes Aereos (SCADTA), the German-backed airline operating in Colombia, paid a visit to Panama in the summer of 1925, the acting secretary of war duly informed the Post Office Department.[25] This correspondence not only represented a continuing exchange of intelligence between these agencies and the Department of State but also formed the backdrop for the creation of Pan American Airways as a bulwark of American commercial, political, and military interests in South America. H. H. Arnold claimed that he had provided the impetus for Pan Am's formation.

Late in 1924, while serving as chief of the information section under General Mason Patrick, Hap Arnold began hearing disturbing reports of SCADTA's Colombian operations. The airline's planes, mechanics, and pilots were all German, and a major route up the Magdalena River in Colombia ran ominously close to the Canal Zone. Arnold, Patrick, and military officers in the Canal Zone all became alarmed. When SCADTA seemed on the verge of winning a concession to fly mail from Central America to the United States by way of Cuba, Arnold determined to block the venture. Enlisting the aid of Major Carl Spaatz and two more confidants, including John Montgomery, a former Navy officer, Arnold and his cohorts received unofficial encouragement from the Post Office Department, enlisted solid financial support, charted promising routes into South America, and eventually returned to the Post Office Department in the autumn of 1925 with a prospectus for Pan American, Incorporated. When SCADTA finally made official overtures for its interamerican airmail service, Arnold claimed that the Post Office Department had rebuffed them on the basis of Pan American's prospectus. The War Department remained mostly unaware of the extent of this sub-rosa enterprise. At one point, Arnold, Spaatz, and others intended to resign from the Air Service in order to run their nascent airline (with Arnold as president and general manager). The charges and countercharges in the wake of the Billy Mitchell trial led to second thoughts about resigning under fire, as Arnold put it, leaving Montgomery to keep the project alive.[26]

SCADTA actually came close to winning the contracts it sought. Through the personal efforts of Dr. Peter Paul von Bauer, an Austrian of German-Czech background who dominated the airline, SCADTA attracted considerable interest from some officials within the Post Office Department and the Department of Commerce. Although von Bauer reported significant United States investment in his proposed interamerican airmail line, many bureaucrats in Washington harbored strong reservations about Teutonic domination of an airline near the

Canal Zone that would also erode American commercial interests in the region. Influential figures in the War Department obviously looked askance at SCADTA's proposals for new routes, and aggressive entrepreneurs in the United States soon offered an alternative to groups who sought improved aerial communications to Latin America. SCADTA needed airmail contracts, but they went to a United States airline—Pan American.

Pan American eventually spread its wings under the guidance of Juan Trippe, an aviation enthusiast well connected with influential bureaucrats and eastern financiers. When the Post Office Department formally opened the bidding for the Key West–Havana route in 1927, Trippe adroitly outmaneuvered several rivals, and the original Pan American group sold out to Trippe, who renamed it Pan American Airways, familiarly known as Pan Am. Before, during, and after these machinations, Trippe's government and business contacts won him the benediction of the Post Office Department, which foresaw Pan Am as the "chosen instrument" for United States foreign air routes, and insulated Pan Am from other American competitors in order to make it a strong contender against European aeronautical interests throughout Latin Amercia.[27]

Herbert Hoover also emerged as an important figure in the development of commercial relations and subsequent aerial links to Latin America. During his term as secretary of commerce, disbursements for the promotion of foreign commerce in Latin America jumped from $30,000 to $338,000.[28] When Pan Am began operations, on October 27, 1927, from Key West to Havana, company officials acknowledged the encouragement given them by Hoover as secretary of commerce.[29] Hoover subsequently won the presidency at a peak of United States investment activity in South America. South American governments received billions of dollars in loans, and American bankers warmed to the idea of improved communications to an area where the United States commercially competed with the Germans, British, and French.[30] Coupled with the emerging formulation of the United States' Good Neighbor policy, Hoover regarded aviation, especially Pan Am, as a dual agent of diplomacy and commerce. As president-elect, Hoover toured Latin America late in 1928, emphasizing America's new posture as a good neighbor and probing the wider potential of interamerican aviation. Among other items on his diplomatic agenda, Hoover discussed airline routes with the chief executive of each country visited, and received an outline from each concerning the rights of an American flag line. With relevant information and specifics garnered at these high levels, Hoover extended an invaluable service to America's "chosen instrument" airline. Speaking of his discussions with Latin American heads of state, Hoover asserted in his *Memoirs*, "These conversations furnished the foundations for the establishment of the Pan American Airways."[31]

It can be argued that Hoover overestimated the significance of his own tour. Certainly, Pan Am's operatives were already at work in various Latin American countries, negotiating partnerships with some existing air service concessions and acquiring others outright. Nevertheless, Hoover's endorsement of Pan Am obviously helped, and his administration continued to accommodate Pan Am, just as the previous one had. With this kind of unassailable patronage, Pan Am flourished, drawing all of Latin America closer to the United States in terms of communication and travel time. The company augmented its original equipment of Fokker trimotors with Sikorsky S-38 flying boats and other long-range flying boats as operations expanded. The inaugural run between Key West and Miami, begun in 1927, was only 110 miles, but with good management, as well as a virtual monopoly on foreign airmail contracts, the company's route mileage soared. On January 1, 1929, Pan Am covered 261 miles, grew to 5,275 miles by March, and expanded to 11,075 by August, with 4,500 more miles to be added soon. In the first six months of 1929, Pan Am flew 1,000,000 passenger miles, carried 7,000 patrons, and delivered 250,000 pounds of mail with an efficiency average of 99.85 percent—the highest of any American carrier. Pan Am was not just an airmail route. In an area of primitive land transportation and intermittent sea transport, the ability of the airline to save days and even weeks of travel made it a vital element in a new era of interamerican commerce. Comparing air routes to ship routes, the trip from Miami to Santiago, Cuba, was reduced by thirty-three and a half hours. Panama could be reached in two days instead of twelve. Mail to Chile was delivered in nine days as compared to twenty; the three-and-a-half-week ordeal by boat and burro to Tegucigalpa, Honduras, could be made in a day and a half by air. Two years after commencement of operations, Pan Am had advanced from a 110-mile shuttle service to become an international carrier delivering passengers, mail, newspapers, specialized cargo, and government correspondence to twelve countries over a route that tied together two continents.[32] During the depression, Pan Am's business continued to rise, and its social significance expanded. Gross revenues climbed 150 percent from 1930 to 1934, permitting Pan Am to retire its debts and still show an annual profit of $1,000,000. In 1930 only 3 percent of United States mail to Latin America (excluding Mexico and Cuba) went by air, but by 1939 the figure had risen to 16.5 percent.[33]

International airline routes between the United States and other countries brought into sharper focus the unresolved problems of international regulations raised at the Paris Peace Conference in 1919. In spite of the advice of influential legal experts and organizations, the United States government declined to ratify the International Air Convention of 1919, even though American delegates in Paris signed the document. The spectacular Lindbergh and Chamberlin-Levine flights in 1927 raised new questions about the international control of aviation, and additional aerial conquests in 1928 increased the recognition of aviation as a new component in international relations. Lindbergh's Latin American tour, the Arctic flights of Wilkins, *Zeppelin* passenger trips over the Atlantic, the transatlantic flight of the German monoplane *Bremen*, the world flights of Australia's Kingsford-Smith as well as the Frenchmen Coste and Le Brix—all underscored the necessity to reach agreement on the worldwide scope of aeronautics.[34]

An Air-Age World

The United States undertook a start along these lines in signing the Pan American Convention on Civil Aviation at Havana on February 15, 1928, seven days after Lindbergh landed in the Cuban city at the end of his thirteen-nation circuit of Latin America. The Pan American Convention included agreements on the sovereignty of air space, registration, inspection, and related matters. The United States evidenced a growing awareness of international aviation when Congress passed a joint resolution authorizing President Coolidge to issue invitations to foreign governments to convene in Washington in order to exchange views on various aspects of aviation and honor the twenty-fifth anniversary of the Wright brothers' flight. The International Civil

Aeronautics Conference, in Washington, December 12–14, 1928, was an auspicious gathering, a milestone in international aviation, and had a great propaganda value. Unfortunately, nothing concrete in the way of international regulation resulted from the meeting. Problems of the regulation of military flights, crew standards, emergency rescue and signal procedure, and the future issue of United States–Europe commercial flights remained unresolved. With the exception of a bilateral agreement in 1929 involving Colombian air routes in the Canal Zone, among other topics, the United States did not enter into any meaningful international regulation of aeronautics until 1947, when President Truman signed the agreement admitting the United States to the newly formed International Civil Aeronautics Organization. In the meantime, international American aviation rested on ad hoc negotiations, limited regional agreements, and informal discussions, often through the American embassy in Switzerland in conjunction with the League of Nations.[35]

Despite the failure to come to grips with international regulation, reassessments of aviation at the close of the twenties included a realization of the practical issues of national security—as well as its promise as a vehicle of peace—in terms of the growing social, cultural, and geographical implications of international aeronautics. After the successful bombing tests in 1921 that sank the German cruiser *Frankfort* and the battleship *Ostfriesland*, Billy Mitchell constantly argued his theories on aerial warfare in magazines and books. "The former isolation of the United States is a thing of the past," he warned in *Winged Defense*. Any conventional protection of the Atlantic and Pacific vanished with the advent of aircraft possessing speed and range to make the entire country vulnerable to planes. These did not have to pierce any geographic barriers such as rugged coasts or fight any preliminary skirmishes to force their way into a strategic pass; the whole continent, with its industries and population, lay exposed.[36] Mitchell's warnings, unheeded by many, seemed more credible after the flurry of long-distance flights in 1927 and 1928.

After Lindbergh's transatlantic crossing, the *New Republic* commented that many leading authorities agreed that future wars could be won by controlling the air, and that aeronautics should be supported for reasons of national defense.[37] Stuart Chase adopted a somewhat paradoxical and fatalistic point of view concerning the role of the airplane and the hope for a peaceful world. *Men and Machines* included a chapter on "The Two-Hour War," an account of the existing capability of an aerial armada to liquidate whole nations by means of chemical bombs dropped from planes. Planes offered a virtually foolproof delivery system, Chase said, because enough of them were bound to be able to penetrate antiaircraft and other defensive systems to create a wasteland. Cost was not a prohibitive factor either, since airplanes were comparatively cheap. It was possible to build a fleet large enough to do the job without breaking the national budget. In one last burst of malign optimism, Chase saw a ray of hope in the event that two opposing nations or coalitions should liquidate each other in a future war. As the surviving noncombatants viewed the fait accompli, "the neutral world will be in a sufficient state of shock to see that this sort of thing must stop. Forever. The surviving West," reasoned Chase, "together with the East, will then ban the machine [airplane] from war—which means, of course, the banishment of war. . . . Or so the conclusion hangs, neatly balanced between the hope and the belief, within my mind."[38]

Heywood Broun also expressed regret that the primary importance of the airplane remained its use as a weapon of destruction in war. "At the moment the score stands against the new invention," Broun stated. "There is blood upon the fuselage." Yet some positive aspects of aviation offered encouragment for the future. "It would be silly to deny that the airplane may serve to enrich life and living," Broun continued. "It can wipe out boundaries and mountain chains for warlike purposes, but this same conquest of the wide spaces could serve to emphasize a feeling of international solidarity. The vision of a united world is no longer fantastic. . . . In another century there will remain no such thing as an isolated people." The problem was that political theory lagged behind technological progress. America's "cornfed statesmen" were behind the times when they invoked Washington's Farewell Address to justify a position of isolation. Broun suggested calling a holiday in technological progress until the politicians were able to catch up.[39] At the end of the twenties, most people probably shared Broun's opinion about the positive effects of aviation. As Harry Guggenheim expressed it, the geographical barriers of rivers, seas, mountains, and deserts separating the peoples of the world had been eliminated by aircraft, giving mankind a new freedom that erased the misunderstandings and prejudices undermining human relations.[40]

In 1930 the Aero Educational Research Organization named Warren Jefferson Davis's *Air Conquest* the best contribution to aviation literature in the preceding year. The editorial board wrote that it had been impressed by the way Davis presented aviation against "a background of idealistic purpose—the opening up of a new international horizon through the breaking down of national barriers."[41] One of the key themes of Davis's book concerned his reflections on the nature of European airlines—especially German ones. Recognizing the extent and international coverage of German air routes, he scoffed at the idea that they would ever be used for aggressive purposes. Building them up, said Davis, had taken too much sacrifice and energy. Germany would never countenance the possibility of seeing them destroyed by war. At any rate, the role of aircraft in blurring national boundaries and nationalities was creating international good will that would last forever. An air trip over the European continent mingled people of all nationalities, Davis wrote; looking down from the speeding plane, everyone could very clearly see the close relationships of countries and the interlocking diversity of European resources, transportation, and industry. Aviation made an anachronism of boundaries and prejudices. Further, Davis added, when he commented on this fact to his fellow passengers, they all agreed with him. He asserted that the years 1928–29 had been the pivotal stage when the concept of aviation changed from one of war to one of peace, and expressed the opinion that commercial airlines to the Orient would serve to reduce the mounting tensions between America and Japan.[42]

Unhappily, international tensions of the next decade erupted into conflicts among the nations Davis wrote about. Aviation emerged as a fearsome weapon of destruction. Nevertheless, it is worth remembering that so many writers of the era remained fascinated by aircraft in a peaceful context. Invariably, the recurrent theme was the effect of speed in transportation and communication. One of the chapters of Hornell Hart's *Technique of Social Progress* (1931) was entitled "Indexes of Technical Mastery." By way of graphic illustration, Hart included a chart to portray the rate of increase of communications and the effect on civilization from 1900 to 1929. Hart added a figure showing miles flown on air routes to dramatize the downward trend of railroad passenger travel caused by auto and plane travel. Statistics given by Hart dramatically emphasized the progressive shrinkage of the world caused by improved means of transportation—from Magellan's 1,090 days to circumnavigate the globe in 1522, to the *Graf Zeppelin's* twenty-one days in 1929, to Wiley Post and Harold Gatty's less than nine days by airplane in 1931. These achievements in transportation promised a tremendous rate of increase in communication. "Communication is the very life blood of culture itself," Hart emphasized. "If technological progress has stimulated communication, it has facilitated that collective functioning through which the life of the individual expands into world-wide sweep."[43] In effect, the late twenties and early thirties marked the passing of civilization into the air-age world for many sophisticated observers.

The universal sky destroyed the traditional geography of time-distances influenced by land and sea barriers, and required a new type of air-age map. Two-dimensional maps had inherent limitations as to true shape, size, location, and distance. Some of these aspects were necessarily distorted in order to obtain the advantages of others, for each map had its special advantages when designed for a particular need. The Mercator map was highly useful for a mariner in charting one or a series of straight-line courses. For an ocean-basin geography, the Mercator map was an admirable navigational aid, but it was not suited to the navigational capability of aircraft, whose straight-line courses were not limited to the availability of a navigable body of water. One of the most suitable maps for the air age was the azimuthal (directional) equidistant map, in which parallels appeared as equally spaced circles along the meridians, as in the familiar polar projection. On such a map, all air routes from one city to another appeared as straight lines with their true directions preserved. To travel from Los Angeles to Moscow, a plane would not fly east, as one would suppose from a Mercator map, but north over the Arctic. This fact dramatized a new element of geographical relationships brought about by the air age. People who were accustomed to thinking in geographical conceptions based on a Mercator map considered Los Angeles to be closer to Rio de Janeiro than to Moscow. But air-age geography put the Russian capital closer to Los Angeles and forced a reconsideration of the importance of Alaska and the Arctic in plotting air routes.[44] In 1925, the geographical implications of aircraft were recognized and treated by A. P. Berejkoff, a radio engineer for General Electric, in an article appearing in *Aviation*. Berejkoff called his map the "equidistant zenithal projection," resembling the standard azimuthal equidistant map in theory and appearance. Air transport lanes of the future, he pointed out, would follow a "great circle route"[45]—a point worth noting because such a route usually came close to the Arctic.

Such geographical concepts were not new. As early as 1912, Vilhjalmur Stefansson anticipated the Arctic's commercial significance for the air age. He first publicly expressed this idea six years later during a talk to visiting European businessmen in New York City,[46] and explicitly set down his concept in the *National Geographic* in 1922. "The map of the Northern Hemisphere shows that the Arctic Ocean is a huge Mediterranean," he explained. "It lies between the continents somewhat as the Mediterranean lies between Europe and Africa. In the past it has been an impassable Mediterranean. In the near future it will not only become passable, but will become a favorite air route between the continents."[47] Stefansson stressed the fact that trans-Arctic aviation and great circle routes would be significant links between large cities of the modern age, which were increasingly concentrated north of the Tropic of Cancer.[48]

A series of spectacular flights dramatized the potentialities of great circle and polar routes. In the spring of 1926, Commander Richard E. Byrd, veteran of an earlier pioneering aerial exploration of Greenland in 1925, planned the first airplane flight over the North Pole. With Floyd Bennett (another veteran of the Greenland operation) piloting a Fokker monoplane, *The Josephine Ford*, the fliers departed Spitsbergen, reportedly circled the North Pole, and returned on May 9, 1926. Just three days later, the American explorer Lincoln Ellsworth conclusively accomplished the same feat in the dirigible *Norge*, commanded by the intrepid Norwegian polar explorer Roald Amundsen. Between August 23 and October 31, 1929, in an often forgotten aerial feat, a Russian plane followed a great circle route while slicing over the Arctic fastness on a remarkable flight from Moscow to Seattle, proceeding to New York. With pilot Bernt Balchen, Byrd capped this adventurous era of polar conquests with the first flight over the South Pole on November 28/29, 1929. These ventures proved that aircraft could successfully operate within the severe environment of polar regions, and, in particular, brought Arctic great circle routes of the future closer to realization.[49] Pan Am began studying great circle routes across the North Atlantic to Europe as early as 1929; Lindbergh surveyed great circle routes to the Orient via Alaska for Pan Am in 1931. Stefansson, the indefatigable champion of Arctic flying, became associated with Pan Am in 1932 as its adviser for northern operations.[50]

During the following decades of aeronautical development, the importance of the polar Mediterranean described by Stefansson came to have a political as well as commercial significance. As late as 1957, the geographer Hans Weigert commented, "We are still struggling to grasp the changes which Polar aviation has caused in the locational relationships of the powers of the East and West, by turning the Arctic Mediterranean and its frozen lands into a pivot area and strategic center."[51]

As early as the late twenties, it became necessary to consider the entire globe from the standpoint of air transportation. All inhabited parts of the earth were affected by the shrinking world brought about by faster ocean travel, the development of the railroad and the automobile, and accelerated by the airplane. The airplane especially altered the significance of old routes of communication, and prompted the need to consider the relationship of continents in the new light of air-age geography.

Epilogue

In his thoughtful study *A Social History of Engineering*, published in 1961, social historian Walter H. G. Armytage observed, "It is not too much to say that aviation has had a more comprehensive and far-reaching effect on all fields of material endeavour embarked upon by humans than any other previous single development."[1] Emphasizing World War II and the postwar era, Armytage noted a broad range of influences, ranging from high-precision machining, metallurgy, and high-test fuels to surveying. Appealing as his enthusiastic accolade might be to aeronautical partisans, it seems somewhat optimistic. Still, the scope of aeronautical development as early as the decade of the twenties suggests the remarkable diversity of aviation technology and its implications in recent civilization.

Advocates of aviation who were sobered at the harsh demonstration of aviation's potential in World War I were gratified by the practical application of aircraft to a multitude of peacetime uses. At the same time, important steps were taken toward fashioning new air power concepts within the U.S. Army and Navy. Developing increasing organizational and operational sophistication, Army aviation began to assume the outlines of the independent Air Force of later decades; the evolution of the Navy's carrier-based air power revolutionized naval tactics and strategy. United States progress in these and other areas of strictly research and development, while striking, was not necessarily uniquely American; there was a persistent thread of European influence in many aviation developments here in the United States—even within the NACA. During most of the twenties, the NACA seemed to conduct much of its programs with an ear closely attuned to military considerations although reports from most of this research could easily be applied to the civilian sector.[2] In addition to strictly aerodynamic concerns, military collaboration was clearly useful in a wide range of activities, including airmail, crop dusting, radio navigation, international relations, and more.

Although aircraft did not entirely displace older methods of performing various civilian tasks, many jobs were completed with greater dispatch and increased efficiency on a larger scale, as in agricultural dusting and aerial surveys of hydroelectric projects. Aviation provided a more comprehensive framework for the approach to projects in regional planning and promoted a wider view of business programs.

Aircraft affected the pace as well as the scope of life. The speed of both domestic and international airmail and a rising volume of air cargo constituted new factors influencing the tempo and organization of commercial activity, continuing a trend toward decentralization. Even though the passenger statistics for scheduled airlines were modest, the patrons of the airlines were often key executive personnel, and this aspect of commercial aviation undoubtedly had a greater significance than suggested by the figures. Private business flying also had an important bearing on the conduct of business during the twenties.

The development of the aviation industry created new jobs and new challenges of administration and regulation. Aviation influenced such diverse fields as medicine, meteorology, and mechanics. Thoughtful observers such as Stuart Chase considered aircraft as an encouraging example of the new technology—workmanlike, efficient, and graceful. Flight—a delight in itself—broadened the dimensions of people's experience and imagination. Heywood Broun echoed the hopes of many when he spoke of the role of aviation in promoting a new spirit of international good will.

From 1918 to 1929 American aviation progressed through the pioneering era, establishing the pattern of aviation's impact on national security, commerce and industry, communication, travel, geography, and international relations. American, as well as global, society experienced a dramatic transformation from a two-dimensional to a three-dimensional world. Aviation development during the first decade after World War I delineated the framework for the air age. By 1929 aviation was poised at the threshold of a new epoch.

Notes

Abbreviations

Annals	Annals of the American Academy of Political and Social Science
ICAC, *Papers*	International Civil Aeronautics Conference, Papers
ICAC, *Proceedings*	International Civil Aeronautics Conference, Proceedings
NASM	National Air and Space Museum, Smithsonian Institution
OHC	Oral History Collection, Columbia University
SAE Journal	Society of Automotive Engineers Journal

Prologue

1. *New York Times*, February 18, 1929
2. For a convenient, lavishly illustrated overview of these developments, *The American Heritage History of Flight* continues to be a valuable reference.
3. Mark Sullivan, *Our Times: The United States, 1900–25*, 4: 215–16.
4. Charles A. Lindbergh, *The Spirit of St. Louis*, p. 547.
5. Raymond B. Prescott, "Law of Growth in Forecasting Demand," *American Statistical Association Journal* 18 (December 1922): 471-79.
6. Robert R. Doane, "Rate of Growth of the Aircraft Industry," *Aviation* 28 (April 12, 1930): 755–57.
7. Harry Frank Guggenheim, *The Seven Skies*, p. 116.

Chapter One. Air Power

1. Alfred Goldberg, ed., *A History of The United States Air Force, 1907–1957*, pp. 30–31; Irving Brinton Holley, Jr., *Ideas and Weapons*, pp. 141–46.

2. Holley, *Ideas*, pp. 136–39; Wesley F. Craven and James L. Cate, eds., *The Army Air Forces in World War II*, 1: 36–37.

3. Craven and Cate, *Army Air Forces*, 1: 18–19, 43–46.

4. Holley, *Ideas*, pp. 159–68, 183–84.

5. Ibid, p. 149; Craven and Cate, *Army Air Forces*, 1: 23–24; Goldberg, *History*, pp. 29–32. The quotation is from the latter.

6. Interview of Carl Spaatz, in the Arnold Collection, Oral History Collection of Columbia University (cited hereinafter as OHC); letter, Henry Wallace to the Secretary of War, May 2, 1921, in the Henry H. Arnold Papers, Library of Congress, Washington, D.C., Box 2; Henry H. Arnold, *Global Mission*, pp. 92, 95.

7. Record flights of the era are conveniently listed in Eugene M. Emme, *Aeronautics and Astronautics, 1915–1960*. Several major aerial adventures of the decade are excerpted in James F. Sunderman, ed., *Early Air Pioneers, 1862–1935*. For contemporary accounts of the T-2 flight and the first global flight, respectively, see John A. Macready, "Non-Stop Flight across America," *National Geographic* 46 (July 1924): 1–83; and Lowell Thomas, *The First World Flight*.

8. The literature on Mitchell, his advocacy of air power, and his court-martial is extensive. For a scholarly assessment of the 1921 bombing trials, see Samuel F. Wells, "William Mitchell and the *Ostfriesland*: A Study in Military Reform," *Historian* 26 (Autumn 1964): 538–62. For authoritative recent studies of Mitchell, see Alfred E. Hurley, *Billy Mitchell: Crusader for Air Power*; and Burke Davis, *The Billy Mitchell Affair*. The Mitchell quote is from Goldberg, *History*, p. 32.

9. Interviews of Carl Spaatz, Ira Eaker, and Donald Douglas, Sr., in Arnold Collection, OHC. See also Benjamin D. Foulois, *From the Wright Brothers to the Astronauts: The Memoirs of Major General Benjamin D. Foulois*, a highly opinionated book.

10. Craven and Cate, *Army Air Forces*, 1: 27–33; Goldberg, *History*, pp. 36–37; interview, Ira Eaker, OHC. The basic similarities of the Lampert and Morrow committees on the issue of unified air services are noted by Frederick C. Thayer, Jr., *Air Transport Policy and National Security*, pp. 31–32. On aircraft procurement in particular, see Edwin H. Rutkowski, *The Politics of Military Aviation Procurement, 1926–1934*. The clearest summary of procurement and related aspects is still Irving Brinton Holley, *Buying Aircraft: Material Procurement for the Army Air Forces*, especially pp. 43–134.

11. Theodore P. Wright, "Wings for Transportation," Smithsonian Institution *Annual Report* (1941), pp. 503–83; Goldberg, *History*, pp. 34–37. For details of the evolution of flight testing as a technical discipline, see Rich-

ard P. Hallion, *Test Pilots: The Frontiersmen of Flight*, especially chapters 3 and 4.

12. Arnold, *Global Mission*, p. 129; Goldberg, *History*, p. 37. For accurate, illustrated plates of military aircraft of the era, including succinct but highly informative discussion of each, see Kenneth Munson, *Fighters and Bombers, 1914–1939*. 2 vols.

13. Arnold, *Global Mission*, pp. 125, 130–31.

14. Archibald D. Turnbull and Clifford L. Lord, *History of United States Naval Aviation*, pp. 119–44.

15. The best general review of naval aviation of the era is still Turnbull and Lord, *History*. During the twenties, the Navy operated two dirigibles, *Shenandoah* and *Los Angeles*, followed by the *Akron* and *Macon* of the thirties. For military purposes, these remarkable behemoths of aeronautical engineering were marginally effective at best. For a concise, pointed summary, see Richard K. Smith, "The Airship in America, 1904–1976," in Eugene M. Emme, ed., *Two Hundred Years of Flight in America: A Bicentennial Survey*, pp. 69–108.

16. The flight of the NC flying boats is told by Richard K. Smith, *First Across: The Navy's Transatlantic Flight of 1919*; Grover Loening's comments are in Loening, *Take Off into Greatness: How American Aviation Grew So Big So Fast*, p. 120.

17. Martin Caidin, *Golden Wings: Pictorial History of the U.S. Navy and Marine Corps in the Air*, pp. 32–41.

18. Turnbull and Lord, *History*, pp. 216–17; Elretta Sudsbury, *Jackrabbits to Jets: The History of North Island, San Diego, California*, p. 120; Neill Macaulay, *The Sandino Affair*, pp. 101, 115–19, 152–53; Peter C. Smith, *The History of Dive Bombing*, pp. 16–30.

19. Interview of Ford O. Rogers, OHC.

20. Macaulay, *Sandino*, pp. 80–81, 152–53, 252–56, 268. For additional comment on Marine aviation of the era, see John A. DeChand, *Devilbirds: The Story of United States Marine Corps Aviation in World War II*; Robert Sherrod, *History of Marine Corps Aviation in World War II*.

21. Turnbull and Lord, *History*, pp. 186–92, et seq.

22. Charles M. Melhorn, *Two-Block Fox: The Rise of the Aircraft Carrier, 1911–1929*, pp. 25–26, 29–38; Wells, "Mitchell and the *Ostfriesland*," pp. 556, 560–61.

23. Melhorn, *Two-Block Fox*, pp. 29–38, 79–81; Turnbull and Lord, *History*, pp. 205–15; Gareth Pawlowski, *Flat-Tops and Fledglings: A History of American Aircraft Carriers*, pp. 17–20.

24. Melhorn, *Two-Block Fox*, p. 86. Melhorn gives an extended discussion of the strategic issues, pp. 77 et seq.

25. Ibid., pp. 94–95. For a sampling of news comment, see "Our First Big Plane Carrier," *Literary Digest* 85 (April 18, 1925): 11.
26. Pawlowski, *Flat-Tops*, pp. 25–36; Joseph A. Skiera, ed., *Aircraft Carriers in Peace and War*, pp. 18–20; interview of Felix Stump, OHC.
27. Turnbull and Lord, *History*, pp. 228–37.
28. Ibid., p. 237; Melhorn, *Two-Block Fox*, pp. 98–101. Quotation from the latter, p. 101.
29. Turnbull and Lord, *History*, pp. 270–72; Melhorn, *Two-Block Fox*, pp. 112–15.
30. For an excellent survey of the origins and significance of aerial warfare, see Robin Higham, *Air Power: A Concise History*. Higham summarizes the interwar years on pp. 59–87. For his theory of the wave cycle of development, see pp. 3–8. A recent study of U.S. military aviation is DeWitt S. Copp, *A Few Great Captains: The Men and Events that Shaped the Development of U.S. Air Power*. The book includes considerable detail on the personal lives and foibles of principal figures in American military aviation through 1939. Approximately one-third of the book (pp. 3–130) surveys the era 1914–1929.
31. Emme, *Aeronautics and Astronautics*, pp. 13, 15, 18, 19. Using the *Lexington* as an alternate power source made national headlines. See, for example, clipping from the *New York Herald Tribune* (October 8, 1929), in files of the National Air and Space Museum, "Miscellaneous: Carriers—Military—U.S.A."

Chapter Two. Airmail and Airlines

1. Thomas C. Cochran, *The American Business System: A Historical Perspective, 1900–1955*, pp. 14, 44, 52.
2. Frank E. Hill, "Enter Aerial Commerce," *New Republic* 18 (February 1, 1919): 21–23.
3. Donald W. Douglas, "Airplane as a Commercial Possibility," *Scientific American* 1 (April 1920): 339–43. The vested interests of individuals such as Douglas may have encouraged somewhat more lavish claims than warranted by the status of aircraft development at the time. Nevertheless, their forecasts revealed remarkable clarity in terms of what actually developed.
4. V. C. Clark, "Air Transportation and the Businessman," *Journal of the Society of Automotive Engineers* 7 (June 1921): 563–69.
5. Henry Ladd Smith, *Airways: The History of Commercial Aviation in the United States*, pp. 52, 56–57; Carl H. Scheele, *A Short History of the Mail Service*, p. 151.

6. Smith, *Airways*, p. 57; E. P. Warner, *The Early History of Air Transportation*, pp. 7–9. For an interesting, if subjective, account of the early struggles of the airmail service, see Benjamin B. Lipsner, *The Airmail: Jennies to Jets*. As a captain in the Air Service, Lipsner organized and directed the first airmail operations. For a review of the details surrounding these events, see Eldon Wilson Downs, "Contributions of U.S. Army Aviation to Uses and Operations of Aircraft" (Ph.D. dissertation, University of Wisconsin, 1959), especially Chapter I.

7. H. H. Arnold, *Global Mission*, p. 71.

8. Lipsner, *Airmail*, pp. 1–20.

9. U.S. Civil Aeronautics Board, *Handbook of Airline Statistics*, p. 442.

10. Thomas Hart Kennedy, *An Introduction to the Economics of Air Transportation*, pp. 34–35.

11. Lipsner, *Airmail*, pp. 6, 75–77; Alexis Klotz, *Three Years off This Earth*, pp. 60, 30.

12. Paul T. David, *Economics of Air Mail Transportation*. For an account of the woes of the original U.S. Air Service DH-4, copied from the model supplied by the British firm to the Royal Air Force, see I. B. Holley, Jr., *Ideas and Weapons*. This American version also incorporated a spelling change, dropping one "l" from the English designer's name Geoffrey de Havilland, to make the American designation "de Haviland DH-4."

13. C. Fayette Taylor, "Aircraft Propulsion: A Review of Aircraft Powerplants," Smithsonian Institution *Annual Report* (1962), pp. 259–62. Taylor classified the Liberty as one of the more important engines of the 1910–18 period.

14. Irving W. Glover, "The Air Mail," in Frank A. Tichenor, ed., "Aviation," *Annals of the American Academy of Political and Social Science* 131 (May 1927): 44–45. Smith, *Airways*, is critical of the surplus DH-4 operations, charging that the modification cost of $2,000 was money wasted on an obsolete type (p. 74).

15. U.S. Civil Aeronautics Board, *Handbook*, pp. 443–44.

16. U.S. Congress, House, Select Committee of Inquiry into the Operations of the U.S. Air Service, Hearings (68th Cong., 2d sess., 1925), testimony of Raymond E. Jones, pp. 903–4. Cited hereafter as Hearings, U.S. Air Service.

17. Harold Bixby, "Aviation Project," OHC, I.

18. R. E. G. Davies, *Airlines of the United States since 1914*, pp. 21–22.

19. Glover, "Air Mail," p. 45. The Army experiments are examined at length in Downs, "Contributions," pp. 171–208.

20. Lipsner, *Airmail*, pp. 203–5; Page Shamburger, *Tracks across the Sky: The Story of the Pioneers of the U.S. Air Mail*, pp. 105–6. Photographs

of this equipment appear in J. P. Van Zandt, "On the Trail of the Air Mail," *National Geographic* 49 (January 1926): 1–61. Expenses for the lighted airway totaled about $500,000 (Smith, *Airways*, p. 78), and it has been estimated that the net cost of the government's Air Mail operations from 1918 to 1927 totaled $12 million (see David, *Economics*, pp. 48–49).

21. Interview of Dean Smith, OHC; Van Zandt, "Trail," pp. 10–12.

22. Warner, *Early History*, p. 27. On European lines of the twenties, see R. E. G. Davies, *A History of the World's Airlines*, pp. 6–218. W. David Lewis and Wesley P. Newton, "Paul Henderson," in John A. Garraty, ed., *Dictionary of American Biography: Supplement Five, 1951–1955*, pp. 294–95.

23. For a discussion, see Peter W. Brooks, *The Modern Airliner: Its Origins and Development*, especially pp. 43–44, 77.

24. *New York Times*, December 7, 1924.

25. Hearings, U.S. Air Service, testimony of Raymond E. Jones, pp. 903–4; testimony of Francis H. Sisson, p. 969. For additional evidence of the use of airmail by banks, see U.S., Congress, House, Committee on Interstate and Foreign Commerce, Aircraft, Hearings before the President's Aircraft Board (1925), testimony of William J. Glover, I, 270–71.

26. For the background of the Air Mail Act and the Air Commerce Act, consult Laurence Frederick Schmeckebier, *The Aeronautics Branch, Department of Commerce: Its History, Activities, and Organization*; for the development of the airlines, see Smith, *Airways*, pp. 84–104, 151–55, 383–92. The government's U.S. Air Mail Service made its last flight in 1927. The formative years of the Aeronautics Branch are thoroughly assessed in Donald R. Whitnah, *Safer Skyways: Federal Control of Aviation, 1926–1966*, esp. pp. 1–85.

27. Warner, *Early History*, pp. 49–51.

28. For a convenient chronology of airplane designs as they were incorporated by the airlines, see U.S. Civil Aeronautics Board, *Handbook*, pp. 490–96.

29. For photographs and details of American planes of the twenties, see Joseph Juptner, *U.S. Civil Aircraft*. Engine design and fuel research are discussed in Taylor, "Aircraft Propulsion," pp. 267–77, and by Robert Schlaifer and S. D. Heron, *Development of Aircraft Engines and Fuels*, pp. 156–98, 575–99. Awareness of wing loading as a design factor is analyzed in Edward P. Warner, *Technical Development and Its Effect on Air Transportation*, pp. 7–11. In this study, Warner points out that even though high-octane fuels, engine cowlings, and stressed-skin construction were

introduced in the twenties, they were not normally utilized in commercial operations until the following decade (pp. 15–31).

30. The best summary of United's early days is still Frank J. Taylor, *High Horizons*, pp. 1–72.

31. For details of Boeing's evolution, see, Harold Mansfield, *Vision: A Saga of the Sky*, pp. 1–86.

32. The books by Taylor and Mansfield, cited above, appear to be the basis for most discussions of United and Boeing. They are still informative, even though both were written by partisans of their respective companies. Smith, *Airways*, is an older study with good insight. Recent books that cover airline development and the role of manufacturers include Carl Solberg, *Conquest of the Skies: A History of Commercial Aviation in America*, pp. 30–62, 100–137; and Oliver E. Allen, *The Airline Builders*. The latter, part of the excellent Time-Life series on the history of flight, concentrates on the era of 1919–1941, and includes a graphic genealogical chart of airline development.

33. Arnold, *Mission*, pp. 125–26.

34. *New York Times*, September 17, 1927.

35. Vernon Schweitzer, in the *Journal of Commerce*, cited in "How the Air Mail Saves Money for the Banks," *Literary Digest* 98 (July 21, 1928): 57–58.

36. Paul H. Henderson, "Business at Airplane Speed," *Magazine of Business* 55 (February 1929): 141.

37. *New York Times*, December 17, 1924; P. G. Johnson, "Aviation's Varied Uses in Business," *Magazine of Business* 55 (May 1929): 600, 602.

38. U.S. Civil Aeronautics Authority, "Air Commerce to Stimulate Nation's Business," *Air Commerce Bulletin* 1 (December 2, 1929): 5–6; U.S. Bureau of Air Commerce, *Aeronautics Bulletin* 1 (April 1, 1934): 4.

39. Letter from William P. MacCracken to the Daniel Guggenheim Fund for the Promotion of Aeronautics, October 23, 1927, in the Guggenheim Papers (Library of Congress, Washington, D.C.), Box 1. The fund helped sponsor Lindbergh's tour.

40. Charles A. Lindbergh, *The Spirit of St. Louis* (New York, 1953) p. 9; Bixby interview, OHC.

41. David, *Economics*, pp. 181–82.

42. Richard Rea Bennett, *Aviation: Its Commercial and Financial Aspects*, p. 4.

43. Smith, *Airways*, p. 72; Warner, *Early History*, p. 25; "Aviation," *Encyclopedia of the Social Sciences*, 2: 343.

44. Lipsner, *Airmail*, pp. 32–37.

45. Van Zandt, "Trail," pp. 1–8.
46. Shamburger, *Tracks*, pp. 66–67; Smith interview, OHC; Lipsner, *Airmail*, p. 35.
47. Shamburger, *Tracks*, pp. 64–65; Van Zandt, "Trail," p. 60; Byron Moore, *The First Five Million Miles*, pp. 2–3; Dean C. Smith, *By the Seat of My Pants*, pp. 135–36.
48. Smith, *Airways*, p. 233; Moore, *First Five*, p. 4; Smith, *Seat*, pp. 139–40, 143; Interview of Dean Smith and Benny Howard, OHC.
49. George E. Hopkins, *The Airline Pilots: A Story in Elite Unionization*, pp. 5–34.
50. Ladislas d'Orcy, "Winged Transportation: A Survey of Commercial Air Services," *Scientific American* 124 (February 26, 1921): 168–69; J. P. Van Zandt, "Looking Down on Europe," *National Geographic* 48 (March 1925): 264, 274; Davies, *World's Airlines*, pp. 9, 39.
51. Richard P. Hallion, *Legacy of Flight: The Guggenheim Contribution to American Aviation*, pp. 8–10.
52. Kennedy, *Economics of Air Transportation*, pp. 69–70, 74–77.
53. Ibid., pp. 74, 83.
54. Cochran, *American Business System*, p. 45.
55. Davies, *Airlines of the United States*, pp. 4–6; Ladislas d'Orcy, "The Dawn of American Commercial Aviation," *Scientific American* 123 (November 27, 1920): 546.
56. D'Orcy, "Dawn," p. 555.
57. Kennedy, *Economics of Air Transportation*, pp. 52–53.
58. Wesley Winans Stout, "Aviation Comes out of A Tail Spin," *Saturday Evening Post* 190 (May 8, 1926): 141.
59. Archibald Black, *The Story of Flying*, p. 129.
60. Stout, "Aviation . . . Tail Spin," p. 141. For a more specific assessment of Aeromarine's corporate and financial arrangements, see William M. Leary, "At the Dawn of Commercial Aviation: Inglis M. Uppercu and Aeromarine Airways," *Business History Review* 53 (Summer 1979): 180–93.
61. Albert E. Blomquist, *Outline of Air Transport Practice*, p. 6. Davies, *Airlines*, discusses Aeromarine and other early efforts, pp. 4–15, and there is an informative tabular summary on p. 582.
62. U.S. Civil Aviation Board, *Handbook*, p. 445. The issue of government airmail contracts as "subsidies" paid to United States airlines seems to be a matter of interpretation (see Smith, *Airways*, pp. 89–93). Nevertheless, federal funds have played a large role in United States aviation development. Although Warner admits that comparisons between European and American commercial lines are complex, he notes that in 1930 United States lines received up to 70 percent of their revenues from federal out-

lays equivalent to subsidies, as opposed to 75 percent for European lines (see Warner, *Early History*, p. 64).

63. For an assessment of this indirect and unwieldy air-rail combination operated by Transcontinental Air Transport and the Pennsylvania Railroad, see Smith, *Airways*, pp. 144–46.

64. The late twenties were a period of rapidly shifting corporate alignments, with airlines operating a surprising assortment of aircraft types. The most convenient source for a discussion of finances and corporate struggles, as well as for photographs and descriptions of airline equipment, is Davies, *Airlines*, especially pp. 34–152. The Davies book also includes route maps, and extensive appendixes cover a miscellany of operational data. Financial and corporate aspects of the period are analyzed in John B. Rae, *Climb to Greatness: The American Aircraft Industry, 1920–1960*; and in Smith, *Airways*.

65. Warner, *Technical Development*, pp. 11–13.

66. Roland B. E. Ullman, "Flying on Business," *Review of Reviews* 77 (April 1928): 416–17.

67. Myron M. Stearns, "All Aboard by Air: Transcontinental Passenger Service," *World's Work* 58 (April 1929): 39–41.

68. Frederick Arthur Poole, Jr., *Records of an Airplane Passenger in 1928 and 1929*.

69. Advertisement in *Review of Reviews* 79 (March 1929): 105.

70. U.S. Bureau of Air Commerce *Aeronautics Bulletin*, 1 (April 1, 1934): 4. The development of American international airlines comprises a separate story. The main factor in the twenties was the Caribbean operations of Pan American Airways, treated in Henry Ladd Smith, *Airways Abroad: The Story of American World Air Routes*, pp. 3–61, and discussed in detail by Matthew Josephson, *Empire of the Air: Juan Trippe and the Struggle for World Airways*. In addition, one should consult two valuable monographs sponsored by the Council on foreign Relations: Oliver James Lissitzyn, *International Air Transport and National Policy*, and William A. M. Burden, *The Struggle for Airways in Latin America*. A recent study is Wesley P. Newton, *The Perilous Sky: U.S. Aviation Diplomacy and Latin America, 1919–1931*.

71. The President's Committee on Social Trends was inclined to regard air passenger traffic for the twenties as "inconsiderable," but concluded, "The rapidity of growth in air travel is significant for what it may forecast" (*Recent Social Trends in the United States* 1: 183–84).

72. Aeronautical Chamber of Commerce, *Aircraft Yearbook* (1930), pp. 28–29. Although Europe at the end of the 1920s had greater route mileage and carried much more express, American commercial aviation led other

nations in virtually every other category including passengers, which came to a total of 166,700 for Europe as a whole (see *Encyclopedia of the Social Sciences*, 2: 354–55). According to Warner, European passenger totals included far more tourist fares than those in the United States (*Early History*, pp. 35, 65). At one point, the Boeing system claimed that 70 percent of its fares were business passengers, according to P. G. Johnson, "Aviation's Varied Uses in Business," *Magazine of Business* 55 (May 1929): 535.

73. Paul Peter Willis, *Your Future in the Air*, p. 33. The growth of scheduled airline passenger miles through the depression years was relatively strong, from 92,880 in 1930 to 754,748 in 1939, with the annual increase normally ranging between 13 percent and 44 percent (U.S. Civil Aeronautics Board, *Handbook*, pp. 52–53). Moreover, the rate of growth of airline passenger miles was at least comparable to that of railroad passenger miles during expansion periods and markedly better during parallel contraction periods (1931–32 and 1936–37); see Thor Hultgren, *American Transportation in Prosperity and Depression*, pp. 135, 361.

74. Robert E. M. Cowie, "Flying Freight," *Magazine of Business* 54 (September 1928): 241–44; National Air Transport, *Bulletin Board* (August 19, 1927), pp. 1–2, and (September 1, 1927), pp. 1–4. Copies of the latter are in the library of Ohio State University, Columbus.

75. Paul H. Henderson, "The Airplane—A New Tool of Business," *Magazine of Business* 52 (September 1927): 259.

76. "Where Time Is Money," *Factory and Industrial Management* 75 (June 1928): 1190–92.

77. *New York Times*, November 24, 1929; James V. Bernardo, *Aviation in the Modern World*, p. 3.

78. In spite of the increasing traffic and interest in air express, the combined air express revenues of United Air Lines' predecessors, including NAT, show that air shipments did not develop an important source of income for the airlines. Express accounted for 1.74 percent of revenues in 1928, passengers for 4.26 percent, and mail for the remaining 94 percent. Although gross airline receipts doubled to about $8 million in 1929, express dropped to less than 1 percent of the total, according to the study made by the law firm Mayer, Meyer, Austrian, and Platt, *Corporate and Legal History of United Air Lines, 1925–1945*, p. 309.

79. U.S. Bureau of Air Commerce, *Aeronautics Bulletin*, No. 1 (April 1, 1934), p. 4; Earl Reeves, *Aviation's Place in Tomorrow's Business*, pp. 73–74; "Cargo-by-Air: Fifteen-Year-Old Reality," *Air Transportation* 1 (October 1942): 6.

80. Paul Henderson, "Air Transportation, Its Origin, Growth, and Outlook

for the Future," *Aeronautic Review* 8 (January 1930): 17. Cost was not the only problem. Additional drawbacks of early service were limitations of weight and shape as well as restrictions that excluded live animals, highly fragile items, and explosives (see John H. Frederick and Arthur D. Lewis, "History of Air Express," *Journal of Air Law and Commerce* 12 (July 1941): 203–31). For a brief review of Ford's aviation venture, see Allan Nevins and Frank E. Hill, *Ford: Expansion and Challenge, 1915–1933*, pp. 238–48.

81. Peter Altman, "History of Aviation in the State of Michigan," *Michigan Historical Magazine* 22 (1938): 180; Homer H. Shannon, "Breaks Records with Express Traffic," *Airway Age* 11 (September 1930): 1195–98. The ARE soon closed the gap. In 1933 ARE and its new rival, General Air Express (formed by six independent airlines), shared 85 percent of the air express business. The remainder was carried by nonaffiliated companies such as Kohler. See Wayne L. McMillen, "Air Express Service in the United States," *Journal of Land and Public Utility Economics* 11 (August 1935): 266–67.

82. Two significant recent books contain material on airline developments of the 1920s. Carl Solberg, *Conquest of the Skies: A History of Commercial Aviation in America*, pp. 13–121, covers airmail, dirigibles, domestic airlines, and early overseas ventures. W. David Lewis and Wesley Phillips Newton, *Delta: The History of an Airline*, stands out as the first comprehensive history of a commercial American airline to be written by professional historians; Delta's origins in the 1920s are covered in pp. 5–29.

Chapter Three. From Barnstorming to Business Flying

1. Lester J. Maitland, *Knights of the Air*, p. 233. The ubiquitous JN-4 Jenny is noted in virtually every compendium of American aircraft types. See, for example, National Aeronautics and Space Administration, Langley Research Center, *Progress in Aircraft Design since 1903*, p. 12.
2. M. W. Royse, "The Air Tramp," *New York Times* (December 11, 1921).
3. Hugh W. Nevin, "A History of Aviation in Lancaster County," *Lancaster County Historical Society Papers* 39 (1935): 33.
4. Charles A. Lindbergh, *We*, pp. 39–42.
5. Ibid., pp. 67, 85.
6. Ibid., pp. 97–98.
7. Interview of Aron (Duke) Krantz, OHC.
8. Elsbeth E. Freudenthal, *The Aviation Business: From Kitty Hawk to Wall Street*, pp. 67–68.

9. Howard Mingos, "America Takes the Lead in Aviation," *World's Work* 51 (April 1926): 636.

10. Maitland, *Knights*, pp. 234–35.

11. Typed manuscript of the President's Aircraft Board: Morrow Board (1925), Library of Congress, Manuscripts Division, Morrow Board Papers, Box 8, p. 53. Cited hereinafter as Morrow Board Papers.

12. Richard P. Hallion, *Legacy of Flight: The Guggenheim Contribution to American Aviation*, p. 6. For a popular history of the barnstorming tradition and its practitioners, see Don Dwiggins, *The Barnstormers: Flying Daredevils of the Roaring Twenties*.

13. Peter Altman, "History of Aviation in the State of Michigan," *Michigan History Magazine* 22 (1938): 184.

14. *New York Times*, August 3, 1924.

15. Harry Frank Guggenheim, *The Seven Skies*, p. 56; Daniel Guggenheim Fund for the Promotion of Aeronautics, *Bulletin*, No. 3 (January 7, 1927), pp. 1–3.

16. Morrow Board Papers, Box 8, p. 53.

17. Letter, Earl Osborn to Herbert Hoover (January 9, 1925), in the Herbert Hoover Presidential Library (West Branch, Iowa), Box 64.

18. Albert E. Blomquist, *Outline of Air Transport Practice*, p. 10.

19. Archibald Black, *The Story of Flying*, pp. 124–25.

20. Aeronautical Chamber of Commerce of America, *Aircraft Yearbook* (1926), pp. 43–65.

21. "Business Side of Flying," *New Republic* 51 (July 20, 1927): 215–16.

22. Marian Templeton Place, *Tall Timber Pilots*, pp. 15–33.

23. Interview of Noel Wien, OHC, and attached manuscript, "Wien Alaska Airlines: Its History," p. 5.

24. Archibald Williams, *Conquering the Air: The Romance of the Development and Use of Aircraft*, p. 301; "Skywriting for Advertising Purposes," *Aviation* 14 (February 5, 1923): 153–54; Alexander Klemin, "Handwriting on the Sky," *Scientific American* 128 (May 1923), p. 323; Paul D. Paddock, "Flying Electric Billboards and Talking Airplanes," *Popular Mechanics* 51 (May 1929): 723–27.

25. Henry Woodhouse, "How the World Found One Hundred Uses for Aeroplanes," *Flying* 9 (September 1920): 497.

26. Russell L. Putman, "When Can a Business Use the Airplane," *Magazine of Business* 55 (June 1929): 654.

27. Interviews of Clarence Jones and Leroy Ponton de Arce, OHC.

28. Morrow Board Papers, Box 7, p. 53.

29. James V. Piersol, "Adapting the Airplane to the Newspaper," *Aero Digest* 18 (January 1931): 35–39, 122; Altman, "History of Aviation . . . Michi-

gan," p. 186; "Airplane Purchased by Baltimore *Sun*," *U.S. Air Service* 4 (October 1920): 16; W. W. Waymack, "Good News," *Palimpsest* 11 (September 1930): 398–403; William F. Ogburn, *The Social Effects of Aviation*, pp. 576–77.

30. "Fighting Forest Fires from the Skies," *Scientific American* 122 (August 2, 1919): 515; "New York's Winged Policemen," *Scientific American* 110 (September 14, 1918): 215; "New York Creates Flying Police Force," *American City* 41 (December 1929): 164.

31. "Aerial Police Unit Starts Operation in New Jersey," *American City* 41 (July 1929): 86; "Coast Guard Air Service Inaugurated," *Aviation* 21 (December 20, 1926): 1033; A. G. West, "The Air Patrol of the Coast Guard," *Aero Digest* 15 (August 1929): 57–58.

32. Interview of Benny Howard and Clarence Jones, OHC; see also *American Heritage History of Flight*, p. 234.

33. Guggenheim Fund, *Bulletin*, p. 3.

34. See, for example, National Business Aircraft Association pamphlet "The Business Aircraft" (ca. 1966).

35. R. L. Putman, "Announcing a Practical Business Test of the Airplane," *Magazine of Business* 52 (September 1927): 263; also "The Shaw Publications Takes to the Air," *Magazine of Business* 52 (October 1927): 401–2, and 52 (December 1927): 754.

36. R. L. Putman, "Twelve Months of Flying for Business," *Magazine of Business* 54 (October 1928): 363–65, 404–6.

37. R. L. Putman, "How the Airplane Will Affect Marketing and Production," *Management Review* 17 (May 1928): 147–56.

38. "Business Has Wings," *Magazine of Business* 52 (October 1927): 414–15.

39. Lawrence P. Smith, "Oil Industry of Southwest Takes the Air When Minutes Mean Dollars," *National Petroleum News* 19 (May 4, 1927): 75–76; see also "Commercial Flying Is Taking Hold in Rocky Mountain Fields," *National Petroleum News* 19 (August 17, 1927): 74–79.

40. *Magazine of Business* 52 (November 1927): 615; and 54 (July 1928): 93.

41. See, for example, National Aeronautics and Space Administration, *Progress in Aircraft Design since 1903*, p. 28.

42. For a technical summary of these and other aircraft of the era, see Joseph P. Juptner, *U.S. Civil Aircraft*.

43. P. G. Johnson, "Aviation's Varied Uses in Business," *Magazine of Business* 55 (May 1929): 602; Myron M. Stearns, "All Aboard by Air: Transcontinental Passenger Service," *World's Work* 58 (April 1929): 34–41.

44. Ward K. Halbert, "Col. Stewart Buys Airplane and Sets Example in Business Flying," *National Petroleum News* 19 (June 1, 1924): 20–23. Since the given figures were not calculated in terms of capitalized values, the

estimates will be somewhat inexact. For additional information on Standard Oil of Indiana and its trimotor, see Paul H. Giddens, *Standard Oil Company, (Indiana): Oil Pioneer of the Middle West*, pp. 300–304.

45. Douglas W. Clephane, "The Business Executive Takes to the Air," *Scientific American* 142 (February 1930): 138–40.

46. "Where Time Is Money," *Factory and Industrial Management* 75 (June 1928): 1191.

47. *Aircraft Yearbook* (1930), pp. 226–32.

48. Thomas D. Crouch, "General Aviation: The Search for a Market, 1910–1976," in Eugene M. Emme, ed., *Two Hundred Years of Flight in America: A Bicentennial Survey*, pp. 117–18.

49. U.S., Congress, House, Committee on Interstate and Foreign Commerce, *Miscellaneous House Hearings* (68th Cong., 1st sess., 1924, No. 13), testimony of Herbert Hoover, p. 21; *Aircraft Yearbook* (1926), pp. 43–65; *Encyclopedia of the Social Sciences*, 2: 352, 354. Official statistics by category for general aviation were first compiled in 1931. In 1931 and 1932 the number of hours flown in business flights amounted to 14 percent and 15 percent, respectively, of the hours for instruction, pleasure, and other purposes. Applying these percentages to the passenger totals for 1929, we can conceivably say that business flying accounted for approximately 420,000 to 450,000 passengers (see U.S. Civil Aeronautics Administration, *Statistical Handbook of Aviation* (1953), pp. 36–37.

Chapter Four. An Aerial Implement

1. U.S. Department of Agriculture, *Weekly Newsletter* 6 (February 26, 1919): 9; R. H. Moulton, "Detective Aeroplane for Discovering Forest Fires and Outlaw Cotton Fields," *Travel* 34 (February 1920): 40.

2. J. S. Houser, "The Airplane in Catalpa Sphinx Control," Ohio Agricultural Experiment Station, *Monthly Bulletin* 7 (1922): 126–36; "The Airplane in Forest Insect Control," Ohio Agricultural Experiment Station, *Forty-First Annual Report, 1921* (1922), pp. xxxii–xxxv; E. P. Felt, "Current Notes," *Journal of Economic Entomology* 14 (October 1921): 459; C. R. Neillie and J. S. Hauser, "Fighting Insects with Airplanes," *National Geographic* 41 (March 1922): 332–38.

3. Eldon W. Downs and George F. Lemmer, "Origins of Aerial Crop Dusting," *Agricultural History* 39 (July 1965): 128–29.

4. B. R. Coad, "Dusting Cotton from Airplanes," U.S. Department of Agriculture Bulletin No. 1204 (January 1924), pp. 1–40.

5. Downs and Lemmer, "Origins," pp. 130–31.

6. H. C. Loeffler, "Aerial Anti-Pest Activities," *World's Health* 7 (February 1926): 66–67.

7. B. R. Coad, "Airplane Dusting of Cotton Fields Proves Effective, Economical," *U.S. Department of Agriculture Yearbook* (1928), pp. 117–20; Joint Committee on Civil Aviation of the U.S. Department of Commerce and the American Council, *Civil Aviation*, pp. 79–82.

8. Roger William Riis, "Commercial Crop Dusting," *Aviation* 181 (May 25, 1925): 573.

9. Orville H. Kneen, "Poison from the Air," *Airway Age* 10 (August 1929): 1219.

10. Ibid., 1218–20.

11. Alan L. Morse, "Airplane Dusting," *Indiana Horticultural Society Transactions* (1925), pp. 34–36; For miscellaneous aspects of Huff-Daland operations and aircraft, see Smithsonian Institution, National Air and Space Museum, Aircraft Files, "Huff Daland." For a summary of continuing aerial dusting experimentation in the twenties and after, see Downs and Lemmer, "Origins," pp. 132–34. Additional details on Huff Daland and its evolution into Delta Air Lines are covered in Lewis and Newton, *Delta*, pp. 10–23.

12. Donald E. Keyhoe, "Seeing America with Lindbergh," *National Geographic* 53 (January 1928): 37, 40.

13. "Airplanes Combat Locust Plague," *U.S. Air Service* 9 (July 1924): 20.

14. W. M. Steele, in *The Manufacturer's Record*, cited in "Fighting Mosquitoes with Airplanes," *Literary Digest* 85 (April 4, 1925): 29.

15. Orville H. Kneen, "The War in the Air—On Mosquitoes," *Airway Age* 11 (July 1930): 1931–33.

16. Howard M. Gore, "Aircraft and the Department of Agriculture," *National Aeronautics Association Review* 3 (May 1925): 68; S. R. Winters, in *Popular Aviation and Aeronautics*, cited in "Plant Protection by Airplane," *Literary Digest* 101 (April 27, 1929): 60–61.

17. "Collecting Insects by Airplane," *Aviation* 22 (May 30, 1927): 1173–74.

18. P. G. Johnson, "Aviation's Varied Uses in Business," *Magazine of Business* 55 (May 1929): 536.

19. U.S. Department of Agriculture, *Weekly Newsletter* 8 (October 22, 1919): 5.

20. Gore, "Aircraft and the Department of Agriculture," p. 68.

21. O. M. Kile, "Crop Reporting by Airplane," *Scientific American* 131 (July 1924): 22–23.

22. Steele, cited in *Literary Digest* 85: 29.

23. Winters, cited in *Literary Digest* 101: 60.

24. Ernest L. Jones, "Possibilities of the Aerial Fish Patrol," *Aviation* 17 (July 7, 1924): 724–25.

25. Edmond Gilligan, "Wings for the Fishing Fleet," *Popular Mechanics* 102 (October 1929): 610–14.

26. B. L. Chicanot, "New Eyes for the Sealing Fleet," *Scientific American* 138 (May 1928): 409–11. The role of the Air Service in various aspects of agriculture and forestry is also discussed in Eldon Wilson Downs, "Contributions of U.S. Army Aviation to Uses and Operation of Aircraft," (Ph.D. dissertation, University of Wisconsin, 1959) pp. 53–139.

27. William F. Ogburn, *The Social Effects of Aviation*, p. 597.

28. "Sowing Seeds by Airplane," *Aviation* 14 (May 21, 1923): 552.

29. Charles V. Stanton, "Seeding of Waste Lands by Airplane," *Aviation* 26 (January 26, 1929): 243–45.

30. S. B. Fracker and A. A. Granovsky, "The Control of the Hemlock Spanworm by Airplane Dusting," *Journal of Economic Entomology* 20 (April 1927): 287–94.

31. U.S. Department of Agriculture, *Weekly Newsletter* 8 (November 12, 1919): 7.

32. Ibid.; Paul G. Redington, "Airplanes and Forest Fires," *Journal of Electricity* 45 (October 15, 1920): 366–67.

33. Cited in "Airplane Fire Patrol Abolished," *Literary Digest* 72 (February 25, 1922): 26.

34. U.S. Civil Aeronautics Authority, *Air Commerce Bulletin* 1 (July 15, 1929): 12.

35. R. M. Kerr, "Airplane Patrol Has Limited Use in Forest Fire Protection in Northeastern Minnesota," *American City* 33 (December 1925): 658–59.

36. U.S. Civil Aeronautics Authority, *Air Commerce Bulletin* 1 (July 15, 1929): 12; Howard R. Flint, "The Airplane in Forestry," *Aviation* 23 (December 26, 1927): 1511–13.

37. Howard R. Flint, "The Fire Eagles," *American Forests* 34 (February 1928): 67–69. See also N. B. Mamer, "Airplanes Are Saving Our Forests," *Aero Digest* 8 (March 1926): 133, 170–71, 176; N. B. Mamer, "Protecting Our Forests from Fire," *Aero Digest* 10 (March 1927): 173, 246–48.

38. U.S. Civil Aeronautics Authority, *Air Commerce Bulletin* 1 (July 15, 1929): 13–14; Marion Templeton Place, *Tall Timber Pilots*, pp. 14, 17.

39. Place, *Tall Timber Pilots*, p. 57.

40. U.S. Civil Aeronautics Authority, *Air Commerce Bulletin* 1 (July 15, 1929): 13–14.

41. G. C. Mattison, *Aerial Survey of the Mississippi River Delta*, U.S. Coast and Geodetic Survey, Topography, Special Publication No. 105 (Washing-

ton, D.C., 1924), p. 1. For an example of early photographic principles based on wartime experience, see Herbert Eugene Ives, *Airplane Photography.*

42. "Methods Used in Aero-Photographic Mapping," *Engineering News-Record* 82 (May 22, 1919): 1000–1004.

43. "Mapping by Airplane," *American Architect* 115 (June 25, 1919): 873–74.

44. Mattison, *Aerial Survey*, pp. 2–4.

45. Ibid., pp. 4–5.

46. Willis Thomas Lee, *The Face of the Earth as Seen from the Air: A Study in the Application of Airplane Photography to Geography*, American Geographical Society, Special Publication No. 4, pp. ix, 1.

47. Ibid., pp. 7–8.

48. Ibid., pp. 27–28, 42.

49. Ibid., pp. 57, 69.

50. Ibid., pp. 54–56.

51. Interview of Reed Chambers, OHC.

52. Byron Moore, *The First Five Million Miles*, pp. 94–95.

53. Stephen B. Sweeney, "Some Economic Aspects of Aircraft Transportation," in "Aviation," *Annals of the American Academy of Political and Social Science*, 131 (May 1927): 179. Cited hereafter as *Annals.*

54. Sherman M. Fairchild, "Winged Surveyors," *Scientific American* 136 (March 1922): 157–60; "Aerial Maps," *Survey* 51 (March 1, 1924): 615–17; Fred Goodcall, "Aerial Photography: A New Business," *Photo-Era* 62 (March 1929): 145–57.

55. "The Making of Greater New York's Air Map," *Aviation* 16 (January 1924): 16–17.

56. Sherman M. Fairchild, "Aerial Mapping of New York City," *American City* 30 (January 1924): 74–75.

57. Nelson P. Lewis, "A New Aid to City Planning," *American City* 26 (March 1922): 209–12.

58. C. G. Krueger, "Application of Aerial Surveying to Watersupply Problems," *American City* 30 (May 1924): 493–94; Sherman M. Fairchild, "Aerial Photography," *Annals*, pp. 49–55. See also other comments by the city engineer of Syracuse, New York, Nelson F. Pitts, Jr., "What Aerial Mapping Has Done for Syracuse," *American City* 37 (September 1927): 354–56; and remarks by the engineer and secretary of the City Planning Commission of Allentown, Pennsylvania, Arthur A. Cassell, "Making and Using Airmaps for City and Regional Planning," *American City* 41 (December 1929): 119–21. A lively controversy over aerial mapping in the *Engineering News-Record* 87 (November 17, 1921): 828, and ibid. 88 (May 4, 1922): 746–47, included United States, Canadian, and Australian

comments that reaffirmed the usefulness of aircraft, although it was agreed they would not entirely displace other methods.

59. "Aerial Pictures in Telephone Study," *Telephony* 85 (August 25, 1923): 14–16.

60. Charles M. Emerson, "Aerial Surveying as Applied to Tax Equalization," *American City* 36 (April 1927): 522–24.

61. *Survey Graphic* 54 (May 1, 1925): 147.

62. Ibid.: 150.

63. Ibid.: 134.

64. Stuart Chase, "Coals to Newcastle," *Survey Graphic* 51 (May 1, 1925): 143–44.

65. Lewis Mumford, "The Fourth Migration," *Survey Graphic* 51 (May 1, 1925): 132.

66. *Journal of Electricity* 45 (October 15, 1920): 352.

67. Ibid.: 386–87; R. C. Starr, "The Airplane in Modern Hydro-Electric Practice," *Journal of Electricity* 45 (October 15, 1920): 357–59.

68. Starr, *Journal of Electricity* 45 (October 15, 1920): 358; H. H. Arnold, "Commercial Possibilities of Aircraft in the West," *Journal of Electricity* (October 15, 1920): 364–65.

69. Ernest W. Dickmann, "Airplane Costs in Hydro-Electric Work," *Journal of Electricity* 45 (October 15, 1920): 362–63.

70. F. A. Allner and J. R. Baker, "Transmission Line Work Aided by Aerial Survey," *Engineering News-Record* 92 (February 28, 1924): 360–63.

71. J. B. Beadle, "Airplane Speeds Up Power Surveys," *Electrical World* 86 (August 15, 1925): 311–14.

72. For a concise summary of the FC-2, see Claudia M. Oakes, compiler, *Aircraft of the National Air and Space Museum.*

73. Ogburn, *Social Effects*, pp. 537–38.

74. "Development of Mining Aviation," *Engineering and Mining Journal* 136 (November 1935): 553–54.

75. Hubert Work, "The Interior Department in the Air," *National Aeronautics Association Review* 3 (February 1925): 21–22.

76. *Engineering and Mining Journal* 136 (November 1935), 537, 554.

77. Kent Sagendorph, "The Airplane Finds Oil," *Aeronautics* 5 (July 1929): 16–18, 90.

78. George Svehla, "A Survey of Civil Aviation in the Southwest," *Aero Digest* 17 (September 1930): 54.

79. Hugh M. Wolfin, *Use of Airplanes in Mining and Petroleum Operations*, U.S. Bureau of Mines, Information Circular No. 6767 (February 1934), p. 11.

80. John L. von Blon, "Alaska Is Mapped from the Air," *Scientific American*

136 (May 1927): 303–5; "Conquering Alaska by Aerial Survey," *Outlook* 144 (November 3, 1926): 294–96.

81. E. F. Burkett, "Mapping Thirteen Thousand Square Miles of Alaska," *Aviation* 27 (December 21, 1929): 1210–13; R. F. Whitehead, "Problems of Aerial Photography in Alaska," *Aviation* 28 (May 24, 1930): 1024–27; "What the Flying Surveyors Found in Alaska," *Literary Digest* 104 (February 22, 1930): 48; Lucy Salamanca, "Photographing the Unknown," *National Republic* 18 (August 1930): 20–24.

Chapter Five. Research and Development

1. "The National Advisory Committee for Aeronautics," *Scientific American* 114 (February 5, 1919): 140. For the origins and background of the NACA, see George W. Gray, *Frontiers of Flight: The Story of NACA Research*.

2. NACA, *Annual Report* (1916), pp. 9–10; James V. Bernardo, *Aviation in the Modern World*, p. 194.

3. Gray, *Frontiers*, pp. 13–15, 34–37.

4. Ibid., p. 113; Edward Pearson Warner, *Technical Development and Its Effect on Air Transportation*, pp. 13–15. See also interview of Fred E. Weick (October 2, 1967), in NASA Historical Archives, Washington, D.C.

5. NACA, *Annual Report* (1929), pp. 4–11; Ludwig Prandtl, "Applications of Modern Hydrodynamics to Aeronautics," NACA, *Report No. 116* (1921).

6. There was growing interest in European aerodynamic research, especially that from Germany. Dr. Alex Roland, of Duke University, is preparing a major reinterpretation of the NACA between 1915 and 1958. My comments here on the NACA are drawn from an extensive, and absorbing, narrative outline that Dr. Roland has generously shared with me. In terms of NACA's overall importance in pioneering roles and in the dissemination of information, I remain in agreement with the U.S. Civil Aeronautics Board, *Handbook of Airline Statistics* (1962), p. 454.

7. Warner, *Technical Development*, p. 1.

8. Authoritative sources for my comments on airframe design include the following: Ronald Miller and David Sawers, *The Technical Development of Modern Aviation*, pp. 53–65; Charles Howard Gibbs-Smith, *The Aeroplane: An Historical Survey of Its Origins and Development*, pp. 96–97, 110; Harold Mansfield, *Vision: A Saga of the Sky*, pp. 44–46; John B. Rae, *Climb to Greatness: The American Aircraft Industry, 1920–1960*, pp. 61–62; and Peter W. Brooks, *The Modern Airliner: Its Origins and Development*. For enlightening comments from people who were close to aeronautical developments of the time, see Warner, *Technical Development*; International Civil Aeronautics Conference *Papers* (Wash-

ington, D.C., 1928), which includes papers by: W. F. Durand, "Historical Sketch of the Development of Aerodynamic Theory"; C. B. Millikan, "Aeronautical Research"; and Lyman Briggs, "Aeronautic Research at the National Bureau of Standards." Cited hereafter as ICAC, *Papers*. See also Joseph Sweetman Ames, "Aeronautic Research," Smithsonian Institution, *Annual Report* (1922), pp. 167–74, and Jerome C. Hunsaker, "Forty Years of Aeronautical Research," Smithsonian Institution, *Annual Report* (1955), pp. 241–71.

9. "Probable Effect of Aeronautic Experience on Automobile Practice," *Society of Automotive Engineers Journal* 4 (April 1919): 237–45. Cited hereafter as *SAE Journal*.

10. Howard C. Marmon, "A Comparison of Airplane and Automobile Engines," *SAE Journal* 4 (April 1919): 237–39.

11. Henry M. Crane, "Possible Effect of Aircraft Engine Development in Automobile Practice," *SAE Journal* 4 (April 1919): 240–42; O. E. Hunt, "Probable Effect on Automobiles of Experience with War Airplanes," *SAE Journal* 4 (April 1919): 243–45.

12. Henry M. Crane, "Automotive Engineering and Its Relation to Aeronautics," ICAC, *Papers*, pp. 81–84.

13. Charles Fayette Taylor, "Aircraft Propulsion: A Review of Aircraft Powerplants," Smithsonian Institution, *Annual Report* (1962), pp. 269–74; Charles L. Lawrance, "The Development of the Airplane Engine in the United States," ICAC, *Papers*, pp. 411–21; Robert Schlaifer and S. D. Heron, *Development of Aircraft Engines and Fuels*, pp. 156–98.

14. Taylor, "Aircraft Propulsion," pp. 283–84. For carburetor improvements, see Schlaifer and Heron, *Development*, pp. 509–44; for propeller research, see Miller and Sawers, *Technical Development*, pp. 71–74. For additional contemporary comment on engine testing and research, see ICAC, *Papers*, especially the essays by George Mead, pp. 399–407, and H. C. Dickinson, pp. 423–29.

15. Schlaifer and Heron, *Development*, pp. 328–29; Miller and Sawers, *Technical Development*, pp. 145–46; Roger E. Bilstein, "Rudolph William Schroeder," in John A. Garraty, ed., *Dictionary of American Biography: Supplement Five, 1951–1955*, pp. 610–11.

16. Matthew Van Winkle, *Aviation Gasoline Manufacture*, pp. 1–3, 8–9.

17. Interview, Benny Howard, OHC. The technique of using mothballs as an aromatic additive (probably ineffectual) was also reported by Schlaifer and Heron, *Development*, p. 582.

18. Schlaifer and Heron, *Development*, p. 559.

19. William Haynes, ed., *American Chemical Industry: A History*, 4: 397–

404; 6: 151–52, 400; Taylor, "Aircraft Propulsion," p. 277; Miller and Sawers, *Technical Development*, pp. 94–97.

20. Miller and Sawers, *Technical Development*, p. 95; Van Winkle, *Aviation Gasoline*, pp. 10–11; Schlaifer and Heron, *Development*, pp. 587–90.

21. George Svehla, "A Survey of Civil Aviation in the Southwest" *Aero Digest* 17 (August 1930): 162, 164.

22. "Aeronautic Education in Colleges and Universities," *Airway Age* 10 (March 1929): 265–69.

23. Interview, Jerome C. Hunsaker, OHC. Another of the earliest texts was written by one of Hunsaker's colleagues at MIT, Edwin Bidwell Wilson, *Aeronautics: A Class Text*.

24. Richard P. Hallion, *Legacy of Flight: The Guggenheim Contribution to American Aviation*, pp. 26–27.

25. "The MIT Aeronautical Course," *Aviation* 19 (July 13, 1925): 42–43.

26. Peter Altman, "History of Aviation in the State of Michigan," *Michigan History Magazine* 22 (1938): 218–19; Felix W. Pawlowski, "Aeronautical Research," ICAC, *Papers*, pp. 435–43; "Aeronautic Education," *Airway Age*, pp. 268–69; Bernardo, *Aviation*, p. 194.

27. For background on the Guggenheims and the Guggenheim Foundation, see Milton Lomask, *Seed Money: The Guggenheim Story*. The complete story of the Fund for the Promotion of Aeronautics is told in Hallion, *Legacy*. Regarding the Guggenheim Fund and aeronautics, see Hallion's superb study for additional details in addition to the other sources cited in this chapter.

28. Alexander Klemin, "Aeronautical Education," *Annals*, pp. 20–22; Lomask, *Seed Money*, pp. 83–85.

29. Alexander Klemin, "Aviation and the University," *Scientific Monthly* 23 (September 1926): 284–87.

30. Klemin, "Aeronautical Education," *Annals*, pp. 20–22; "Aeronautic Education," *Airway Age*, pp. 265–69.

31. Charles W. Lytle, director of industrial co-operation, New York University, to Grover Loening (October 29, 1925), *Loening Papers*, Library of Congress, Box 5; Lytle to L. R. Grumman, General Manager, Loening Aeronautical Engineering Co., (January 10 and January 11, 1929), Box 9.

32. Interview, J. H. Kindelberger, OHC.

33. Interview, Donald Douglas, Sr., OHC.

34. News release dated January 26, 1928, to be issued January 27, 1928, in *Guggenheim Papers*, Library of Congress, Box 1.

35. William F. Durand, "Aeronautical Education," National Education Association of the U.S., *Addresses and Proceedings* (1928), pp. 809–13.

36. W. R. Davis, "The Development of Aviation Medicine," *Military Surgeon* 53 (September 1923): 207–17.

37. A. D. Tuttle and H. G. Armstrong, "Role of Aviation Medicine in the Development of Aviation," *Military Surgeon* 85 (October 1939): 285 ff.

38. Robert J. Benford, *Doctors in the Sky: The Story of the Aero Medical Association*, pp. 7–11; Green Peyton, *Fifty Years of Aerospace Medicine: Its Evolution since the Founding of the United States Air Force School of Aerospace Medicine in January 1918*, pp. 44–68, 70–73; Douglas H. Robinson, *The Dangerous Sky: A History of Aviation Medicine*, pp. 128–29.

39. There are two popular biographies of this remarkable and gifted aeronautical pioneer: Carroll V. Glines, *Jimmy Doolittle: Daredevil Aviator and Scientist*; Lowell Thomas and Edward Jablonski, *Doolittle: A Biography*. For Doolittle's work with the Guggenheim FFL, I have relied on Doolittle's own recapitulation, in James H. Doolittle, "Early Experiments in Instrument Flying," Smithsonian Institution, *Annual Report* (1961), pp. 338–39, 342–43. Quotation from the latter.

40. Doolittle, "Early Experiments," pp. 343–55; interview, James H. Doolittle, OHC; Hallion, *Legacy*, pp. 101–2, 127.

41. Nick A. Komons, *Bonfires to Beacons: Federal Civil Aviation Policy under the Air Commerce Act, 1926–1938*, pp. 147–63; Monte D. Wright, *Most Probable Position: A History of Aerial Navigation to 1941*. The latter is an especially informative study of the background and history of air navigation, including European influences.

42. Tuttle and Armstrong, "Role of Aviation Medicine," pp. 293–96. See also E. C. Schneider, "Human Machine in Aviation," *Yale Review* 11 (April 1922): 594–612; Arthur La Roe, "Two Sciences—Medical and Aeronautical," *Annals*, pp. 124–29.

43. Benford, *Doctors*, pp. 13–22, 89–93; Peyton, *Fifty Years*, pp. 79–80. During the 1950s, as space exploration quickened, the association became the Aerospace Medical Association, and its publication became *Aerospace Medicine*.

44. William Ogburn, *The Social Effects of Aviation*, p. 374. In 1936 the Bureau of Commerce listed seven hundred doctors who were specially trained to check the qualifications of pilots who flew passengers and mail over scheduled routes; by the end of the thirties, many airlines had their own medical and research divisions. The military services and the Civil Aeronautics Authority as well as the Mayo Clinic, Harvard, and Columbia were conducting various studies. See: "Flying Supermen and Superwomen," *Literary Digest* 122 (November 14, 1936): 22; Donald E. Keyhoe, "Living in a Spotlight," *American Mercury* 128 (July 1937): 27.

45. Ogburn, *Social Effects*, p. 670.
46. Willis Ray Gregg, "Chasing Weather Secrets in Airplanes," *Aero Digest* 7 (August 1925): 421–22.
47. Willis Ray Gregg, "Meteorology and Its Application to Flying," *Annals*, pp. 107, 111; Donald R. Whitnah, *A History of the United States Weather Bureau*, p. 200.
48. Gregg, "Meteorology," pp. 110–115.
49. Whitnah, *History*, p. 167.
50. Harry Frank Guggenheim, *The Seven Skies*, pp. 80–82; Lomask, *Seed Money*, pp. 108–112.
51. "Meteorological Education in the United States," *Weatherwise* 6 (October 1953): 130, 136.
52. "A Brief History of the Department of Meteorology at Massachusetts Institute of Technology," *American Meteorological Society Bulletin* 32 (March 1951): 103–4. See also C. R. Smith, *Safety in Air Transportation over the Years*, p. 7. For further contemporary comments on meteorology, see Willis Ray Gregg, *Aeronautical Meteorology*, as well as the presentations by Gregg and others in ICAC, *Papers*, pp. 525–53.
53. For an authoritative and comprehensively illustrated history of rocketry, see Wernher von Braun and F. I. Ordway III, *History of Rocketry and Space Travel*. The "authorized" Goddard biography is by Milton Lehman, *This High Man: The Life of Robert H. Goddard*. On Edward A. Link and flight simulators, see Lloyd L. Kelly, *The Pilot Maker*. In Europe significant steps were made toward development of turbojets in the late 1920s. People and events in this historic trend are thoroughly assessed in Edward W. Constant III, *The Origins of the Turbojet Revolution*. Constant's book also discusses several of the American aerodynamic advances mentioned in this chapter.
54. Hallion, *Legacy*, pp. 158–60.
55. Harold F. Pitcairn, "Autogiro: Its Characteristics and Accomplishments," Smithsonian Institution, *Annual Report* (1930), pp. 265–71.
56. An excellent, balanced summary of the dirigible era is Richard K. Smith, "The Airship in America, 1904–1976," in Eugene M. Emme, ed., *Two Hundred Years of Flight in America: A Bicentennial Survey*, especially pp. 77–87.
57. Leslie Forden, *The Ford Air Tours, 1925–1931*. The Guggenheim Fund sponsored similar tours to take advantage of the publicity in the wake of Byrd's polar attempt and Lindbergh's transatlantic flight. See, for example, Hallion, *Legacy*, pp. 152–58.
58. The air races have generated their own body of historical literature. See, for example, Don Vorderman, *The Great Air Races*.

59. Taylor, "Aircraft Propulsion," p. 264; Schlaifer and Heron, *Development*, pp. 554–58. See also Miller and Sawers, *Technical Development*, pp. 59–60; John W. R. Taylor, Michael J. H. Taylor, and David Mondey, *Air Facts and Feats*, p. 204.

Chapter Six. Industry and Institutions

1. Victor Selden Clark, *History of Manufacturers in the U.S.*, 2: 338.
2. Welman Austin Shrader, *Fifty Years of Flight*, p. 20.
3. U.S. Bureau of the Census, *Historical Statistics of the United States, 1789–1945*, p. 466.
4. U.S. Bureau of Air Commerce, *Aeronautics Bulletin* 1 (April 1, 1934): 9. Only half of the 6,193 planes were sold in 1929. For further discussion of aircraft production, consult Elsbeth E. Freudenthal, *The Aviation Business: From Kitty Hawk to Wall Street*, pp. 117 ff. See also G. R. Simonson, "The Demand for Aircraft and the Aircraft Industry, 1907–1958," *Journal of Economic History* 20 (September 1960): 361–82.
5. U.S. Bureau of the Census, *Historical Statistics of the United States, Colonial Times to 1957*, p. 412. The air transport industry also proved more resilient than the railroad passenger business during the depression years, especially in contraction periods. See Thor Hultgren, *American Transportation in Prosperity and Depression*, pp. 135, 361.
6. "America's First Aircraft Show," *Magazine of Business* 53 (June 1928): 714.
7. "New Industry Emerges," *Magazine of Business* 53 (March 1928): 294–97.
8. Pynchon and Company, *The Aviation Industry*.
9. Archibald Black, ed., *Transport Aviation*, pp. 292 ff.
10. Pask and Walbridge, *The Development of Aviation in the United States*; Pask and Walbridge, *The Development and Outlook of the Fairchild Aviation Corporation and Its Subsidiaries*, p. 16; Library of Congress, Division of Aeronautics, *Aeronautical Periodicals and Serials in the Library of Congress*, p. 1.
11. Commercial National Bank and Trust Company of New York, *Financial Handbook of the American Aviation Industry*, cited in its foreword.
12. Freudenthal, *Aviation Business*, p. 88.
13. Collier's: The National Weekly, *The Aviation Industry and Its Market*.
14. Curtis Publishing Company, *The Aviation Industry*, p. 144.
15. Howard Mingos, "Thus Man Learned to Fly," *Saturday Evening Post* 201 (July 7, 1928): 10 ff; Charles A. Lindbergh, "Air Transport," ibid. 202 (February 1, 1930): 7 ff; Ralph D. Weyerbacher, "The Common Carrier

Hops Off," ibid. 200 (July 30, 1927): 6 ff; Wesley Winans Stout, "Aviation Comes Out of a Tail Spin," ibid. 198 (May 8, 1926): 3 ff. For a concise listing of the above and other articles in the *Saturday Evening Post*, see Curtis Publishing Company, *The Aviation Industry*, pp. 135–39.

16. John B. Rae, *Climb to Greatness: The American Aircraft Industry, 1920–1960*, p. 48.

17. For a concise survey of the developments, see Rae, *Climb*, pp. 39–57. See also Feudenthal, *Aviation Business*, and Simonson, "Demand." A laudatory, contemporary account is Howard Mingos, *The Birth of an Industry*.

18. For a general discussion, see William Glen Cunningham, *The Aircraft Industry: A Study in Industrial Location*, especially chapters 1 and 2. On Wichita, see Rae, *Climb*, pp. 15–16.

19. *Magazine of Business* 54 (October 1928): 403.

20. J. F. Richardson, "First in the Air: Preview of the Pacific Coast's Aviation Future," *Sunset* 59 (December 1927): 12–13.

21. *World's Work* 58 (June 1929): 5.

22. U.S. Bureau of Labor Statistics, "Employment and Production in Airplane Manufacture," *Monthly Labor Review* 2 (August 1929): 336–37.

23. Ellmore A. Champie, *The Federal Turnaround on Aid to Airports, 1926–1938*, pp. 2–5; U.S. Bureau of Air Commerce, *Aeronautics Bulletin*, p. 6. The share of federal funding for airports between 1933 and 1938 amounted to 76.7 percent; municipal, 17.7 percent; private, 3.6 percent. Until 1933, the total funds expended on airports amounted to $146,311,513. In just six years, 1933–1938, total spending amounted to $179,931,598, of which $137,931,950 came from New Deal programs (Champie, *Federal Turnaround*, pp. 5–6).

24. Westinghouse Lamp Company, Illuminating Engineering Bureau, *Airport and Airway Lighting*.

25. Ford Motor Company, Stout Metal Airplane Division, *The New Era of Transportation*, p. 11.

26. Ernest Payton Goodrich, "Airports as a Factor in City Planning," *National Municipal Review*, Supplement 17 (March 1928), p. 181. Other discussions include D. R. Lane, "Recent Developments of Municipal Airports in the West," *American City* 37 (July 27, 1927): 1–5, and H. M. Olmstead, "Airport and the Municipality," *American City* 38 (January 1928): 117–19.

27. Austin F. McDonald, "Airport Problems of American Cities," *Annals of the American Academy of Political and Social Sciences* 151 (September 1930): 263. See also William E. Arthur, "Airports and Landing Fields," *Annals*, pp. 56–57.

28. Archibald Black, ed., *Civil Airports and Airways*; Henry V. Hubbard et al., *Airports: Their Location, Administration, and Legal Basis*; Donald Duke, *Airports and Airways: Cost, Operation, and Maintenance*. See also Lehigh Portland Cement Company, *American Airport Designs*.

29. R. H. Simpson, "Columbus Prepares for Transcontinental Air Lines," *American City* 40 (April 1927): 150; Henry Ladd Smith, *Airways: The History of Commercial Aviation in the United States*, pp. 144–46.

30. Robert E. Emmenegger, Wesley A. Hunting, and Richard L. Sloane, "An Economic History of Port Columbus" (thesis, Ohio State University, 1938), pp. 3–4, 7, 18.

31. C. R. Roseberry, *The Challenging Skies: The Colorful Story of Aviation's Most Exciting Years, 1919–1939*, pp. 232–33. The history of airport development deserves more attention than it has thus far received. One step toward filling this gap in the literature is Paul David Friedman, "Fear of Flying: The Development of Los Angeles International Airport and the Rise of Public Protest over Jet Aircraft Noise" (thesis, University of California, Santa Barbara, 1978). Friedman discusses the development of Los Angeles International Airport in the 1920s, pp. 14–33.

32. Charles H. Holland, "Aviation Insurance," *Annals*, pp. 130–36.

33. Ibid.; Walter C. Crowdus, "Aviation Insurance," *Journal of Air Law* 2 (April 1931): 178–79.

34. "Is Aviation Blocked by Insurance Timidity?" *Literary Digest* 86 (September 5, 1925): 62.

35. "Progress of Aviation Insurance," *Popular Aviation* 10 (January 1932): 39.

36. Alexander Klemin, "American Passenger Air Transport," *Scientific American* 141 (October 1929): 361; G. L. Lloyd, "Aviation Insurance in America," International Civil Aeronautics Conference, *Papers*, p. 93. Cited hereafter as ICAC, *Papers*. See also Joint Committee on Civil Aviation, *Civil Aviation*, pp. 160–75; Black, *Transport Aviation*, pp. 303 ff; Ray A. Dunn, *Aviation and Life Insurance*, a study written for the Guggenheim Fund.

37. E. E. Slosson, "Commercial Aviation," *Scientific Monthly* 21 (November 1925): 555–57.

38. W. P. MacCracken, "The Growth of Aeronautical Law in America," *Journal of Air Law* 1 (October 1930): 416–17.

39. Albert E. Blomquist, *Outline of Air Transport Practice*, p. 5.

40. Edward P. Warner, "Commercial Use of Airplanes," *Boston Society Civil Engineers Journal* 9 (December 1922): 300. For a discussion of the formation and operation of the convention, see Pierre Etienne Plandin, "International Air Convention of October 13, 1919," ICAC, *Papers*, pp. 97–111; Kenneth W. Colegrove, *International Control of Aviation*, pp. 53–

65. Eventually, twenty-six nations signed, although the United States never did.

41. Joint Committee on Civil Aviation, *Civil Aviation*, pp. 99–121.

42. Lawrence Frederick Schmeckebier, *The Aeronautics Branch, Department of Commerce: Its History, Activities, and Organization*, pp. 7–9.

43. Nick A. Komons, *Bonfires to Beacons: Federal Civil Aviation Policy under the Air Commerce Act, 1926–1938*, chapters 1–8, especially pp. 21–159. See also Donald R. Whitnah, *Safer Skyways: Federal Control of Aviation, 1926–1966*.

44. News item, *Chicago Daily Tribune*, June 12, 1929; letter of John W. Wigmore to Jerry Land, June 28, 1929—both in Guggenheim Papers, Box 4.

45. Letter of Reed Landis to Jerry Land, July 1, 1929; letter of Jerry Land to Reed Landis, July 9, 1929—both in Guggenheim Papers, Box 4.

46. Letter of Harry F. Guggenheim to John W. Wigmore, July 23, 1929; item from *Northwestern University Bulletin*, no. 11 (November 11, 1929)—both in Guggenheim Papers, Box 4.

47. Komons, *Bonfires*, pp. 26, 54–55; Howard Mingos, *The Birth of an Industry*. The latter is a self-laudatory but informative account of the ACC.

48. Joint Committee on Civil Aviation, *Civil Aviation*; "Aviation" issue of the *Annals*.

49. ICAC, *Papers*, and *Proceedings*.

Chapter Seven. Symbolism and Imagery

1. Matthew Baigell, *Thomas Hart Benton*, pp. 73, 78–79, 87.

2. Charles A. Beard and Mary R. Beard, *The Rise of American Civilization*, pp. 744–45.

3. Edwin E. Slosson, in Preston William Slosson, *The Great Crusade and After, 1914–1928*, p. 403. Slosson's father, Edwin, wrote chapter 14 as a special essay, "Science, Mistress and Handmaid," in which he devoted several pages to the general progress of aviation in the twenties.

4. The Bella C. Landauer Collection of Aeronautical Music is now housed in the Admiral DeWitt Clinton Ramsey Room, National Air and Space Museum, Washington, cited hereafter as NASM. In addition to having a delightful time rummaging through the collection itself, I benefited from several newspaper and magazine clippings housed with the collection. I also relied on John Vinton, ed., *Dictionary of Contemporary Music* for comments on Antheil and Weill; the comment from the *Musical Courier* is cited in Dixon Wecter, *The Hero in America*, p. 435.

5. United States Copyright Office, *Motion Pictures, 1912–1939*, p. 10; Guy

Gilpatrick, *Guy Gilpatrick's Flying Stories*, p. 65; Albert Loening to C. G. Grey (December 15, 1919), in the Grover Loening Papers, Library of Congress, Box 4.

6. See, for example, Leslie Halliwell, ed., *The Filmgoer's Companion.*

7. "The Air Mail," *Aero Digest* 6 (April 1925): 224.

8. Columbia Pictures press release, *Flight* (1928), in Arts Files, NASM.

9. Edward V. Rickenbacker, *Rickenbacker*, p. 161; *Mutt and Jeff* clipping (1929) in Ira Eaker Papers, Library of Congress, Washington, D.C., Box 35; miscellaneous editorial cartoons in Arts Files, NASM.

10. The Ford ads regularly appeared in issues of the *Literary Digest* during 1928. The campaign is discussed and illustrated in Peter Paul Willis, *Your Future in the Air*, pp. 12–14. The *Literary Digest* solicitation appeared in vol. 100 (February 23, 1929), p. 83.

11. *Country Life* 56 (October 1929): 92–93.

12. S. Fred Roach, Jr., "Vision of the Future: Aspects of Will Rogers' Support of Commercial Aviation during the 1920s and 1930s," a paper presented at the Missouri Valley Historical Conference, Omaha, Neb. (March 1978), copy in my files.

13. *Literary Digest* 65 (May 22, 1920): 109; *World's Work* 58 (April 1929): 138; *American City* 41 (December 1929): 138; *Magazine of Business* 55 (April 1929): 363.

14. In addition to the evidence adduced from the *Reader's Guide*, a descriptive brochure in the Landauer Collection (NASM) discusses Mrs. Landauer's accumulation of early children's books and dime novels on kites and aviation, dating from 1744. The NASM holdings also include a wide selection of juvenile literature, housed in the Ramsey Room. There is also a good selection of aeronautical juvenilia in the Ross-Barnett Aeronautical Collection, Denver Public Library, Denver, Colorado. My reference to the *Boy Scout Handbook* is taken from Roderick Nash, *The Nervous Generation: American Thought, 1917–1930*, p. 135.

15. Daniel Sayre, "After *We* the Deluge," *Bookman* 68 (January 1929): 584–87.

16. Ruth Leigh, "Aviation and the Book Business," *Publishers Weekly* 116 (October 5, 1929): 1715–18. In one of the books published by the Ronald Press, Richard Rea Bennett's *Aviation: Its Commercial and Financial Aspects*, an unnumbered page just inside the cover listed twenty-three titles on engines, design, construction, and the like in Ronald Press's "Aeronautic Series."

17. Lee McCann, "Travel via the Skyway," *Country Life* 56 (October 1929): 98.

18. *Aviation Town and Country Club Magazine* 1 (December 1923); 2 (January 1924): 7.
19. *Sportsman Pilot* 1 (March 1929): 11.
20. Lester D. Gardner, "Aviation Country Clubs," *Sportsman Pilot* 1: 25.
21. Interview of Ruth Nichols, OHC.
22. See, for example, Claudia M. Oakes, *United States Women in Aviation through World War I*, Smithsonian Studies in Air and Space, Number 2, p. 43.
23. Paul A. Carter, *Another Part of the Twenties*, especially chapter 6, pp. 103–22.
24. Louis M. Starr, "Earhart, Amelia," *Dictionary of American Biography*, 22 (1958): 163–64. Most of the recent studies of Earhart's career focus on her last flight and disappearance over the Pacific in 1937. Before her untimely death, she wrote her own autobiography, *The Fun of It: Random Records of My Own Flying and of Women in Aviation.*
25. Carter, *Another Part*, p. xi. For samples of press comment on Amelia Earhart, see "A Woman Hops the Atlantic," *Literary Digest* 97 (June 30, 1928): 8–9; O. O. McIntyre, "I Want You to Meet a Real American Girl," *Cosmopolitan* 85 (November 1928): 21; T. J. C. Martyn, "Women Fliers of the Uncharted Skies," *New York Times* (August 10, 1930).
26. Charles E. Planck, *Women with Wings.*
27. Interview, Ruth Nichols, OHC; Martyn, "Women Fliers."
28. Grover C. Loening, "Making the Airplane a Utility," *Society of Automotive Engineers Journal* 4 (June 1919): 489.
29. "America from the Air," *National Geographic* 46 (July 1924): 84–92.
30. K. A. Taylor, "Riding High," *Sunset* 63 (August 1929): 20–21. For other descriptions of the delights of aerial travel, see O. Graeve, "Editor Discovers America," *Delineator* 116 (January 1930): 4; Joseph S. Edgerton, "Seeing America from TAT," *Aero Review* 7 (August 1929): 11–15.
31. J. Parker Van Zandt, "On the Trail of the Air Mail," *National Geographic* 49 (January 1926): 46.
32. Ibid., 57–58.
33. Charles A. Lindbergh, *The Spirit of St. Louis*, pp. 227–28.
34. Dean C. Smith, *By the Seat of My Pants*, p. 140. In his *Civilizing the Machine: Technology and Republican Values in America, 1776–1900*, historian John Kasson suggests that Lindbergh, like many firsthand participants, experienced the thrill of flight only as a novice, and "soon felt separated from his ecstatic initial vision by his very experience and technical expertise" (p. 116). Although many active technological professionals (trainmen, riverboat captains, aircraft pilots) must inevitably accept

the practical realities and humdrum of tending their machines, it may be that aviators at least did not become quite as jaded as Kasson thought.

35. "Editorial Paragraphs," *Independent* 117 (August 28, 1926): 225.

36. "The Nation Looks Skyward," *Independent* 119 (November 5, 1927): 444.

37. Roderick McKenzie, "Spatial Distance," *Sociology and Social Research* 13 (July–August 1929): 540, 542.

38. Heywood Broun, "It Seems to Heywood Broun," *Nation* 129 (September 4, 1929): 241.

39. Will Durant, "Is Progress a Delusion?" *Harper's Weekly* 153 (November 1926): 748.

40. Rose Henderson, "Art and the Aeronaut," *International Studio* 89 (June 1924): 194.

41. Babette Deutsch, "The Future of Poetry," *New Republic* 60 (August 21, 1929): 12–13.

42. Gilbert Seldes, "Transatlantic," *New Republic* 51 (June 1, 1927): 47.

43. Stuart Chase, *Men and Machines*, p. 178.

44. Ibid., p. 102.

45. Ibid., p. 144.

46. Lewis Mumford, *Technics and Civilization*, pp. 239, 266.

47. Ibid., p. 231; caption for commentary on plate XI. Although the book was published in 1934, Mumford had written the first draft in 1930.

48. John W. Ward, "The Meaning of Lindbergh's Flight," *American Quarterly* 10 (Spring 1958): 14–16.

49. John Erskine, "Flight," *Century* 114 (September 1927): 514–15. This aspect of Lindbergh's flight is also discussed by Kenneth S. Davis in *The Hero: Charles A. Lindbergh and the American Dream*, pp. 243–44.

Chapter Eight. International Skyways

1. G. Douglas Wardrop, "War Aviation in Retrospect: Commercial Aviation in Prospect," *Journal of the Engineers Club* 36 (April 1919): 147–49.

2. Interview of Gill Robb Wilson, Interview of Eddie Rickenbacker, OHC.

3. Evan John David, "Commercial Flying," *Society of Automotive Engineers Journal* 4 (March 1919): 200–202. Similar views were expressed by W. H. Smith, "Via the Air-Line, Now: The New Skyways of the World," *Forum* 61 (April 1919): 417–29; "Aviation and World Brotherhood," *Living Age* 302 (September 6, 1919): 591–94.

4. The Navy seaplane NC-4 flew from New York City to Plymouth, England, via Newfoundland, the Azores, and Portugal, May 8–11, 1919; the

British twin-engine Vickers bomber flew nonstop from Newfoundland to Ireland, June 14/15, 1919.

5. Lowell Jackson Thomas, *The First World Flight*, p. 3.

6. Mason M. Patrick, "Military Aircraft and Their Use in Warfare," in Eugene M. Emme, ed., *The Impact of Airpower: National Security and World Politics*, pp. 47, 50.

7. Mason M. Patrick, "The World from Above," *Aero Digest* 6 (January 1925): 14–16, 47; Mason M. Patrick, *The United States in the Air*, pp. 126–27.

8. Harry Frank Guggenheim, *The Seven Skies*, pp. 68–69.

9. J. J. Jusserand, "Lindbergh in Paris," *Review of Reviews* 76 (July 1927): 35–36.

10. Herrick described these feelings in the foreword he wrote for Lindbergh's *We*, pp. 5–12, especially p. 10.

11. Robert H. Ferrell, *Peace in Their Time: The Origins of the Kellogg-Briand Pact*, pp. 83–85.

12. Edward S. Martin, "Re-Discovering Europe," *Harper's* 155 (August 1927): 389–92. See also Kenneth S. Davis, *The Hero: Charles A. Lindbergh and the American Dream*, p. 207.

13. Cited in "America and Germany Reunited by Air," *Literary Digest* 93 (June 18, 1927): 5–7.

14. E. W. Burgess, "Communication," in William O. Ogburn, ed., *Social Changes in 1928*, pp. 1077–78. For discussions of earlier Army flights in Latin America, see Wesley Phillips Newton, *The Perilous Sky: U.S. Aviation Diplomacy and Latin America, 1919–1931*, pp. 44, 50–52, 85–99.

15. Harold Nicholson, *Dwight Morrow*, pp. 306–14.

16. Charles A. Lindbergh, "To Bogotá and Back by Air," *National Geographic* 53 (May 1928): 529–602.

17. Charles W. Hackett, "Success of Lindbergh's Good Will Mission to Mexico," *Current History* 27 (February 1928): 727–29. Morrow had adopted a very fruitful attitude of friendship, respect, and trust toward the Calles government. Another of his moves was to invite Will Rogers, who was still in Mexico City at Lindbergh's arrival.

18. Russell Owen, "Lindbergh's Historic Central American Flight," *Current History* 28 (April 1928): 89–96.

19. "Southward Air Trade Outlooks," *Outlook* 148 (January 18, 1928): 98–99; "We Discover Central America," *Review of Reviews* 77 (February 1928): 141–43; the latter issue carried a number of cartoons from sources across the United States that supported Lindbergh's Latin American flight (pp. 134–35).

20. *New York Times*, May 10, 1928.

21. James Warner Bellah, "Linking the Americas," *Saturday Evening Post* 201 (April 20, 1929): 6–7, 82.

22. William A. M. Burden, *The Struggle for Airways in Latin America*, pp. 15–16.

23. U.S. *Congressional Record*, 68th Congress, 2d Sess., 1925, LXVI, Part 5, pp. 5513–15.

24. C. H. Calhoun in the *New York Times* (February 26, 1928).

25. See, for example, the reports and correspondence of: Raycroft Walsh, Memo for record, February, 1924, citing study order dated August 31, 1923; J. V. Magee and V. C. Burke, "Investigation of Proposed Establishment of Air Mail Service with Central America and The Canal Zone," November 19, 1924; Correspondence, Major J. H. Burns, executive assistant to the secretary of war, to the post master general, August 26–September 9, 1925—all in the National Archives, Records of the Post Office Department, Bureau of the 2d post master general, Division of International Postal Service, "Records Relating to Central American Air Service," Record Group 628, Box 1.

26. These events are outlined in H. H. Arnold's autobiography, *Global Mission*, pp. 114–17, 122. The H. H. Arnold Papers (Box 2) in the Library of Congress contain a miscellany of memos and correspondence from Patrick, Arnold, and Canal Zone officers during the period January–August 1925, expressing concern about SCADTA intentions. See also interview of Mrs. H. H. Arnold, OHC. Until the time of Trippe's takeover of Pan Am, the airline continued to try to entice Arnold to sign on as a managing director. See, for example, letters from John Montgomery to Arnold, July 19, 1927, and July 27, 1927, in the Arnold Papers, Box 2.

27. Henry Ladd Smith, *Airways Abroad: The Story of American World Air Routes*, pp. 6–30. The SCADTA imbroglio and the roles of American bureaucrats for and against it were both subtle and complex. For a more detailed analysis, see Wesley P. Newton, *Perilous Sky: U.S. Aviation Diplomacy and Latin America, 1919–1931*, especially pp. 61–84.

28. "Hoover and the Pan-American Airways," *Aero Analyst* 1 (April 1929): 14.

29. William I. Van Dusen, "The First Million Miles," *Aeronautic Review* 7 (September 1929): 19.

30. Matthew Josephson, *Empire of the Air: Juan Trippe and the Struggle for World Airways*, pp. 43–45, 71.

31. Herbert Hoover, *The Memoirs of Herbert Hoover* 2: 214–45, 334.

32. Earl Reeves, *Aviation's Place in Tomorrow's Business*, pp. 118–20; Van Dusen, "First Million Miles," *Aeronautic Review*, p. 19. Pan Am's own

vigorous activities in route negotiations are discussed in Newton, *Perilous Sky*, especially pp. 161–209.

33. Josephson, *Empire of the Air*, p. 78; Oliver James Lissitzyn, *International Air Transport and National Policy*, p. 341. A later and colorful analysis of the Pan Am story is Robert Daley, *An American Saga: Juan Trippe and His Pan Am Empire*, which covers the 1920s era, pp. 6–82.

34. George H. Houston, "Aeronautics, International Aspects, National Control, Commercial Development, etc.," *Society of Automotive Engineers Journal* 6 (May 1920): 293; C. F. G. Zollman, *Law of the Air*, pp. 4–5; Burgess, "Communication," in Ogburn, ed., *Social Changes in 1928*, pp. 1076–78.

35. For discussion of the Havana proceedings, see Newton, *Perilous Sky*, pp. 151–56; for the Colombian accord, pp. 213–24. The text of the Pan American Convention can be found in Kenneth Wallace Colegrove, *International Control of Aviation*, pp. 173–82. Limited navigation agreements were signed with Canada in 1929, as well as airmail agreements with Austria, Germany, and Belgium, see pp. 234, 236. The ICAC is discussed in Chapter 6, above. Hoover noted league contacts in his *Memoirs* 2: 337. For the background and organization of the ICAO, see Smith, *Airways Abroad*, pp. 163–204.

36. William Mitchell, *Winged Defense*, pp. xi–xiii. See also William Mitchell, *Skyways*, pp. 235–89.

37. "Business Side of Flying," *New Republic* 51 (July 20, 1927): 216.

38. Stuart Chase, *Men and Machines*, pp. 307–17.

39. Heywood Broun, "It Seems to Heywood Broun," *Nation* 129, p. 241.

40. Harry Frank Guggenheim, *The Seven Skies*, pp. 11–12.

41. Warren Jefferson Davis, *Air Conquest*, p. iii.

42. Ibid., pp. 93–95, 222, 223, 230.

43. Hornell Hart, *The Technique of Social Progress*, pp. 78–80.

44. James V. Bernardo, *Aviation in the Modern World*, pp. 23–31.

45. A. P. Berejkoff, "Aerial Map of the World," *Aviation* 19 (August 24, 1925): 208–9.

46. Vilhjalmur Stefansson, *The Northward Course of Empire*, p. iii.

47. Vilhjalmur Stefansson, "The Arctic as an Air Route of the Future," *National Geographic* 42 (August 1922): 205.

48. Vilhjalmur Stefansson, "What Amundsen Has Proved: The Earth Is a Sphere, Not a Cylinder," *World's Work* 52 (July 1926): 241–49. In the introduction to his book *The Northward Course of Empire*, Stefansson acknowledged the fact that S. C. Gilfillan had previously commented on the northern advance of population and urban centers. Cf. S. C. Gilfil-

lan, "The Coldward Course of Progress," *Political Science Quarterly* 35 (September 1920): 393–410.

49. Eugene M. Emme, *Aeronautics and Astronautics, 1915–1960*, p. 25; Byrd's Arctic, polar, and other flights are covered in his autobiographical *Skyward*. But serious discrepancies concerning Byrd's claims for the North Pole flight are convincingly discussed in Richard Montague, *Oceans, Poles, and Airmen.*

50. Graham B. Grosvenor, "The Northward Course of Aviation," in Hans W. Weigert and Vilhjalmur Stefansson, eds., *Compass of the World*, pp. 312–35.

51. Hans Werner Weigert et al., *Principles of Political Geography*, pp. 246–49.

Epilogue

1. Walter H. G. Armytage, *A Social History of Engineering*, p. 269.
2. This issue of military influence on aviation is the subject of a stimulating, unpublished paper by Alex Roland, "The Impact of War upon Aeronautical Progress" (NASA History Office, 1978), in which he surveys the literature and analyzes the role of the NACA in particular.

Bibliography

Archival Holdings and Specialized Collections

Albert F. Simpson Historical Research Center, Air University, Maxwell Air Force Base, Montgomery, Alabama.

Aviation Collection, University of Texas at Austin (now housed at University of Texas, Dallas).

Columbia University, Oral History Research Office, New York, New York.

Denver Public Library, Ross-Barnett Aviation Collection, Denver, Colorado.

Experimental Aircraft Association, Franklin, Wisconsin.

Historical Office, Johnson Space Center, National Aeronautics and Space Administration, Houston, Texas.

Historical Office, National Aeronautics and Space Administration, Washington, D.C.

Herbert Hoover Presidential Library, West Branch, Iowa.

Institute of Aviation, University of Illinois, Urbana.

Library, Air Force Museum, Wright-Patterson Air Force Base, Dayton, Ohio.

Library, Ohio Historical Society, Columbus.

Library, Wisconsin State Historical Society, Madison.

Library of Congress, Washington, D.C.

Medical Library, Ohio State University, Columbus.

Medical Library, University of Wisconsin, Madison.

Milwaukee Public Library, Milwaukee, Wisconsin.

National Air and Space Museum, Smithsonian Institution, Washington, D.C.

National Archives, Washington, D.C.

National Library of Medicine, Bethesda, Maryland.

Transportation History Foundation, Coe Library, University of Wyoming, Laramie.

Periodicals

Addresses and Proceedings of the National Educational Association of the U.S., 1928.
Aero Analyst, 1929.
Aero Digest, 1925–1931.
Aeronautic Review, 1929–1930.
Aeronautics, 1929.
Aerospace Historian, 1962.
Agricultural History, 1965.
Air Power, 1919.
Air Transportation, 1942.
Airway Age, 1929–1930.
American Architect, 1919.
American City, 1922–1929.
American Forests, 1928.
American Mercury, 1929, 1937.
American Meteorological Society Bulletin, 1951.
American Quarterly, 1958.
American Statistical Association Journal, 1922.
Annals of the American Academy of Political and Social Science, 1930.
Aviation, 1923–1930.
Aviation Town and Country Club Magazine, 1923–1924.
Bookman, 1929.
Boston Society of Civil Engineers Journal, 1922.
Bulletin of the Daniel Guggenheim Fund for the Promotion of Aeronautics, 1926–1929.
Business History Review, 1979.
Cosmopolitan, 1928.
Century, 1927.
Country Life, 1929.
Current History, 1928.
Delineator, 1930.
Electrical World, 1925.
Engineering and Mining Journal, 1935.
Engineering News Record, 1919–1924.
Factory and Industrial Management, 1928.
Flying, 1920.
Forum, 1919.
Harper's, 1927.
Harper's Weekly, 1926.

Historian, 1964.

Independent, 1926–1927.

Indiana Horticultural Society Transactions, 1925.

International Studio, 1924.

Journal of Air Law, 1930–1931.

Journal of Air Law and Commerce, 1941.

Journal of Economic Entomology, 1921–1927.

Journal of Electricity, 1920.

Journal of Land and Public Utility Economics, 1935.

Journal of the Engineers Club, 1919.

Lancaster County [Pa.] Historical Society Papers, 1935.

Literary Digest, 1922–1930, 1936.

Living Age, 1919.

Magazine of Business, 1927–1929.

Management Review, 1928.

Mechanical Engineering, 1930.

Michigan History Magazine, 1938.

Military Surgeon, 1923, 1934, 1939.

Nation, 1929.

National Aeronautic Association Review, 1925.

National Air Transport Bulletin Board, 1927–1929.

National Geographic, 1922–1928.

National Municipal Review, 1928.

National Petroleum News, 1924–1927.

National Republic, 1926, 1930.

New Republic, 1919–1929.

Outlook, 1926–1928.

Palimpsest, 1930.

Photo-Era, 1929.

Political Science Quarterly, 1920.

Popular Aviation, 1932.

Publishers Weekly, 1929.

Review of Reviews, 1927–1928.

Royal Aeronautical Society Journal, 1926.

Saturday Evening Post, 1926–1930.

Scientific American, 1916–1930.

Scientific American Supplement, 1919.

Scientific Monthly, 1925–1926.

Society of Automative Engineers Journal, 1919–1921.

Sociology and Social Research, 1928–1929.

Sportsman Pilot, 1924–1929.

Sunset, 1927–1929.
Survey, 1924.
Survey Graphic, 1925.
Telephony, 1923.
Travel, 1920.
U.S. Air Service, 1920–1929.
Weatherwise, 1953.
World's Health, 1926.
World's Work, 1926–1929.
Yale Review, 1922.

Government Publications

"The Airplane in Forest Insect Control." Ohio Agricultural Experiment Station, *Forty-first Annual Report, 1921*.

Champie, Ellmore A. *The Federal Turnaround on Aid to Airports, 1926–1938*. Washington, D.C.: Department of Transportation, Federal Aviation Administration, 1973.

Coad, B. R. "Airplane Dusting of Cotton Fields Proves Effective, Economical." In *U.S. Department of Agriculture Yearbook*, pp. 117–20. Washington, D.C.: Government Printing Office, 1928.

———. "Dusting Cotton from Airplanes." U.S. Department of Agriculture Bulletin No. 1204 (January 1924), 1–40.

Emme, Eugene M. *Aeronautics and Astronautics, 1915–1960*. Washington, D.C.: Government Printing Office, 1961.

Holley, Irving Brinton, Jr. *Buying Aircraft: Material Procurement for the Army Air Forces*. Washington, D.C.: Office of the Chief of Military History, Department of the Army, 1964.

Houser, J. S. "The Airplane in Catalpa Sphinx Control." Ohio Agricultural Experiment Station, *Monthly Bulletin* 7 (1922): 126–36.

International Civil Aeronautics Conference. *Papers*. Washington, D.C.: Government Printing Office, 1928.

International Civil Aeronautics Conference. *Proceedings*. Washington, D.C.: Government Printing Office, 1928.

Komons, Nick A. *Bonfires to Beacons: Federal Civil Aviation Policy under the Air Commerce Act, 1926–1938*. Washington, D.C.: Department of Transportation, Federal Aviation Administration, 1978.

Library of Congress, Division of Aeronautics. *Aeronautical Periodicals and Serials in the Library of Congress*. Washington, D.C.: Library of Congress, 1937.

Mattison, G. C. *Aerial Survey of the Mississippi River Delta*. U.S. Coast and

Geodetic Survey, Topography, Special Publication No. 105. Washington, D.C.: Government Printing Office, 1924.

National Aeronautics and Space Administration, Langley Research Center. *Progress in Aircraft Design since 1903.* Washington, D.C.: Government Printing Office, 1976.

Oakes, Claudia M. *United States Women in Aviation through World War I.* Smithsonian Studies in Air and Space, No. 2. Washington, D.C., 1978.

———, compiler. *Aircraft of the National Air and Space Museum.* Washington, D.C.: National Air and Space Museum, 1976.

Peyton, Green. *Fifty Years of Aerospace Medicine: Its Evolution since the Founding of the United States Air Force School of Aerospace Medicine in January 1918.* Air Force Systems Command Historical Publishing Series, No. 67–180. Brooks Air Force Base, Texas, 1968.

Prandtl, L. "Applications of Modern Hydrodynamics to Aeronautics." U.S. National Advisory Committee for Aeronautics Report No. 116. Washington, D.C.: Government Printing Office, 1921.

Smithsonian Institution. *Annual Report.* Washington, D.C.: Government Printing Office, 1918–1962.

U.S. Bureau of Air Commerce. *Aeronautics Bulletin.* 5 vols. Washington, D.C.: Government Printing Office, 1928–1937.

U.S. Bureau of Labor Statistics. *Monthly Labor Review.* Washington, D.C.: Government Printing Office, 1915.

U.S. Bureau of the Census. *Fifteenth Census of the United States: 1930. Population.* 6 vols. Washington, D.C.: Government Printing Office, 1931–1933.

———. *Historical Statistics of the United States, 1789–1945.* Washington, D.C.: Government Printing Office, 1949.

U.S. Civil Aeronautics Authority. *Air Commerce Bulletin.* 11 vols. Washington, D.C.: Government Printing Office, 1929–1939.

U.S. Civil Aeronautics Board. *Annual Report, 1964.* Washington, D.C.: Government Printing Office, 1964.

———. *Handbook of Airline Statistics.* Washington, D.C.: Government Printing Office, 1960.

U.S. *Congressional Record,* 1919–1929.

U.S. Copyright Office. *Motion Pictures, 1912–1939.* Washington, D.C.: Government Printing Office, 1951.

U.S. Department of Agriculture. *Weekly News Letter.* 9 vols. Washington, D.C.: Government Printing Office, 1913–1921.

U.S. Federal Aviation Agency. *FAA Statistical Handbook of Aviation.* Washington, D.C.: Government Printing Office, 1964.

U.S. Federal Aviation Agency, Eastern Region. *General Aviation and Its Relationship to Industry and Community.* Washington, D.C.: Government Printing Office, 1964.

U.S. National Advisory Committee for Aeronautics. *Annual Report*. Washington, D.C.: Government Printing Office, 1915.

Wolfin, Hugh M. *Use of Airplanes in Mining and Petroleum Operations*. U.S. Bureau of Mines, Information Circular No. 6767. Washington, D.C.: Government Printing Office, 1934.

Books

Aerospace Industries Association of America. *Aerospace Facts and Figures, 1964*. Los Angeles: Aero Publishers, 1964.

Aircraft Yearbook. Aeronautical Chamber of Commerce of America, 1919–1930.

Air Transport Association. *Facts and Figures about Air Transportation, 1962*. Washington, D.C.: Air Transport Association of America, 1962.

Allen, Oliver E. *The Airline Builders*. Alexandria, Va.: Time-Life Books, 1981.

American Heritage History of Flight. New York: American Heritage, 1962.

Armytage, Walter H. G. *A Social History of Engineering*. Cambridge, Mass.: MIT Press, 1961.

Arnold, Henry H. *Global Mission*. New York: Harper, 1942.

Aviation. May 1927 issue of *Annals of the American Academy of Political and Social Science*.

Baigell, Matthew. *Thomas Hart Benton*. New York: Abrams, 1975.

Beard, Charles A., and Mary R. Beard. *The Rise of American Civilization*. New York: Macmillan, 1934.

Benford, Robert J. *Doctors in the Sky: The Story of the Aero Medical Association*. Springfield, Ill.: Chas. C. Thomas, 1955.

Bennett, Richard Rea. *Aviation: Its Commercial and Financial Aspects*. New York: Ronald Press, 1929.

Bernardo, James V. *Aviation in the Modern World*. New York: Dutton, 1960.

Black, Archibald, ed. *Civil Airports and Airways*. New York: Simmons-Boardman, 1929.

———. *The Story of Flying*. New York: McGraw-Hill, 1940.

———. *Transport Aviation*. New York: Simmons-Boardman, 1929.

Blomquist, Albert E. *Outline of Air Transport Practice*. New York: Pitman, 1941.

Brooks, Peter W. *The Modern Airliner: Its Origins and Development*. London: Putnam, 1961.

Burden, William A. M. *The Struggle for Airways in Latin America*. New York: Council on Foreign Relations, 1943.

Byrd, Richard E. *Skyward*. New York: Putnam, 1928.

Caidin, Martin. *Golden Wings: Pictorial History of the U.S. Navy and Marine Corps in the Air.* New York: Random House, 1960.

Carter, Paul A. *Another Part of the Twenties.* New York: Columbia University Press, 1977.

Chase, Stuart. *Men and Machines.* New York: Macmillan, 1929.

Clark, Victor Selden. *History of Manufacturers in the U.S.* 3 vols. New York: McGraw Hill, 1929.

Cleveland, Reginald M. *America Fledges Wings.* New York: Pitman, 1942.

Cochran, Thomas C. *The American Business System: A Historical Perspective, 1900–1955.* New York: Harper Torchbooks, 1962.

Colegrove, Kenneth Wallace. *International Control of Aviation.* Boston: World Peace Foundation, 1930.

Collier's: The National Weekly. *The Aviation Industry and Its Market: Past Progress, Present Trends, and Future Sales.* New York: Crowell, 1930.

Commercial National Bank and Trust Company of New York. *Financial Handbook of the American Aviation Industry.* New York: Commercial National Bank and Trust Company of New York, 1929.

Constant, Edward W. *The Origins of the Turbojet Revolution.* Baltimore: Johns Hopkins University Press, 1980.

Copp, DeWitt S. *A Few Great Captains: The Men and Events that Shaped the Development of U.S. Air Power.* Garden City, N.Y.: Doubleday, 1980.

Craven, Wesley F., and James L. Cate, eds. *The Army Air Forces in World War II.* 7 vols. Chicago: University of Chicago Press, 1948–1955.

Cunningham, William Glen. *The Aircraft Industry: A Study in Industrial Location.* Los Angeles: Lorrin L. Morrison, 1951.

Curtis Publishing Company. *The Aviation Industry.* Philadelphia: Curtis Publishing Company, 1930.

Daley, Robert. *An American Saga: Juan Trippe and His Pan Am Empire.* New York: Random House, 1980.

David, Paul T. *Economics of Air Mail Transportation.* Washington, D.C.: Brookings Institution, 1934.

Davies, R. E. G. *Airlines of the United States since 1914.* London: Putnam, 1972.

———. *History of the World's Airlines.* London: Oxford University Press, 1974.

Davis, Burke. *The Billy Mitchell Affair.* New York: Random House, 1967.

Davis, Kenneth S. *The Hero: Charles A. Lindbergh and the American Dream.* Garden City, N.Y.: Doubleday, 1959.

Davis, Warren Jefferson. *Air Conquest.* Los Angeles: Parker, Stone, 1930.

De Chand, John A. *Devilbirds: The Story of United States Marine Corps Aviation in World War II.* New York: Harper, 1947.

Duke, Donald G. *Airports and Airways: Cost, Operation and Maintenance.* New York: Ronald Press, 1927.

Dunn, Ray A. *Aviation and Life Insurance.* New York: Daniel Guggenheim Fund for the Promotion of Aeronautics, 1930.

Dwiggins, Don. *The Barnstormers: Flying Daredevils of the Roaring Twenties.* New York: Grosset and Dunlap, 1968.

Earhart, Amelia. *The Fun of It: Random Records of My Own Flying and of Women in Aviation.* New York: Harcourt, 1932.

Emme, Eugene M., ed. *The Impact of Air Power: National Security and World Politics.* Princeton: Van Nostrand, 1959.

————, ed. *Two Hundred Years of Flight in America: A Bicentennial Survey.* San Diego: American Astronautical Society, 1977.

Ferrell, Robert H. *Peace in Their Time: The Origins of the Kellogg-Briand Pact.* New Haven: Yale University Press, 1952.

Ford Motor Company, Stout Metal Airplane Division. *The New Era of Transportation.* Detroit: Ford Motor Company, 1927.

Forden, Lesley. *The Ford Air Tours, 1925–1931.* Alameda, Calif.: Nottingham Press, 1973.

Foulois, Benjamin D. *From the Wright Brothers to the Astronauts: The Memoirs of Major General Benjamin D. Foulois.* New York: McGraw-Hill, 1968.

Freudenthal, Elsbeth E. *The Aviation Business: From Kitty Hawk to Wall Street.* New York: Vanguard, 1940.

Garraty, John A., ed. *Dictionary of American Biography: Supplement Five, 1951–1955.* New York: Scribner's, 1977.

Gibbs-Smith, Charles Howard. *The Aeroplane: An Historical Survey of Its Origins and Development.* London: Her Majesty's Stationery Office, 1960.

Giddens, Paul H. *Standard Oil Company (Indiana): Oil Pioneer of the Middle West.* New York: Appleton-Century-Croft, 1955.

Gilfillan, S. C. *The Sociology of Invention.* Chicago: Follett, 1935.

Gilpatrick, Guy. *Guy Gilpatrick's Flying Stories.* New York: Dutton, 1946.

Glines, Carroll V. *Jimmy Doolittle: Daredevil Aviator and Scientist.* New York: Macmillan, 1972.

Goldberg, Alfred, ed. *A History of the United States Air Force, 1907–1957.* Princeton: Van Nostrand, 1957.

Gray, George W. *Frontiers of Flight: The Story of NACA Research.* New York: Knopf, 1948.

Gregg, Willis Ray. *Aeronautical Meteorology.* New York: Ronald Press, 1930.

Guggenheim, Harry Frank. *The Seven Skies.* New York: Putnam, 1930.

Hallion, Richard P. *Legacy of Flight: The Guggenheim Contribution to American Aviation.* Seattle: University of Washington Press, 1977.

————. *Test Pilots: The Frontiersmen of Flight.* Garden City, N.Y.: Doubleday, 1981.

Halliwell, Leslie, ed. *The Filmgoer's Companion.* 6th ed. New York: Hill and Wang, 1977.

Hanle, Paul A. *Bringing Aerodynamics to America.* Cambridge, Mass.: MIT Press, 1982.

Hart, Hornell. *The Technique of Social Press.* New York: Holt, 1931.

Haynes, William, ed. *American Chemical Industry: A History.* 6 vols. New York: Van Nostrand, 1945–1954.

Higham, Robin. *Air Power: A Concise History.* New York: St. Martin's, 1972.

Holley, Irving Brinton, Jr. *Ideas and Weapons.* New Haven: Yale University Press, 1953.

Hoover, Herbert. *The Memoirs of Herbert Hoover.* 3 vols. New York: Macmillan, 1951–1952.

Hopkins, George E. *The Airline Pilots: A Study in Elite Unionization.* Cambridge, Mass.: Harvard University Press, 1971.

Hubbard, Henry V., et al. *Airports: Their Location, Administration, and Legal Basis.* Cambridge, Mass.: Harvard University Press, 1930.

Hultgren, Thor. *American Transportation in Prosperity and Depression.* New York: National Bureau of Economic Research, 1948.

Hurley, Alfred E. *Billy Mitchell: Crusader for Air Power.* New York: Franklin Watts, 1964.

Ives, Herbert Eugene. *Airplane Photography.* Philadelphia: Lippincott, 1920.

Joint Committee on Civil Aviation of the U.S. Department of Commerce and the American Engineering Council. *Civil Aviation.* New York: McGraw Hill, 1926.

Josephson, Matthew. *Empire of the Air: Juan Trippe and the Struggle for World Airways.* New York: Harcourt, Brace, 1944.

Juptner, Joseph J. *U.S. Civil Aircraft.* 9 vols. Los Angeles: Aero Publishers, 1962–1982.

Kasson, John F. *Civilizing the Machine: Technology and Republican Values in America, 1776–1900.* New York: Grossman, 1976.

Kelly, Lloyd L. *The Pilot Maker.* New York: Grosset and Dunlap, 1970.

Kennedy, Thomas Hart. *An Introduction to the Economics of Air Transportation.* New York: Macmillan, 1924.

Klotz, Alexis. *Three Years Off This Earth.* Garden City, N.Y.: Doubleday, 1960.

Lee, Willis Thomas. *The Face of the Earth as Seen from the Air: A Study in the Application of Airplane Photography to Geography.* American Geographical Society Special Publication No. 4. New York, 1922.

Lehigh Portland Cement Company. *American Airport Designs*. New York: Lehigh Portland Cement Company, 1930.

Lehman, Milton. *This High Man: The Life of Robert H. Goddard*. New York: Farrar, Straus, 1963.

Lewis, W. David, and Wesley Phillips Newton. *Delta: The History of an Airline*. Athens: University of Georgia Press, 1979.

Lindbergh, Charles A. *The Spirit of St. Louis*. New York: Scribner's, 1953.

———. *We*. New York: Putnam, 1927.

Lipsner, Benjamin B. *The Airmail: Jennies to Jets*. Chicago: Wilcox and Follett, 1951.

Lissitzyn, Oliver James. *International Air Transport and National Policy*. New York: Council on Foreign Relations, 1942.

Loening, Grover. *Take Off into Greatness: How American Aviation Grew So Big So Fast*. New York: Putnam, 1968.

Lomask, Milton. *Seed Money: The Guggenheim Story*. New York: Farrar, Straus, 1964.

Macaulay, Neill. *The Sandino Affair*. Chicago: Quadrangle Books, 1967.

Maitland, Lester J. *Knights of the Air*. Garden City, N.Y.: Doubleday, Doran, 1929.

Mansfield, Harold. *Vision: A Saga of the Sky*. New York: Duell, Sloan, and Pearce, 1956.

Mayer, Meyer, Austrian, and Platt. *Corporate and Legal History of United Air Lines, 1925–1945*. Chicago: Twentieth Century Press, 1953.

Melhorn, Charles M. *Two-Block Fox: The Rise of the Aircraft Carrier, 1911–1929*. Annapolis: Naval Institute Press, 1974.

Miller, Ronald, and David Sawers. *The Technical Development of Modern Aviation*. New York: Praeger, 1970.

Mingos, Howard. *The Birth of an Industry*. New York: W. B. Conkey, 1930.

Mitchell, William. *Skyways*. Philadelphia: Lippincott, 1930.

———. *Winged Defense*. New York: Putnam, 1925.

Montague, Richard. *Oceans, Poles, and Airmen*. New York: Random House, 1971.

Moore, Byron. *The First Five Million Miles*. New York: Harper, 1955.

Mumford, Lewis. *Technics and Civilization*. New York: Harcourt, Brace, 1934.

Munson, Kenneth. *Fighters and Bombers, 1914–1939*. 2 vols. New York: Macmillan, 1970.

Nash, Roderick. *The Nervous Generation: American Thought, 1917–1930*. Chicago: Rand McNally, 1970.

Nevins, Allan, and Frank E. Hill. *Ford: Expansion and Challenge, 1915–1933*. New York: Scribner's, 1957.

Newton, Wesley, P. *The Perilous Sky: U.S. Aviation Diplomacy and Latin America, 1913–1931*. Coral Gables, Fla.: University of Miami Press, 1978.

Nicholson, Harold. *Dwight Morrow*. New York: Harcourt, Brace, 1935.

Ogburn, William F. *The Social Effects of Aviation*. Boston: Houghton Mifflin, 1946.

————, ed. *Social Changes in 1928*. Chicago: University of Chicago Press, 1928.

Pask and Walbridge Company. *The Development of Aviation in the United States*. New York: Pask and Walbridge, 1928.

————. *The Development and Outlook of the Fairchild Aviation Corporation and Its Subsidiaries*. New York: Pask and Walbridge, 1928.

Patrick, Mason M. *The United States in the Air*. Garden City, N.Y.: Doubleday, Doran, 1928.

Pawlowski, Gareth. *Flat-Tops and Fledglings: A History of American Aircraft Carriers*. New York: A. S. Barnes, 1971.

Place, Marian Templeton. *Tall Timber Pilots*. New York: Viking, 1953.

Planck, Charles E. *Women with Wings*. New York: Harper, 1942.

Poole, Frederick Arthur, Jr. *Records of an Airplane Passenger in 1928 and 1929*. Chicago: privately printed, 1929.

President's Committee on Social Trends. *Recent Social Trends in the United States*. 2 vols. New York: McGraw Hill, 1933.

Pynchon and Company. *The Aviation Industry*. New York: Pynchon and Company, 1928.

Rae, John B. *Climb to Greatness: The American Aircraft Industry, 1920–1960*. Cambridge, Mass.: MIT Press, 1968.

Reeves, Earl. *Aviation's Place in Tomorrow's Business*. New York: Forbes, 1930.

Rickenbacker, Edward V. *Rickenbacker*. Englewood Cliffs, N.J.: Prentice-Hall, 1967.

Robinson, Douglas H. *The Dangerous Sky: A History of Aviation Medicine*. Seattle: University of Washington Press, 1973.

Roseberry, C. R. *The Challenging Skies: The Colorful Story of Aviation's Most Exciting Years, 1919–1939*. Garden City, N.Y.: Doubleday, 1966.

Rutkowski, Edwin H. *The Politics of Military Aviation Procurement, 1926–1934: A Study in the Political Assertion of Consensual Values*. Columbus: Ohio State University Press, 1967.

Schlaifer, Robert, and S. D. Heron. *Development of Aircraft Engines and Fuels*. Cambridge, Mass.: Harvard Graduate School of Business Administration, 1950.

Scheele, Carl H. *A Short History of the Mail Service*. Washington, D.C.: Smithsonian Institution Press, 1970.

Schmeckebier, Laurence Frederick. *The Aeronautics Branch, Department of Commerce: Its History, Activities and Organization*. Washington, D.C.: Brookings Institution, 1930.

Seligman, Edwin R. A., ed. *Encyclopedia of the Social Sciences.* 15 vols. New York: Macmillan, 1930–1935.

Shamburger, Page. *Tracks Across the Sky: The Story of the Pioneers of the U.S. Air Mail.* Philadelphia: Lippincott, 1964.

Sherrod, Robert. *History of Marine Corps Aviation in World War II.* Washington, D.C.: Combat Forces Press, 1952.

Shrader, Welman Austin. *Fifty Years of Flight.* Cleveland: Eaton Manufacturing Company, 1953.

Skiera, Joseph A., ed. *Aircraft Carriers in Peace and War.* New York: Franklin Watts, 1965.

Slosson, Preston William. *The Great Crusade and After, 1914–1928.* New York: Macmillan, 1930.

Smith, C. R. *Safety in Air Transportation Over the Years.* New York: Wings Club, 1971.

Smith, Dean C. *By the Seat of My Pants.* Boston: Little, Brown, 1961.

Smith, Henry Ladd. *Airways: The History of Commercial Aviation in the United States.* New York: Knopf, 1942.

———. *Airways Abroad: The Story of American World Air Routes.* Madison: University of Wisconsin Press, 1950.

Smith, Peter C. *The History of Dive Bombing.* Annapolis: Nautical and Aviation Publishing Company, 1981.

Smith, Richard K. *First Across: The Navy's Transatlantic Flight of 1919.* Annapolis: Naval Institute Press, 1972.

Solberg, Carl. *Conquest of the Skies: A History of Commercial Aviation in America.* Boston: Little, Brown, 1979.

Stefansson, Vilhjalmur. *The Northward Course of Empire.* New York: Macmillan, 1924.

Sudsberry, Elretta. *Jackrabbits to Jets: The History of North Island, San Diego, California.* San Diego: Neyenesch Printers, 1967.

Sullivan, Mark. *Our Times: The United States, 1900–25.* 6 vols. New York: Scribner's, 1926–1935.

Sunderman, James F., ed. *Early Air Pioneers, 1962–1935.* New York: Franklin Watts, 1961.

Taylor, Frank J. *High Horizons.* New York: McGraw-Hill, 1951.

Taylor, John W. R., J. H. Taylor, and David Mondey, eds. *Air Facts and Feats.* New York: Bantam Books, 1979.

Thayer, Frederick C., Jr. *Air Transport Policy and National Security: A Political, Economic, and Military Analysis.* Chapel Hill: University of North Carolina Press, 1966.

Thomas, Lowell Jackson. *The First World Flight.* Boston: Houghton Mifflin, 1925.

Thomas, Lowell, and Edward Jablonski. *Doolittle: A Biography*. Garden City, N.Y.: Doubleday, 1976.

Turnbull, Archibald D., and Clifford L. Lord. *History of United States Naval Aviation*. New Haven: Yale University Press, 1949.

Van Winkle, Matthew. *Aviation Gasoline Manufacture*. New York: McGraw-Hill, 1944.

Vinton, John, ed. *Dictionary of Contemporary Music*. New York: Dutton, 1974.

von Braun, Wernher, and F. I. Ordway III. *History of Rocketry and Space Travel*. New York: Crowell, 1969.

Vorderman, Don. *The Great Air Races*. Garden City, N.Y.: Doubleday, 1969.

Warner, Edward P. *The Early History of Air Transportation*. York, Pa.: Maple Press, 1937.

―――. *Technical Development and Its Effect on Air Transportation*. York, Pa.: Maple Press, 1937.

Wecter, Dixon. *The Hero in America*. New York: Scribner's, 1941.

Weigert, Hans Werner, Henry Brodie, Edward W. Doherty, John R. Fernstrom, Eric Fischer, and Dudley Kirk. *Principles of Political Geography*. New York: Appleton-Century-Croft, 1957.

Weigert, Hans Werner, and Vilhjalmur Stefansson, eds. *Compass of the World*. New York: Macmillan, 1944.

Westinghouse Lamp Company, Illuminating Engineering Bureau. *Airport and Airway Lighting*. New York: Westinghouse Lamp Company, 1926.

Whitnah, Donald R. *A History of the United States Weather Bureau*. Urbana: University of Illinois Press, 1961.

―――. *Safer Skyways: Federal Control of Aviation, 1926–1966*. Ames: Iowa State University Press, 1966.

Williams, Archibald. *Conquering the Air: The Romance of the Development and Use of Aircraft*. New York: Nelson, 1928.

Willis, Paul Peter. *Your Future in the Air*. New York: Prentice-Hall, 1940.

Wilson, Edwin Bidwell. *Aeronautics: A Class Text*. New York: Wiley, 1920.

Wright, Monte D. *Most Probable Position: A History of Aerial Navigation to 1941*. Lawrence: University of Kansas Press, 1973.

Zollman, C. F. G. *Law of the Air*. Milwaukee: Bruce, 1927.

Unpublished Studies

Downs, Eldon Wilson. "Contributions of U.S. Army Aviation to Uses and Operation of Aircraft." Ph.D. dissertation, University of Wisconsin, Madison, 1959.

Emmeneger, Robert E., Wesley A. Hunting, and Richard L. Sloane, "An

Economic History of Port Columbus." Bachelor of Civil Engineering thesis, Ohio State University, Columbus, 1938.

Friedman, Paul. "Fear of Flying: The Development of Los Angeles International Airport and the Rise of Public Protest over Jet Aircraft Noise." M.A. thesis, University of California, Santa Barbara, 1978.

Roach, S. Fred, Jr. "Vision of the Future: Aspects of Will Rogers' Support of Commercial Aviation during the 1920s and 1930s." Paper presented at the Missouri Valley Historical Conference. Omaha, Nebr., 1978.

Roland, Alex. "The Impact of War upon Aeronautical Progress." Copy in the files of the History Office, National Aeronautics and Space Administration, Washington, D.C., 1978.

Roland, Alex. "A Narrative Outline of the National Advisory Committee for Aeronautics, 1915–1958." Copy in the files of the History Office, National Aeronautics and Space Administration, Washington, D.C., n.d.

Index